Kidnapping

Kidnapping

An Investigator's Guide to Profiling

Diana M. Concannon

Bruce Fain

Dianna Fain

Alan B. Honeycutt

Jana Price-Sharps

Matthew Sharps

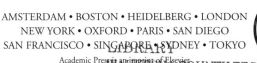

AMSTERDAM • BOSTON • HEIDELBERG • LONDON
NEW YORK • OXFORD • PARIS • SAN DIEGO
SAN FRANCISCO • SINGAPORE • SYDNEY • TOKYO
Academic Press is an imprint of Elsevier

ELSEVIER

Acquisitions Editor: Jennifer Soucy
Associate Developmental Editor: Kelly Weaver
Project Manager: Sarah M. Hajduk
Marketing Manager: Kristin Banach
Cover Design: Eric DeCicco
Cover image: istockphoto.com

Academic Press is an imprint of Elsevier
30 Corporate Drive, Suite 400, Burlington, MA 01803, USA
525 B Street, Suite 1900, San Diego, California 92101-4495, USA
84 Theobald's Road, London WC1X 8RR, UK

This book is printed on acid-free paper. ∞

Library of Congress Cataloging-in-Publication Data
Kidnapping : an investigator's guide to profiling / Diana M. Concannon ... [et al.].
    p. cm.
  Includes index.
  ISBN-13: 978-0-12-374031-1 (hardcover : alk. paper) 1. Kidnapping–United States.
I. Concannon, Diana M.
  HV6598.K53 2008
  363.25'9540973–dc22

2007050686

British Library Cataloguing-in-Publication Data
A catalogue record for this book is available from the British Library.

ISBN: 978-0-12-374031-1

For information on all Academic Press publications
visit our Web site at www.books.elsevier.com

Printed in the United States of America
08 09 10 9 8 7 6 5 4 3 2 1

Table of Contents

Biographies:
Author, Evaluators,
and Contributors

Evaluator and author **Diana M. Concannon** holds a doctorate degree in forensic psychology and is certified as a Professional Certified Investigator by the American Society for Industrial Security. She has worked extensively with individuals who have been victims of violence, as well as with those who have perpetrated violence. She has conducted risk and psychological assessments on paroled sex offenders for the State of California Department of Corrections and Rehabilitation and has lectured on topics including the ethics of the Sexually Violent Predator Act, the effects of stalking upon health care workers and situational awareness and personal safety. She also consults with businesses and organizations on workplace violence prevention and disaster preparedness.

Evaluator **Bruce Fain** is a Detective with the Fresno City Police Department. He has been employed by the Department for 35 years, is a Detective/Specialist, and has worked in numerous divisions within the department.

Evaluator **Dianna Fain** is a Crime Analyst for the Fresno Police Department. She has been a Crime Analyst for approximately 10 years. She received her education from Sacramento State University, and is certified in Crime Intelligence and Analysis by the State of California, and is the Treasurer of the Central Valley Crime and Intelligence Analysts Association.

Evaluator the **Honorable Alan B. Honeycutt** is a Judge of the Superior Court of California, County of Los Angeles. Judge Honeycutt presides over a criminal trial calendar in the Torrance Court House. He is a former reserve police officer and City Prosecutor for the City of Redondo Beach. Judge Honeycutt is a frequent lecturer in the area of criminal and constitutional law. He has previously served as the Chair of the Criminal Justice Section of the Los Angeles County Bar.

Contributor **Mike Gillette** is a leading threat management specialist for high-risk persons and organizations. His leading-edge behavioral analysis and conflict resolution techniques have been put to use in a variety of industries. He has authored counter-terrorism training curricula for government agencies and is a frequent presenter at professional conferences on the topics of violence management and personal safety. Mike is an Executive Vice President for Infinite Contingencies Group based in Las Vegas, Nevada. Mike is active as a close-protection specialist and provides services for some of the world's wealthiest businessmen. His previous professional experience has spanned the fields of law enforcement, military service, and the martial arts.

Contributor **Brad Parker** is director of Defend University, a research and development group dedicated to the exploration of leading-edge techniques and strategies for self-defense, security, and defensive tactics. Brad is currently responsible for security for the Arizona Sports and Tourism Authority and managing the executive protection unit of a security services provider. He has more than 20 years of martial arts experience and 15 years of law enforcement experience. In addition, he is a state-licensed Private Investigator, former Gang Enforcement Training Unit instructor, and former Emergency Medical Technician.

Contributor **Jana Price-Sharps**, Ed.D., is a professor of clinical psychology at Alliant International University's Forensic Psychology Program. She has conducted and published numerous studies on the effects of substance abuse on executive functioning. Jana is also consulting psychologist to the Fresno Police Department.

Contributor **Matthew Sharps**, Ph.D., is Professor of Psychology, California State University, Fresno, and serves on the adjunct faculty of Alliant University. He received his master's degree in clinical psychology from UCLA, and his master's and doctorate in developmental psychology from the University of Colorado, specializing in adult cognitive development and cognition. He is the author of numerous published articles and papers and of the book *Aging, Representation, and Thought: Gestalt and Feature-Intensive Processing*, in which he details his Cognitive Asynchrony theory of visual cognitive aging and his Gestalt/Feature-Intensive Processing theory of general cognitive representation. His research has been funded by the National Institutes of Health; he has won numerous teaching awards; and he has taught and conducted research at the University of Colorado, the University of Wyoming, Stockholm University, and the University Foundation of Thailand. He has served as an expert witness or consultant in over 150 criminal cases, and his current research addresses cognitive processing and representation in high-risk circumstances, eyewitness identification, and forensic cognitive psychology.

Contributor **Malinda Wheeler** has been a Registered Nurse for 26 years, holding a variety of positions. She received her bachelor's degree in nursing from Niagara University, New York, her master's degree as a Clinical Nurse Specialist in Critical Care from UCLA, and her Family Nurse Practitioner certificate from California State University, Long Beach. Malinda was a Professor of Nursing for Long Beach City College for 10 years and has worked as a Family Nurse Practitioner in various settings. For the past 14 years, Malinda has been the owner and director of Forensic Nurse Specialists, Inc., a private practice/business that provides forensic evidentiary examinations 24 hours per day to law enforcement for victims of sexual assault and domestic violence. She holds several contracts with cities, counties, universities, and hospital systems. Forensic Nurse Specialists currently provides services to over 55 law enforcement agencies in the Los Angeles and Orange County area. She is nationally certified as a pediatric, adolescent, and adult sexual assault nurse examiner. Malinda is past member on the Board of Directors for the International Association of Forensic Nurses and is Founding President of the Southern California Chapter of IAFN. She was co-chair of the Los Angeles Sexual Assault Coordinating Council for 4 years and helped established certification requirements for all SART Centers in Los Angeles County. Currently, Malinda is a board member with the Forensic Nurse Certification Board and Pomona Children's Advocacy Center (CAC), and a child forensic interviewer with the CAC. She has helped develop curriculum for the state law enforcement educational requirements on sexual assault and domestic violence. Malinda has lectured extensively on sexual assault, domestic violence, and drug-facilitated sexual assault.

Preface

On the evening of July 24, 2002, I watched the televised funeral of Samantha Runnion, a 5-year-old girl who was kidnapped, sexually assaulted, and left for dead on a California hiking trail. I listened as CNN's Aaron Brown spoke with restrained passion of the "summer of child abduction," the feared legacy of 2002's sunny season.

In Colorado, 14-year-old Elizabeth Smart remained missing. Seven-year-old Erica Pratt miraculously escaped from the Philadelphia home in which she had been held. The trial of those who murdered 7-year-old Danielle van Dam was concluding in a San Diego courtroom.

Nightly, the pain and terror of these children's families aired over television and radio stations. Parents sacrificed their right to privacy for the need to keep their story before the public and the one or two citizens who might provide information related to their child's whereabouts. Or the whereabouts of their child's body.

Their suffering was beyond what any parent should have to bear.

I had witnessed this hellacious form of parental anguish firsthand: When I was 5, my youngest brother disappeared in a mall teeming with families capitalizing on Washington's Birthday bargains and clamoring for free cherry trees. My parents braved the consumer rush by anchoring their four children in hand-holding formation between them. My mother paused outside Woolworth's, releasing my sister's hand, unintentionally signaling that my sister could do so with me, and me with my brothers. My mother assumed that my father still held us. My father had assumed the same about her.

Within a matter of minutes, my 16-month-old brother was swept away, and my mother was screaming. She planted her remaining children before a display case, yelling at me, her eldest, to make sure everyone stayed put before grabbing at every passerby. She frantically called my brother's name while my father sought a security guard.

At the suggestion of a level-headed older woman, my mother sought an employee who could call my brother's name over a public address system.

I watched my mother's frantic departure and tracked her return with my father. I heard my brother's name and our location announced over the P.A. I watched my mother's cries turn into sobs.

A security guard joined us a few moments later with a little boy who was not my brother.

My parents continued their frantic search. When they returned to the display case, my mother looked just beyond me and started screaming anew. Something in her tone had changed, and I followed her movements as she bent down and scooped my theretofore missing brother into her arms.

He had found us before we had seen him.

More than three decades later, I asked my mother about the incident, wondering if she had thought that anyone had actually taken my brother. We lived, after all, in a "good" neighborhood, during a simpler time.

"Of course, I did," she responded. "People have been taking kids forever."

So, too, have kidnappers had a long history of taking adults.

Over time kidnapping has mutated, spawning new and horrendous variations that complicate the prevention endeavors and investigative responses of law enforcement and security professionals.

A new typology that identifies the defining characteristics of kidnapping subtypes could assist in these efforts.

Chapter one

Introduction

CHAPTER CONTENTS

A PREVIOUS TYPOLOGY OF KIDNAPPING

In 1978, sociologist Ernest Kahlar Alix evaluated kidnapping from a sociohistorical method, defined as a study of past events from a sociological perspective. His analysis, which was primarily based on an evaluation of *New York Times* reports of kidnappings during the prior century, yielded 15 different proposed kidnapping subtypes. More than half of Alix's subtypes involved a financial element, such as ransom, extortion, or prostitution. As a result of the analysis, Alix focused his attention on ransom kidnapping, which he identified as "the most visible among the types of unlawful takings."

PSYCHOLOGY AND CRIMINAL ANALYSIS

In the intervening decades since Alix's typology, the motivations and modus operandi of kidnappers have broadened, and a wider range of kidnapping types has gained significant visibility. Simultaneously, cooperative advances in psychology and law offer a new approach to analyzing kidnapping, including its categorization, prevention, and investigation.

The intersection of law and psychology, termed *forensic psychology*, has grown in application in the last half of the twentieth century and into the twenty-first. Forensic psychology encompasses both the practice of psychology within settings such as prisons and parole offices, as well as research endeavors that focus on human behavior as it relates to legal processes. The latter includes such activities as providing support to traumatized victims and assisting attorneys in jury selection.

It also includes research into criminal behaviors, such as kidnapping. This research is frequently called *profiling*.

Profiling owes its origination to Dr. James A. Brussel who, in the 1950s, helped investigators apprehend the Mad Bomber. Prior to Brussel's involvement, police had been unsuccessful in identifying the individual responsible for more than 30 New York City bombings, including those against the landmark Grand Central Station and Radio City Music Hall.

After reviewing available evidence and photos of the bombed sites, Brussel identified several characteristics which he believed the suspect would possess. The offender, Brussel claimed, was a paranoid, overweight man of middle years. He was foreign born. He was single, lived with a sibling in Connecticut, and was a disgruntled current or former employee of the city's power company. Brussel, the legend goes, also indicated that the suspect would likely wear a buttoned, double-breasted suit.

Shortly after receiving Brussel's report, police arrested George Metesky, a heavy-set, foreign-born, middle-aged man who lived with his two sisters in the city of Waterbury, Connecticut. Metesky, a former employee of the Consolidated Edison power company, dressed himself in a buttoned, double-breasted suit for his ride to the police station.

Twenty years later, the Federal Bureau of Investigation furthered the application of psychology to crime-solving at its Behavioral Science Unit. The legendary work of professionals such as Howard Teten, Pat Mullany, Roy Hazelwood, John Douglas, and Robert Ressler involved what Douglas calls an inductive process, i.e., "observing particular elements of a crime and drawing larger conclusions from them." Based on interviews with hundreds of convicted criminals and a review of thousands of pieces of crime scene evidence, these behavioral scientists (as they are called), identified patterns of behavior and behavioral characteristics common to perpetrators of similar crimes. These FBI professionals became known as *profilers*, and their work, *profiling*.

In the decades since the FBI's initial forays into profiling, the term has been applied to a broad spectrum of activities. The creation of grid patterns to help locate a suspect's residence or place of employment, for example, are known as *geographic profiles*. Stereotyping by certain members of the law enforcement community—and more recently by transportation officials—has been called *racial profiling*.

Brent Turvey lists six additional qualifiers by which profiling has been labeled, including *behavioral profiling*, *crime-scene profiling*, *criminal-personality profiling*, *offender profiling*, *psychological profiling* and, the term he has chosen to adopt, *criminal profiling*.

As opposed to the inductive methods of the FBI, Turvey employs a deductive method, which he defines as "a set of offender characteristics that are reasoned from the convergence of physical and behavioral-evidence patterns within a crime or a series of related crimes." His comprehensive criminal profile, inclusive of wound pattern analysis, victimology, crime scene characteristics, and modus operandi (m.o.), is an evolution in the use of profiling as an investigative tool.

The deductive profile employed by Turvey will lead to a specific suspect in a particular case. As with the logic on which it is based, if the reasoning used in the deductive profile is sound, the conclusion reached—i.e., the suspect identified—will be accurate.

The inductive profile will yield the most likely suspect type based on the actions of criminals who have committed similar crimes in the past. Inductive profiling, as Robert Depue, former head of the FBI Behavioral Science Unit has stated, "doesn't identify individuals—just types of people."

The inductive profile is not foolproof; no matter how many times similar crimes are committed in similar ways, it is possible that an individual criminal will deviate from the norm. The value of inductive profiling lies in its ability to assist investigators to develop a case by pointing to the most likely scenario, and allowing a more efficient allocation of limited resources.

Kidnapping: An Investigator's Guide to Profiling employed the inductive profiling approach to derive the kidnapping subtypes presented in this book.

METHODOLOGY

Kidnapping: An Investigator's Guide to Profiling is based on a three-part analysis of 100 randomly selected kidnapping cases that survived Supreme Court appeal. These cases were chosen to ensure that the crime in each case survived challenges that questioned whether the offense committed was, in fact, kidnapping, as opposed to a different crime such as murder or sexual assault.

During the first part of the analysis, I joined with three other reviewers involved in law enforcement, including a crime analyst, detective, and city prosecutor. We independently reviewed the 100 cases and responded to a specially designed questionnaire that required placing each case in one of seven proposed subtypes. These subtypes, and their definitions, are as follows:

- *Domestic Kidnapping*, defined as an intra-family kidnapping to further custody when the legal right is absent.
- *Political Kidnapping*, defined as kidnapping to further a political agenda.
- *Predatory Kidnapping—Adult Victim*, defined as the kidnapping of an adult to satisfy the lust of the offender.
- *Predatory Kidnapping—Child Victim*, defined as the kidnapping of a minor to satisfy the lust of the offender.
- *Profit Kidnapping*, defined as kidnapping for actual or perceived gain.
- *Revenge Kidnapping*, defined as a kidnapping which is perpetrated by an irrational individual who kidnaps to rectify a real or perceived wrong.
- *Staged Kidnapping*, defined as kidnapping which is feigned to distract from another crime or undisclosed situation.

Inter-rater reliability—the level of agreement between the different reviewers—was measured with a Pearson Correlation which yielded correlation coefficients beyond $p = .001$. The results of this analysis are included in Table 1.1. When the reviewers disagreed, a subtype was adopted if three of the four reviewers reached agreement. This occurred in all of the 20 instances in which the reviewers were not in total accord.

One of the seven subtypes—Staged Kidnapping—was represented in only three of the 100 cases. This was predicted, as those who stage a kidnapping are typically convicted of the crime that the "kidnapping" was designed to obscure, or are charged with making a false

Table 1.1 Subtype Inter-Rater Reliability

	Reviewer A	Reviewer B	Reviewer C	Reviewer D
Reviewer A	1.00	.815*	.932*	.928*
Reviewer B	.815*	1.00	.861*	.853*
Reviewer C	.932*	.861*	1.00	.973*
Reviewer D	.928*	.853*	.973*	1.00

*Correlation is significant at the 0.01 level (2-tailed).

statement if no other crime has occurred. Nonetheless, information from the three cases, as well as from notorious staged kidnappings, was assessed to provide a greater understanding of this phenomena.

An additional proposed subtype, the Political Kidnapping, was also absent from the cases evaluated. This reflects the fact that such cases are not typically tried in the United States courts. The prevalence of this type of kidnapping, particularly in recent conflicts such as the Iraqi War, predicated the inclusion of the subtype. In place of court transcripts, Political Kidnappings were evaluated based on news accounts and information provided by security professionals involved in such kidnappings.

In the second part of the analysis, inter-rater reliability was again examined for answers to six elements that were deemed to be subjective in nature. Reviewers were asked to determine if an element was true or false for each case. Reviewers could also indicate whether the case material did not provide adequate information to offer a response. The specific elements, as presented on the questionnaire, are as follows:

- The victim was preselected/presurveilled.
- The victim was chosen randomly or opportunistically.
- The victim was low risk, i.e., not likely to be immediately missed or reported as missing.
- The victim was high risk, i.e., likely to be immediately missed or reported as missing.
- The level of force used during the abduction was beyond that necessary to facilitate captivity.
- The offender partook in ritualistic behaviors against the victim (taking souvenirs, cannibalistic behaviors, bizarre mutilation, etc.)
- The offender took steps to conceal his crime.

Inter-rater reliability was significant on only two of the subjective elements: (1) the victim was chosen randomly or opportunistically, and (2) the victim was low risk, i.e., not likely to be missed or reported as missing. Details of the subjective element inter-rater reliability are included in Table 1.2.

Table 1.2 The Victim Was Preselected/Presurveilled

	Reviewer A	Reviewer B	Reviewer C	Reviewer D
Reviewer A	1.00	.057	.135	.379*
Reviewer B	.057	1.00	.362*	.317*
Reviewer C	.135	.362*	1.00	.153
Reviewer D	.379*	.317*	.153	1.00

The victim was chosen randomly or opportunistically.

	Reviewer A	Reviewer B	Reviewer C	Reviewer D
Reviewer A	1.00	.512*	.499*	.665*
Reviewer B	.512*	1.00	.394*	.546*
Reviewer C	.499*	.394*	1.00	.466*
Reviewer D	.665*	.546*	.466*	1.00

The victim was low risk, i.e., not likely to be immediately missed or reported missing.

	Reviewer A	Reviewer B	Reviewer C	Reviewer D
Reviewer A	1.00	.380*	.684*	.438*
Reviewer B	.380*	1.00	.370*	.424*
Reviewer C	.684*	.370*	1.00	.320*
Reviewer D	.438*	.424*	.320*	1.00

The victim was high risk, i.e., likely to be immediately missed or reported as missing.

	Reviewer A	Reviewer B	Reviewer C	Reviewer D
Reviewer A	1.00	−.167	.562*	.339*
Reviewer B	−.167	1.00	−.136	.241**
Reviewer C	.562*	−.136	1.00	.167
Reviewer D	.339*	.241**	.167	1.00

The level of force used during the abduction was beyond that necessary to facilitate captivity.

Continued...

Table 1.2 The Victim Was Preselected/Presurveilled—continued

	Reviewer A	Reviewer B	Reviewer C	Reviewer D
Reviewer A	1.00	.518	−.058	.143
Reviewer B	.518*	1.00	.025	.089
Reviewer C	−.058	.025	1.00	.167
Reviewer D	.143	.089	.167	1.00

The offender partook in ritualistic behaviors against the victim (taking souvenirs, cannibalistic behaviors, bizarre mutilations).

	Reviewer A	Reviewer B	Reviewer C	Reviewer D
Reviewer A	1.00	.134	−.014	.320*
Reviewer B	.134	1.00	.094	−.013
Reviewer C	−.014	.094	1.00	−.028
Reviewer D	.320*	−.013	−.028	1.00

The offender took steps to conceal his crime.

	Reviewer A	Reviewer B	Reviewer C	Reviewer D
Reviewer A	1.00	−.116	.005	−.296*
Reviewer B	−.116	1.00	.196	.184
Reviewer C	.005	.196	1.00	.166
Reviewer D	−.296*	.184	.166	1.00

*Correlation is significant at the 0.01 level (2-tailed).
**Correlation is significant at the 0.05 level (2-tailed).

The two subjective elements for which there was significant reviewer agreement were added to 39 additional, objective elements (such as whether the victim was over 18 years of age, whether the abduction was perpetrated by more than one offender, etc.) for the final aspect of the analysis.

As with the subjective elements, these objective elements were rated as "true," "false," or "information not available." Each subjective and objective element was placed in one of four subcategories:

- *Victimology and Offender Characteristics:* Demographic data pertaining to the victim(s) and offender(s).
- *Abduction Site:* General information regarding the site of the kidnapping.

- *Modus Operandi:* The behaviors exhibited by the offender to commit the offense, as well as any behaviors exhibited by the offender that go beyond those necessary to commit the offense.
- *Outcome:* The result of the kidnapping, including any key elements that led to the offender's apprehension and conviction.

Each element was evaluated within the proposed kidnapping subtypes to identify those that were significant to the subtype. A specific overview of the elements by subcategory is included in Table 1.3.

Table 1.3 Kidnapping Characteristics

Victimology & Offender Characteristics	1. The victim was under 18 years of age.
	2. The victim and the offender were strangers to one another.
	3. The victim and the offender had a relationship prior to the abduction.
	4. The offender and the victim were of different genders.
	5. The offender and the victim are of different ethnicities.
	6. The victim was low risk, i.e., not likely to be immediately missed or reported as missing.
	7. The offender was unemployed at the time of the abduction.
	8. The offender was employed at the time of the abduction.
Abduction Site	1. The abduction occurred in a public place.
	2. The victim was abducted from a private location (such as home, school, workplace).
Modus Operandi	1. The abduction was perpetrated by more than one offender.
	2. The victim was chosen randomly or opportunistically.
	3. Physical force was used to abduct the victim.
	4. The victim was abducted following verbal threats of harm to himself or herself and/or others.
	5. The victim's abduction was the result of persuasion or deception.
	6. The offender used a firearm to facilitate the abduction.
	7. The offender used a knife to facilitate the abduction.
	8. The offender used a weapon, other than a knife or a firearm, or did not use a weapon, to facilitate the abduction.
	9. The offender sexually assaulted the victim during the abduction.
	10. The offender physically assaulted the victim during the abduction in a manner that did result in death.
	11. The offender physically assaulted the victim during the abduction in a manner that did not result in death.
	12. The offender did not assault or physically harm the victim during the abduction.

Continued...

Table 1.3 Kidnapping Characteristics—continued

	13. The offender transported the victim during the abduction.
	14. The offender did not transport the victim during the abduction.
	15. The offender exhibited obvious psychotic symptoms (delusions, hallucinations, etc.).
	16. The offender held the victim captive for greater than 24 hours.
	17. The offender held the victim captive for less than 24 hours.
	18. The kidnapping occurred in the morning (midnight–8 a.m.).
	19. The kidnapping occurred during the day (8 a.m.–4 p.m.).
	20. The kidnapping occurred in the evening/at night (4 p.m.–midnight).
	21. More than one victim was abducted.
Outcome	1. The abduction was witnessed.
	2. The victim was released by the offender.
	3. The victim escaped.
	4. The victim was released following law enforcement intervention.
	5. The victim was not found.
	6. The victim was found dead.
	7. The victim was discovered in a public place.
	8. The victim was discovered in a private place (a home, school or workplace).
	9. Witness testimony contributed to the offender's apprehension/conviction.
	10. Physical evidence contributed to the offender's apprehension/conviction.
	11. Accomplice statements contributed to the offender's apprehension/conviction.
	12. Victim testimony contributed to the abductor's apprehension/conviction.

The results of the three-part analysis are detailed in the chapters that follow. Each chapter explores the elements associated with a kidnapping subtype and provides examples of the cases that embody it. Based on the analysis, each chapter also offers a section titled "Implications for Prevention and Investigation," designed to offer law enforcement and security professionals suggestions for the practical application of the presented material.

Additionally, the second chapter offers a brief overview of the history of United States kidnapping laws, offering insight into the frequently ambiguous evolution of this crime.

CONCLUSION

As author and investigator Patricia Cornwell has eloquently observed, "there are no facile explanations or infallible sequences of cause and effort. But the compass of human nature can point a certain way...."

Kidnapping: An Investigator's Guide to Profiling navigates the motivations, behaviors, and characteristics of various kidnapper subtypes to help law enforcement, victims, and all those who are affected by this heinous crime.

REFERENCES

Alix, Ernest Kahlar. (1978). *Ransom Kidnapping in America, 1874–1974.* Carbondale, IL: Southern Illinois University Press.

Bartol, C. R., and Bartol, A. M. (1999). *History of Forensic Psychology.* New York: John Wiley.

Cornwell, Patricia. (2002). *Portrait of a Killer: Jack the Ripper, Case Closed.* New York: Penguin Putman, Inc.

Depue, Roger L. (2005). *Between Good and Evil: A Master Profiler's Hunt for Society's Most Violent Predators.* New York: Time Warner Book Group.

Douglas, John, and Olshaker, Mark. (1995). *Mind Hunter: Inside the FBI's Elite Serial Crime Unit.* New York: Pocket Books.

Turvey, Brent. (1999). *Criminal Profiling: An Introduction to Behavioral Evidence Analysis.* California: Academic Press.

The History of U.S. Kidnapping Laws

In February 1932, aviator Charles Lindbergh was an icon of hope during the American economic depression. Five years earlier, he enthralled millions by becoming the first man to successfully fly solo across the Atlantic. His courage and fortitude in the face of enormous difficulty served as a metaphor to which many would cling, rendering him "the last hero" of his generation.

The following month, he would embody the ubiquitous despair of the time.

On the night of March 1, 1932, Charles and his wife Anne Morrow Lindbergh relaxed in their newly constructed New Jersey mansion. They built their home for privacy from a world that was aggressively curious about their lives, and about their 20-month-old son Charles Augustus Lindbergh, Jr. "Little Lindy," as the press dubbed the toddler, was suffering from a cold. His nursemaid placed him in his crib at 8:00 p.m.

Two hours later, the crib was empty.

Muddy footprints were found on the floor of the child's room, and a homemade ladder with a broken rung was found a short distance from the house. Beside the nursery window from which Little Lindy was presumably taken, Lindbergh found a ransom note demanding $50,000.

Two days later, a liaison for Lindbergh delivered the ransom to a "man with a triangle face" who arranged a meeting in a cemetery. Lindbergh and several law enforcement agents listened from nearby as the ransom was exchanged for a note that indicated the baby was on a boat off Cape Cod. Intense searches of the area failed to find a boat or the baby.

Two months after the kidnapping, truck driver William Allen pulled to the side of a New Jersey road four miles from the Lindbergh home. He stumbled across a mound of dirt and leaves which barely concealed the remains of a small body.

A coroner identified the body as that of Charles A. Lindbergh, Jr., who died from "external violence" to the head. The death most likely occurred shortly after the kidnapping.

THE FEDERAL KIDNAPPING ACT

The Lindbergh kidnapping was the most publicized of many abductions that occurred in the 1930s. "Child snatching" was commonly utilized by criminals to supply large employers with cheap labor. Kidnapping was also a tool of revenge wielded by the many gangsters who thrived during this era.

In most states, kidnapping remained a misdemanor, and a bill to make it a federal crime was stalled in Congress. Law enforcement was hamstrung by savvy criminals who took their victims across state lines, knowing that idosyncratic and sometimes conflicting state laws rendered a nationwide manhunt difficult.

With the death of the son of America's hero, Congress quickly enacted the Federal Kidnapping Act of 1932, known as the "Lindbergh Act." The act sought to offer a universal definition of kidnapping, which it defined as

> any person who shall have been unlawfully seized, confined, inveigled, decoyed, kidnapped, abducted, or carried away by any means whatsoever and held for ransom or reward, except, in the case of a minor, by a parent thereof.

Within 2 years, legislators and the judiciary realized that kidnapping refused to conform to a static definition. Over the successive decades, lawmakers, the courts, and even outraged citizens would try to legislate a crime that continually enveloped new victims, new motivations, and new modus operandi.

In 1934, the phrase "and held for ransom or reward" was changed to read "and held for ransom or reward or otherwise" to reflect nonmonetary motivations.

During that same year, Congress enacted a provision that allowed authorities to presume that interstate or foreign transportation occurred if a kidnapping victim was not released within 7 days. The presumption allowed federal authorities to investigate cases in which proof of interstate commerce was absent. In 1956, the period without release was reduced from 7 days to 24 hours. The provision was again modified as part of The National Child Search Assistance Act of 1990. This last amendment prohibits law enforcement agencies from having any waiting period before accepting a missing child report and allows immediate federal involvement in such cases.

Federal jurisdiction was further expanded in 1988 to apply to kidnappings in which a victim is murdered prior to interstate travel as long as the victim was alive when transportation began.

Abduction of a minor child by a parent, usually associated with child custody disputes, is specifically exempted under the Federal Kidnapping Act. In 1993, the International Parental Kidnapping Crime Act made it a federal crime to remove a child from the United States with the intent to obstruct the lawful exercise of parental rights. In 1994, Congress limited the act's definition of "parent" to one who has legal custody.

With each new provision and amendment, lawmakers attempted to keep pace with kidnapping's evolving nature. The courts strove to do likewise with an evermore diverse population of kidnappers.

KIDNAPPING CASE LAW

Two years after the "or otherwise" provision was added to the "for ransom or reward" clause of the Federal Kidnapping Act, convicted kidnappers argued that their reasons for taking another did not match lawmaker intentions. The definition of "or otherwise" and the distinction between kidnapping and other crimes such as rape and murder have been two of the issues consistently raised by the convicted to overturn their convictions.

The Definition of "Or Otherwise"

When the Federal Kidnapping Act was first enacted, kidnapping was defined as an unlawful abduction committed for the purpose of extracting a ransom or reward. Two years later, the act was amended to prohibit abductions committed for "ransom or reward or otherwise."

In 1936, the Supreme Court agreed to hear the first case that tested the "or otherwise" provision.

Gooch v. United States

Gooch was approached in Paris, Texas, by two law enforcement officers who sought to arrest him. Gooch resisted, disarmed the officers, and transported them from Texas to Oklahoma, where he released them. Gooch was later convicted of kidnapping the officers, and sentenced to hang.

In his Supreme Court appeal, Gooch claimed that he should not have been convicted of kidnapping because his actions were designed to avoid arrest and did not fall under the "ransom or reward or otherwise" clause of the Federal Kidnapping Act.

The Court disagreed, asserting that "holding an officer to prevent the captor's arrest is something done with the expectation of benefit to the transgressor." The Court likened the benefit Gooch sought to derive from his actions to that sought by the kidnapper for ransom. The Court upheld Gooch's conviction.

The Court likewise upheld the convictions of kidnappers whose motivations ranged from bizarre to pathetic, as illustrated in *United States v. Parker et al.* and *United States v. Walker*, respectively.

United States v. Parker et al.

Detective Ellis H. Parker conspired with several accomplices to kidnap a man named Paul H. Wendel. The men sought to bring Wendel from his home in New York City to New Jersey. Once there, they would coerce him to confess to the kidnapping and murder of Charles Lindbergh, Jr.

At the time, the New Jersey Court of Pardons was reviewing an appeal application by Bruno Richard Hauptmann, the man convicted for the murder of the Lindbergh child.

Parker and his colleagues did not seek Wendel's "confession" for the purpose of freeing Hauptmann. They had no evidence that Wendel was involved in the Lindbergh crime. Rather, Parker conspired to kidnap Wendel, the Court found, to obtain a false confession that would "enhance the reputation of Ellis H. Parker as a successful and competent detective" whose services would be "in great demand."

Such a motive, Parker argued after his conviction, was not envisioned by the "ransom or reward or otherwise" clause of the Federal Kidnapping Act.

As in Gooch, the Court disagreed: "We think that Congress by the phrase 'or otherwise' intended to include any object of a kidnapping which the perpetrator might consider of sufficient benefit to himself to induce him to undertake it."

As demonstrated in *United States v. Walker*, a kidnapper's objective can also include a pathetic attempt at love.

United States v. Walker

On July 19, 1996, John Furfay Walker and Jolene Dilley began a relationship. Days later, on July 25, the two were together at the Regal Inn in Salt Lake City. Jolene told Walker that she was going to leave to see her children. Walker refused to let her go and pinned her to the bed. With his free hand, Walker smashed a beer bottle on the end of a table and threatened to kill himself if Jolene attempted to leave. He then took the broken bottle and scratched a "J" on his wrist, saying, "See, this proves I love you."

"What you have to do in order for me not to kill you," Walker then informed Jolene, "is go with me in your car for 12 hours out and 12 hours back, a total of 24 hours, to give me time to talk you into staying with me."

Jolene consumed two beers and two Xanax tablets and accompanied Walker to Idaho.

During their travels, Walker pulled over at several rest stops, threatening Jolene each time. As they continued driving, Walker told Jolene that she was "the worst kind of girl there could be."

"You're not going to take me back, are you?" Jolene finally demanded.

"No, and not only that, but I'm going to tear your f____g heart out like you did to mine," Walker replied.

Jolene attempted to grab the steering wheel and car keys. Walker punched her in the face. Jolene kicked the gear shift, undid her seat belt, jumped from the car, and successfully stopped an oncoming motorist.

Walker sped away. He was later apprehended and convicted of kidnapping.

On appeal, Walker claimed that there was no way he could have known his conduct violated the "or otherwise" purpose of the kidnapping statute.

As in Gooch and Parker, the Court disagreed and Walker's conviction was upheld.

KIDNAPPING AS A DISTINCT CRIME

The act of abducting another against his or her will is a common element in crimes ranging from robbery to rape to murder. In several decisions, the Court has sought to distinguish kidnapping from other criminal acts.

United States v. Wolford

On June 5, 1969, Lawrence B. Wolford and two accomplices approached Rufus Wilson, Jr. and a coworker as the two men returned to their delivery truck. One of the Wolford's accomplices put what Rufus believed to be a gun to his back. The accomplice told Rufus and his coworker they were going "for a little ride." The second accomplice took the truck, while Wolford and the first accomplice forced Rufus and his coworker into the back seat of a car, holding them at gunpoint. Wolford drove with his victims for less than an hour before releasing them. During that time, the accomplice stole the truck's cargo, which consisted of $13,000 worth of alcoholic beverages.

Wolford and his accomplices were convicted of kidnapping. On appeal, they claimed that they were wrongfully charged: Their abduction of Rufus, they argued, was a part of their robbery and not a separate crime.

Wolford's claim had been successful in other cases, such as in *Prince v. United States* and *California v. Daniels*. In these cases, the Courts found that the charge of kidnapping was included in the defendants' indictments as a result of "prosecutorial zeal," rather than because the distinct crime of kidnapping had occurred.

The Court ruled that the same overzealness was not evident in Wolford's conviction:

> The forcible detention of Wilson both in time and place went far beyond the momentary detention necessarily associated with every robbery, and his removal to Rock Creek Park at gunpoint substantially increased the risk of harm over and above that incident to the offense of armed robbery.

These two elements—confining or transporting a victim when unnecessary to commit a separate crime and doing so in a manner that posed additional risk to the victim—became standards that federal and many state courts adopted to determine if the crime of kidnapping had occurred.

These standards, the Court determined, were not met in the *Government of the Virgin Islands v. Berry*.

Government of the Virgin Islands v. Berry

On March 8, 1978, Luis Raul Morales was walking home when Warren Berry and an accomplice approached and offered him nearly $400 worth of marijuana. Berry told Luis that he could sell the marijuana and pay Berry the following day. Luis sold the marijuana but spent the money elsewhere. When Berry approached him the following day, Luis reported that he did not have the money, but that he could get money from his brother. Luis entered a car with Berry and the accomplice, and the three men drove to a bar where Luis's brother worked. Luis's brother could give Luis only $100. Luis took the money and turned it over to Berry, stating that he'd give Berry the remaining money the following day. Luis reentered the car, asking Berry to take him to a second bar.

Instead of doing so, Berry and his accomplice took Luis to a beach, where the three men exited the car. Berry told Luis to take off his clothes and go for a swim. As Luis started to do so, Berry ordered his accomplice to take a shotgun from the car. Luis went swimming until Berry told him to return. Berry informed Luis that he wanted his money by 10:00 a.m. the following morning. If he did not receive the money, Berry said, he would kill Luis. Berry and his accomplice took Luis's clothing, leaving him to walk naked from the beach. Sometime later, Luis contacted the police, and Berry and the accomplice were subsequently charged and convicted of kidnapping and robbery.

As in *Wolford*, Berry claimed that there was insufficient evidence to support a kidnapping charge against him. Unlike in *Wolford*, the Court agreed, finding that "confinement occurred during the commission of those other offenses [robbery and extortion]" and that the degree of confinement was "no greater than that which is inherent in the commission of those crimes."

In defining the elements that constitute the crime of kidnapping, the Court adopted the two standards articulated in *Wolford*, i.e., whether the detention or asportation was inherent to a separate offense and whether the asportation or detention created a significant danger to the victim independent of that posted by the separate offense.

The Court also added the duration of the detention or asportation as an additional factor to be considered.

These standards have served as the basis for federal—and many state—kidnapping convictions. Though effective in ensuring that incarcerated kidnappers remain so, the Court's guidelines did little to assist in preventing kidnappings or in apprehending kidnappers.

Following a rash of horrific abductions of children, members of the public took matters into their own hands and successfully advocated for legal reforms designed to facilitate the prevention of kidnappings, when possible, and apprehension of kidnappers, when not.

THE NATIONAL CENTER FOR MISSING AND EXPLOITED CHILDREN

On July 27, 1981, 6-year-old Adam Walsh and his mother, Reve, embarked on a day of errands, including a trip to the local Sears store to take advantage of a sale on lamps. Adam was left to watch several children play a new computer game during the approximately 10 minutes his mother spoke with a sales associate in the nearby lighting department.

When Adam's mother completed her transaction, she went to retrieve her son. Adam was gone.

Police applied standard investigative techniques to what was at the time an unusual crime. Alerts and bulletins were disseminated only on a local level. Friends and relatives were the primary suspects, to the exclusion of other potential offenders. Resources were limited to those of the city's police department, as national criminal data banks tracked stolen cars but not missing persons.

Less than a month following his disappearance, Adam's severed head was found by two fishermen in a canal 100 miles north of his hometown. Adam's body has never been found.

For more than 2 years after Adam's murder, his parents—Reve and John Walsh—pioneered an unprecedented public and government lobbying effort to find their son's kidnapper. John Walsh became host of *America's Most Wanted*, a highly effective television show that seeks the public's assistance in locating missing children and apprehending criminals.

The Walshes, along with U.S. Congressional staffer Jay Howell, child advocate John Rabun, and others, also founded the National Center for Missing and Exploited Children (NCMEC) in 1984.

NCMEC is a private organization that works in partnership with the government to support the prevention of abducted, endangered, and sexually exploited children. The Center's services include operating a CyberTipline that the public may use to report Internet-related child sexual exploitation; providing technical assistance to individuals and law enforcement agencies in the prevention, investigation, prosecution, and treatment of cases involving missing and exploited children; and serving as an informational clearinghouse.

NCMEC also distributes missing children's photographs to a network of photo partners. Through this effort, one in every six of the children featured is recovered.

Among its other services, the NCMEC also provides lawmakers with information regarding effective abduction prevention legislation. Resulting legislative initiatives include the Jacob Wetterling Act, Megan's Law, and the Amber Alert system.

THE JACOB WETTERLING ACT AND MEGAN'S LAW

In 1989, 11-year-old Jacob Wetterling, along with his 10-year-old brother Trevor and 11-year-old friend Aaron, were approached by a masked man as they rode their bicycles home from a local Minnesota convenience store. The man stepped out of a driveway with a gun, ordered the children to throw their bikes into a ditch, and made them lie face down on the ground. After asking the boys their ages, the masked man told Jacob's brother and friend to run into the woods and not look back or he would shoot them. The masked man took Jacob. He has never been apprehended. Jacob has never been found.

Five years after Jacob's disapparence, Congress passed an act bearing his name. The Jacob Wetterling Crimes Against Children and Sexually Violent Offender Registration Program stated that "the designated state law enforcement agency and any local law enforcement agency authorized by the state agency may release relevant information that is necessary to protect the public concerning a specific person."

Later in 1996, the tragic death of 7-year-old Megan Nicole Kanka would cause lawmakers to amend the Jacob Wetterling Act to require states to release such information.

On July 29, 1994, Megan was lured to the home of her New Jersey neighbor. She was promised a puppy. Instead, she was brutally raped, strangled, and suffocated by a two-time convicted sex offender named Jesse Timmendequas. In 1981, Timmendequas was convicted of an attack on a 5-year-old child and an attempted sexual assault on a 7-year-old. Timmendequas lived across the street from Megan's home in a house he shared with two other paroled sex offenders.

Within 3 months of Megan's death, New Jersey passed the first version of what has become known as Megan's Law. Within 2 years, the federal government amended the Jacob Wetterling Act to read that state and local law enforcment "shall" rather than "may" release relevant information concerning convicted sex offenders to protect the public. All 50 states subsequently adopted some version of a sex offender registry, whereby members of the public can learn of a paroled sex offender's current residence, as well as demographic characteristics and offense history.

THE AMBER ALERT SYSTEM

On January 14, 1996, 9-year-old Amber Hagerman was riding her bike on a Saturday afternoon when a witness watched a man in a black pickup grab her by the arm and take the screaming child into his truck. Less than a week later, Amber's body was found in a nearby creek bed, her throat cut.

In response to Amber's murder, outraged community members contacted Dallas radio stations, suggesting that stations broadcast "alerts" during child abductions. The alerts could disseminate key information to community members who would, in turn, be on the lookout for the abducted child and his or her kidnapper. The goal was to potentially avert tragedies such as the one that befell Amber.

The Dallas/Fort Worth Association of Radio Managers coordinated with law enforcement to establish the first America's Missing: Broadcasting Emergency Response (AMBER) alert system.

In 2003, the federal government passed a nationwide Amber Alert law. Amber Alert interventions include the interruption of regular radio and television programming to provide information on an abducted child and his or her kidnapper, including the make and model of the kidnapper's vehicle. Several states also post this data on electric highway signs and disseminate alerts through wireless communication devices, such as mobile phones.

Law enforcement will issue Amber Alerts for abducted children under age 17 who are deemed to be in imminent danger of serious bodily injury or harm. As of 2006, the Amber Alert system has been responsible for the recovery of 233 children.

The passage of kidnapping laws, the Court's precedents in defining the laws; the creation of the National Center for Missing and Exploited Children; and initiatives such as the Jacob Wetterling Act, Megan's Law, and the Amber Alert system have greatly contributed to the apprehension and conviction of kidnappers.

The development of a new typology that profiles the varied elements of this diverse crime can further aid efforts to effectively deal with kidnappings and their perpetrators.

Milestones in Federal Kidnapping Legislation

1932: Federal Kidnapping Act—also known as the "Lindbergh Act" is passed by Congress.

1934: Act amended to include kidnappings executed for reasons other than ransom or reward. Allowed the presumption that a kidnapping crossed state lines if the victim was not released within 7 days.

1956: Waiting period for presumption of kidnapping reduced from 7 days to 24 hours.

1972: Federal jurisdiction expanded to include kidnappings that occur within U.S. maritime or aircraft jurisdiction, or occur against individuals who are internationally protected.

1981: The National Center for Missing and Exploited Children established.

1984: Federal jurisdiction expanded to DEA agents and employees kidnapped during the performance of their work.

Continued...

Milestones in Federal Kidnapping Legislation—continued

1994: Definition of "parent" in the Federal Kidnapping Act redefined to exclude individuals whose parental rights have been legally severed.

1994: The Jacob Wetterling Act passed.

1996: Federal Megan's Law passed.

1998: Definition of federal kidnapping expanded to include the transportion of a murdered victim across state lines, if the victim was alive when the transportation commenced.

2003: National Ambert Alert system law passed.

2006: Adam Walsh Child Protection Act passed. Empowers the National Center for Missing and Exploited Children and the United States Marshall Services to work in tandem to apprehend sex offenders who do not comply with registry laws.

The Federal Kidnapping Act

(a) Whoever unlawfully seizes, confines, inveigles, decoys, kidnaps, abducts, or carries away and holds for ransom or reward or otherwise any person, except in the case of a minor by the parent thereof, when —

(1) the person is willfully transported in interstate or foreign commerce, regardless of whether the person was alive when transported across a State boundary or if the person was alive when the transportation began;

(2) any such act against the person is done within the special maritime and territorial jurisdiction of the United States;

(3) any such act against the person is done within the special aircraft jurisdiction of the United States as defined in section 46501 of title 49;

(4) the person is a foreign official, an internationally protected person, or an official guest as those terms are defined in section 1116(b) of this title; or

(5) the person is among those officers and employees described in section 1114 of this title and any such act against the person is done while the person is engaged in, or on account of, the performance of official duties, shall be punished by imprisonment for any term of years or for life and, if the death of any person results, shall be punished by death or life imprisonment.

(b) With respect to subsection (a)(1), above, the failure to release the victim within twenty-four hours after he shall have been unlawfully seized, confined, inveigled, decoyed, kidnapped, abducted, or carried away shall create a rebuttable presumption that such person has been transported to interstate or foreign commerce. Notwithstanding the preceding sentence, the fact that the presumption under this section has not yet taken effect does not preclude a Federal investigation of a possible violation of this section before the 24-hour period has ended.

(c) If two or more persons conspire to violate this section and one or more of such persons do any overt act to effect the object of the conspiracy, each shall be punished by imprisonment for any term of years or for life.

(d) Whoever attempts to violate subsection (a) shall be punished by imprisonment for not more than twenty years.

(e) If the victim of an offense under subsection (a) is an internationally protected person outside the United States, the United States may exercise jurisdiction over the offense if (1) the victim is a representative, officer, employee, or agent of the United States, (2) an offender is a national of the United States, or (3) an offender is afterwards found in the United States. As used in this subsection, the United States includes all areas under the jurisdiction of the United States including any of the places within the provisions of sections 5 and 7 of this title and section 46501(2) of title 49. For purposes of this subsection, the term "national of the United States" has the meaning prescribed in section 101(a)(22) of the Immigration and Nationality Act (8 U.S.C. 1101(a)(22)).

(f) In the course of enforcement of subsection (a)(4) and any other sections prohibiting a conspiracy or attempt to violate subsection (a)(4), the Attorney General may request assistance from any Federal, State, or local agency, including the Army, Navy, and Air Force, any statute, rule, or regulation to the contrary notwithstanding.

(g) Special Rule for Certain Offenses Involving Children. —

    (1) To whom applicable. — If —

        (A) the victim of an offense under this section has not attained the age of eighteen years; and

        (B) the offender —

            (i) has attained such age; and

            (ii) is not —

                (I) a parent;

                (II) a grandparent;

                (III) a brother;

Continued...

(IV) a sister;

(V) an aunt;

(VI) an uncle; or

(VII) an individual having legal custody of the victim; the sentence under this section for such offense shall be subject to paragraph (2) of this subsection.

(2) Guidelines. — The United States Sentencing Commission is directed to amend the existing guidelines for the offense of "kidnapping, abduction, or unlawful restraint," by including the following additional specific offense characteristics: If the victim was intentionally maltreated (i.e., denied either food or medical care) to a life-threatening degree, increase by 4 levels; if the victim was sexually exploited (i.e., abused, used involuntarily for pornographic purposes) increase by 3 levels; if the victim was placed in the care or custody of another person who does not have a legal right to such care or custody of the child either in exchange for money or other consideration, increase by 3 levels; if the defendant allowed the child to be subjected to any of the conduct specified in this section by another person, then increase by 2 levels.

(h) As used in this section, the term "parent" does not include a person whose parental rights with respect to the victim of an offense under this section have been terminated by a final court order.

REFERENCES

Gooch v. United States, 297 U.S. 124.

Government of the Virgin Islands v. Berry, 604 F.2d 221.

Jacob Wetterling Crimes Against Children and Sexually Violent Offender Registration Program, 42 U.S.C. 14071.

Prosecutorial Remedies and Other Tools to End the Exploitation of Children Today Act of 2003, Title III, Section 301.

United States v. Parker et al., 103 F.2d 857.

United States v. Walker, 137 F.3d 1217.

United States v. Wolford, 144 U.S. App. D.C. 1.

Ross, Walter S. (1964). *The Last Hero: Charles A. Lindbergh*. New York: Harper & Row.

Chapter | three

Domestic Kidnapping

CHAPTER CONTENTS

WHAT DEFINES THE DOMESTIC KIDNAPPING?

The domestic kidnapping involves an abduction by or on behalf of an individual with whom the victim has or had a familial or romantic relationship. The domestic kidnapper may abduct a former spouse or partner and/or the children of the former spouse or partner. He or she is typically motivated by a need to control or to punish.

The characteristics of the domestic kidnapping are detailed in Table 3.1. The domestic kidnapping is illustrated by the cases of Fazal Raheman, Cleother Tidwell, and Riddick Lamont Bowe.

Table 3.1 Elements of the Domestic Kidnapping

Victimology & Offender Characteristics	1. The victim was under 18 years of age.	33%
	2. The victim and the offender were strangers to one another.	0%
	3. The victim and the offender had a relationship prior to the abduction.	100%
	4. The offender and the victim were of different genders.	80%
	5. The offender and the victim are of different ethnicities.	NA*
	6. The victim was low risk, i.e., not likely to be immediately missed or reported as missing.	0%
	7. The offender was unemployed at the time of the abduction.	NA*
	8. The offender was employed at the time of the abduction.	NA*
Abduction Site	1. The abduction occurred in a public place.	27%
	2. The victim was abducted from a private location (such as home, school, workplace).	73%
Modus Operandi	1. The abduction was perpetrated by more than one offender.	27%
	2. The victim was chosen randomly or opportunistically.	0%
	3. Physical force was used to abduct the victim.	60%
	4. The victim was abducted following verbal threats of harm to himself or herself and/or others.	40%
	5. The victim's abduction was the result of persuasion or deception.	33%
	6. The offender used a firearm to facilitate the abduction.	60%
	7. The offender used a knife to facilitate the abduction.	20%
	8. The offender used a weapon, other than a knife or a firearm, or did not use a weapon, to facilitate the abduction.	27%
	9. The offender sexually assaulted the victim during the abduction.	33%
	10. The offender physically assaulted the victim during the abduction in a manner that did result in death.	33%
	11. The offender physically assaulted the victim during the abduction in a manner that did not result in death.	53%
	12. The offender did not assault or physically harm the victim during the abduction (excludes sexual assault).	13%
	13. The offender transported the victim during the abduction.	87%
	14. The offender did not transport the victim during the abduction.	13%
	15. The offender exhibited obvious psychotic symptoms (delusions, hallucinations, etc.).	7%

Continued...

Table 3.1 Elements of the Domestic Kidnapping—continued

	16. The offender held the victim captive for greater than 24 hours.	53%
	17. The offender held the victim captive for less than 24 hours.	40%
	18. The kidnapping occurred in the morning (midnight–8 a.m.).	33%
	19. The kidnapping occurred during the day (8 a.m.–4 p.m.).	13%
	20. The kidnapping occurred in the evening/at night (4 p.m.–midnight).	27%
	21. More than one victim was abducted.	20%
Outcome	1. The abduction was witnessed.	53%
	2. The victim was released by the offender.	7%
	3. The victim escaped.	20%
	4. The victim was released following law enforcement intervention.	40%
	5. The victim was not found.	0%
	6. The victim was found dead.	33%
	7. The victim was discovered in a public place.	33%
	8. The victim was discovered in a private place (a home, school, or workplace).	67%
	9. Witness testimony contributed to the offender's apprehension/ conviction (not limited to event witnesses).	87%
	10. Physical evidence contributed to the offender's apprehension/ conviction.	53%
	11. Accomplice statements contributed to the offender's apprehension/conviction.	13%
	12. Victim testimony contributed to the abductor's apprehension/ conviction.	67%

*NA-Insufficient data to render determination.

Fazal Raheman

In May 1990, the victim, Saihba, married Fazal Raheman in India before returning to Massachusetts where Raheman was employed. In 1992, the two became permanent residents of the United States. By 1996, they had given birth to an American-born girl and Indian-born boy. Their son became a naturalized American citizen within 2 years of his birth.

In 1997, Raheman threatened to send the couple's children to India to live with his mother in response to the victim's growing independence. Instead, the victim took her children and moved to a Cambridge apartment.

The relocation did not deter Raheman from his continued threats to take away the couple's children. When the victim counter-threatened to contact law enforcement, Raheman warned that he would turn into "a lethal weapon." The victim did not back down and again told Raheman that she would report him to law enforcement.

Raheman changed tactics and verbally committed to refraining from taking the children to India, demanding that, in return, the victim not take him "in front of a judge." The victim continued negotiations with her estranged husband.

In the interim, Raheman continued his harassment covertly. Unbeknownst to the victim, Raheman had a miniature video camera installed in her bedroom. He hired a private investigator to follow and videotape her. He asked his nephew to move into her apartment building and spy on her. During the first 10 days of November 1997, Raheman recorded more than 100 hours of the victim's private telephone conversations.

Raheman's actions were not confined to watching. On November 14, 1997, Raheman traveled to India. There, he enrolled his daughter in a local school. He filed for custody of his children, claiming that his wife was involved in an adulterous relationship. When he returned to the states, Raheman bought three additional airline tickets to India—one for himself, two for his children. The tickets for his children were one way.

On November 26, 1997, Raheman arranged to take his children for an outing to a museum. He met the victim at her apartment and informed her that he would return that evening. Instead, he kept the children overnight. The next day, Raheman took his two children and departed for India.

Per a prearranged plan, one of Raheman's cousins telephoned the victim once Raheman was in flight with their children. Immediately thereafter, the victim telephoned police to report the kidnapping. The victim had not pursued legal separation from her husband, nor had she sought legal custody of her children. Two days after the abduction, the victim obtained an emergency custody order from the Massachusetts Probate Court. The Massachusetts police read the order to Raheman over the telephone. In response, Raheman obtained his own custody order from the Nagpur Family Court in India.

Between November 1997 and August 1998, the victim enlisted federal assistance in several failed attempts to obtain physical custody of her children. In late August, she expanded her request for assistance to the Indian authorities, traveling to India to plead her case. Raheman fought her efforts, filing criminal charges against her. Before Indian authorities could apprehend her, the victim returned to the United States. For the next 2 years, the victim continued her attempts to obtain custody of her children. Raheman continued to actively thwart her efforts. In September 1999, he obtained a second custody order from the Indian courts based on a provision in Islamic law that grants a father full custody if the mother lives a significant distance away.

On July 25, 2001, nearly 4 years after his abduction of their children, Raheman was indicted by a federal grand jury on one count of international parental kidnapping. When he returned to the United States later that year, Raheman was arrested. Shortly thereafter, he was convicted for the kidnapping and for his illegal wiretapping of the victim's telephone line. He was ordered to return the children to the victim's custody.

Cleother Tidwell

At approximately 2:00 a.m. on March 21, 1993, the victim, Linda, returned from work and found Cleother Tidwell in her Chicago apartment. The victim and Tidwell had a previous romantic relationship during which they lived together. The victim had terminated the relationship several months prior, and Tidwell had moved out. When the victim entered the apartment, Tidwell asked her to go for a walk with him. The victim refused. In response, Tidwell pulled out a gun and pointed it at her head, stating, "You can either stay here dead, or you can go with me alive."

Under duress, the victim accompanied Tidwell from the apartment. Tidwell walked her to his car and drove her to a room he rented. "This is how things are going to be now," he made her say aloud. He sexually assaulted her before falling asleep.

The following morning, Tidwell informed the victim that he was going out, and gave her the option of joining him or staying. She opted for the latter until Tidwell threatened to tie her up for the length of his outing. Tidwell took the victim and his gun and headed to Wisconsin to visit a cousin. When they reached a rest stop, Tidwell told the victim that he would shoot her, along with anyone else in the area, if she tried to escape.

The next time Tidwell asked the victim if she wanted to join him on a trip, she declined. Tidwell asked if she would try to leave if he left her untied. The victim said that she would, and Tidwell tied her hands behind her back and used twine bindings and a chain to anchor her to the bed. He covered her mouth with duct tape.

As soon as Tidwell left, the victim freed her hands and used a lighter to burn away the twine that bound her legs. She escaped the apartment and called law enforcement.

Riddick Lamont Bowe

In 1998, the victim, Judy, took her five children and separated from Riddick Lamont Bowe, her husband of 9 years. She relocated from Fort Washington, Maryland, to Cornelius, North Carolina.

At 10:30 p.m. on February 24, 1998, Bowe called the victim to attempt a reconciliation. During the 90-minute telephone conversation, Bowe ascertained the time that his children left for school each morning. Prior to concluding the call, Bowe informed the victim that he had "a surprise" for her.

Bowe borrowed a Lincoln Navigator from a former employee. He enlisted his brother to assist him in kidnapping the victim and their children. Shortly before 7:00 a.m. on the morning of February 25, 1998, Bowe traveled to where his three eldest children awaited their school bus. After ordering the children into the car, he drove to the victim's home, forced his way inside, and ordered her to ready herself and their two youngest children for the trip back to his Maryland home.

The victim had time to put on a skirt but not a shirt, and grabbed a heavy jacket to cover the pajama top she wore.

"I came prepared," Bowe informed the victim once en route. He showed her a knife, flashlight, duct tape, pepper spray, and handcuffs.

"If I had found you with another man," he informed her, "you'd both be dead."

He stabbed her left breast to emphasize his point.

Once across Virginia state lines, Bowe instructed his brother to pull into a restaurant parking lot. He commanded the victim to use her cell phone to call her lawyer and suspend her pending divorce proceedings. He also demanded that she drop criminal charges she had pressed against Bowe, a former professional boxer, following an earlier assault in Maryland. Bowe ordered the victim to telephone her brother and instruct him to move her furniture from her North Carolina home to Bowe's Maryland residence. Neither the victim's attorney nor her brother answered the phone.

Bowe allowed the victim to use the restaurant restroom. He stood guard outside the door and repeatedly poked his head inside to hurry her. Still in possession of the cell phone used to call her attorney and brother, the victim telephoned her cousin in North Carolina, reported the kidnapping and named the restaurant at which she was stopped. Bleeding from her chest wound, the victim also asked two elderly women who entered the restroom to call the police.

Shortly after Bowe forced the family to return to the car, Virginia police responded to an emergency call from a restaurant employee and stopped the Lincoln Navigator. Tidwell and his brother were arrested, and the victim and her children were released to medical personnel.

CHARACTERISTICS OF THE DOMESTIC KIDNAPPING

Victimology

Domestic kidnappers in the reviewed cases had, predictably, a prior relationship to their victims (100 percent). In 27 percent of the cases reviewed, the kidnapper had an accomplice who, like the kidnapper, believed that the victim(s) belonged with (and to) the abductor.

Domestic kidnappers were typically male and were more likely to abduct adults (67 percent) than they were to abduct children (33 percent). While the cases reviewed did not include kidnappings by females, it should be noted that female-perpetrated domestic kidnappings are rising as courts increasingly recognize paternity rights, and the placement of children with biological mothers is no longer automatic. The Office of Juvenile Justice and Delinquency Prevention's National Incidence Studies of Missing, Abducted, Runaway and Throwaway Children (NISMART-2) estimates that 25 percent of family abductions during 1999 were perpetrated by females.

Abduction Site

The prior relationship between victim and domestic kidnapper typically provided the perpetrator with access to the victim's home. As in the kidnappings perpetrated by Raheman, Tidwell, and Bowe, the majority of domestic kidnappers (73 percent) abducted their victims from private residences. The remaining 27 percent of abductions occurred in locations with unrestricted public access. These were locations commonly frequented by the victim and known to the abductor, or locations at which the victim agreed to meet the abductor, mistakenly believing that the presence of others would deter the kidnapper from violating her liberty.

Modus Operandi

As was true in the case of Raheman (who told his wife that he was taking his children to the museum when he was actually taking them out of the country), 33 percent of the domestic kidnappers used deception or persuasion to further their abductions. The majority of domestic kidnappers were more direct. As in the Tidwell and Bowe cases, domestic kidnappers tended to employ the use of force (60 percent) and/or verbal threats (40 percent) to accomplish their abductions. Tidwell, like 60 percent of domestic kidnappers, used a firearm to threaten his victim into submission. As in the kidnapping perpetrated by Bowe, 20 percent of domestic kidnappers used a knife to facilitate the abduction.

As was true of Raheman, Tidwell, and Bowe, the majority of domestic kidnappers (87 percent) transported their victims during the abduction and held them for greater than 24 hours (53 percent). Of the cases in which the time of abduction was known, they were most commonly perpetrated in the morning (33 percent between the hours of midnight and 8 a.m.), followed by between the hours of 4 p.m. and midnight (27 percent) and between the hours of 8 a.m. and 4 p.m. (13 percent).

During captivity, only 13 percent of victims escaped physical assault. Typically, a lack of physical violence was associated with abductions where the children of the domestic kidnapper were the sole victims. Thirty-three percent of victims were sexually assaulted during the abductions.

Outcome

Law enforcement was pivotal in recovering surviving victims of domestic kidnappings; law enforcement intervention was responsible for the recovery of victims in 40 percent of domestic kidnappings. Twenty percent of domestic kidnappings resolved when the victim escaped, while another 7 percent of victims were released by their abductors. In 33 percent of domestic kidnappings, the victim was murdered.

As in the case of Bowe, witness testimony was critical in the apprehension and conviction of domestic kidnappers in a majority of the cases reviewed (87 percent). Victim testimony contributed to perpetrator apprehension and conviction in 67 percent of cases, followed by physical evidence in 53 percent of cases. Twenty-seven percent of the domestic kidnappers engaged an accomplice; accomplice testimony resulted in the perpetrator's apprehension and conviction in 13 percent of cases.

IMPLICATIONS FOR PREVENTION AND INVESTIGATION

During their relationship, Cleother Tidwell tied his ex-girlfriend to their bed and held her at gunpoint to test her willingness to escape. During their marriage, Fazal Raheman tried to control and curtail his wife's growing independence; when she left, he believed himself entitled to know the content of her phone conversations and her actions within the supposed privacy of her own bedroom. Riddick Bowe physically assaulted his wife during their marriage and stabbed her after their estrangement. He reported that he would have killed her had he found her with another man.

The sexual, psychological, and physical aggression exhibited by Tidwell, Raheman, and Bowe are associated with the domestic violence that often characterizes the pre-abduction relationship. In most jurisdictions, domestic disturbance calls are the most prevalent, and most unpredictable, to which law enforcement responds. When aggression, a need for control, or jealousy continue beyond the relationship's end, domestic kidnapping is one possible outcome. Identifying and interrupting the cycle of violence during domestic disturbance calls is one way to potentially prevent an escalation of aggression.

The Dynamics of Domestic Violence

During the 1980s, community activists worked to ensure that domestic violence (DV) was recognized as a public health issue, rather than treated as a private concern. The success of their efforts—coupled with several highly publicized femicides—resulted in extensive research into the domestic violence dynamic and changes in the way law enforcement responds to DV calls.

Domestic violence is defined as the presence of one or more of the following between current or former spouses or cohabitants:

1. *Physical Violence*, such as punching, choking, kicking, hair pulling, stabbing, and shooting.
2. *Sexual Violence*, including rape, rape with objects, and physical attacks of the genital areas and breasts.
3. *Emotional Violence*, including threats to the victim's life or the lives of the victim's family, coworkers, or friends; forcing the victim to perform degrading acts; and controlling access to money.
4. *Psychological Violence*, such as the constant threat of physical violence through the destruction of the victim's property or harm to the victim's pet.

The presence of physical abuse in a relationship frequently co-occurs with sexual, emotional, and psychological abuse.

The typical course of violence within domestic relationships can be charted. In 1979, psychologist Leonore Walker coined the term *Cycle of Violence* to describe the three phases commonly associated with domestic violence. During the first phase—the Tension Building Phase—tension escalates and the DV perpetrator (commonly labeled the *batterer*) engages in increasingly hostile verbal interactions with his partner. Verbal hostilities escalate to physical violence during the second phase, known as the Acute Battering Phase. As the name implies, the Acute Battering Phase involves physical violence against the victim. The violence may be intentional (i.e., resulting from a desire to control, harm, or intimidate) or impulsive (resulting from a loss of control, frequently due to the disinhibition of alcohol or drug abuse). This is the phase in which the domestic disturbance call will most likely be received. In many states, current law requires law enforcement to make an arrest if there is reasonable cause to believe that a felony or misdemeanor family offense has been committed. Unfortunately, arrests and convictions are frequently followed by the perpetrator's return to the home. The return typically coincides with the third or Honeymoon Phase of the cycle. During this phase, the batterer expresses remorse for his assault and pledges never to harm his victim again.

The potential for law enforcement to interrupt the cycle of violence and to prevent further escalation, including the domestic kidnapping, is facilitated by knowledge of both victim and perpetrator dynamics.

The Effects of Victim Dynamics

As in the domestic kidnapping, the victim of domestic violence is typically female. (Although there is general agreement that DV against men is underreported due to the stigma of male victimization, women are still believed to be DV victims at significantly higher rates than men; the Bureau of Justice Statistics reports that women are five times more likely to be victimized by current and former partners than are men.)

Victims of DV report several common experiences. Typically, a woman's first response to violence at the hands of her intimate partner is shock and confusion. For some women, these emotions quickly dissipate: Violence is rightly attributed to the batterer. The batterer's behavior is truly an anomaly that does not repeat, or the woman separates from or terminates the relationship.

Women who remain in their relationships frequently attribute the cause of violence to factors other than the batterer. The drug or alcohol the batterer ingested prior to his attack is blamed. Social stressors, such as a loss of employment, may be implicated. Some DV victims will also assume blame for the violence perpetrated against them, rationalizing the attack as an appropriate response to reasonable behaviors, such as staying out later than expected, spending money on themselves or their children, or not preparing dinner at a certain time. It is not uncommon for the DV victim to defend her partner's violence to law enforcement responding to DV calls.

The DV victim's pattern of rationalization contributes to her endurance of additional violence. Her decision to remain with her battering partner is further reinforced by the typical batterer's lack of personal responsibility for his actions. Victim and batterer enter a generally unspoken agreement that his behavior is not his fault. The batterer who expresses remorse during the Honeymoon Phase of the Cycle of Violence is perceived as trustworthy: He is demonstrating great integrity by taking responsibility for a violent act that is rationalized as understandable in light of the circumstances that precipitated it.

When continued violence erodes the façade of the batterer's integrity, the pattern of rationalization is reactivated. As the relationship progresses, the victim's ability to separate is further compromised by the control behaviors commonly employed by the batterer, including isolating the victim from her friends and family, denying her access to funds, and threatening a lengthy and expensive child custody battle.

Controlling access to the victim's pre-relationship support system gives the batterer even greater control over the victim's self-perceptions; without the reality check of others, she will believe the rationalizations the couple have devised to justify the violence against her. When in the presence of family or friends, and in the presence of law enforcement, the batterer reinforces the belief that he cannot be to blame by offering a rational and charming contrast to the victim's decompensating emotional state. Members of the victim's support system insist she is fortunate to be with her abuser. She learns that if she terminates her relationship, she—and her children—will be without the emotional or financial support of others. Connecting the victim to community resources or responding to DV calls in concert with a victim advocate can support DV victims to recognize that they do, in fact, have alternatives to the abuse they are enduring.

DV victims who manage to overcome myriad challenges and separate from their batterers face significant post-relationship stressors. Frequently, they must find housing despite a lack of funds, and employment despite a lack of skills. For mothers, these challenges are compounded by the need to care for their children.

The victim of DV who separates from her abuser also faces the heightened threat posed by her ex-partner: The domestic batterer is more likely to escalate his abuse following an estrangement.

As illustrated in the post-relationship behaviors of Raheman, Tidwell, and Bowe, the escalation of violence can include the domestic kidnapping of the victim, the victim's children, or both.

Assessing the risk for an escalation of violence post-relationship is aided by an understanding of batterer dynamics.

The Effects of Batterer Dynamics

Perpetrators of domestic violence share various characteristics that distinguish them from individuals who are non-violent. As in the domestic kidnapping, the domestic violence perpetrator is typically male. He most likely witnessed marital violence as a child, and engaged in peer relationships that were characterized by violence and delinquency.

Consistent exposure to violence during childhood and adolescence has a desensitizing effect; interviews with domestic batterers reveal that they are favorably biased toward violence and view it as a legitimate means to attain their goals. The batterer's bias toward violence appears to inhibit his development of social and problem-solving skills that offer non-violent alternatives to goal attainment. Many batterers have difficulty being assertive and cannot clearly articulate their desires. Unable to tolerate the resulting frustration, the batterer blames his partner for not intuiting his needs; he resorts to the verbal aggression and criticism that frequently characterizes the Tension Building Phase of the Cycle of Violence. The DV perpetrator is also more likely to believe that others are acting in ways that are intentionally hostile. The wife who wants to pursue a career, for example, is perceived as demeaning the batterer's ability to support his family, rather than following her own interests. Any assertion of independence by the partner will be experienced as rejection by the batterer. It is common for feelings of rejection to heighten aggressive impulses; batterers act upon these impulses.

The frequency with which a batterer engages in violence is positively correlated with the severity of his actions: The more frequent his abuse behaviors, the greater the threat he poses to his victim(s).

Researchers Amy Holtzworth-Munroe and Gregory Stuart's characterization of three types of domestic batterers offers practical data for assessing the risk of escalated violence.

The first type, the family-only batterer, was found to be the most common of the three subtypes and represents an estimated 50 percent of domestic violence batterers. As the name implies, the family-only batterer is typically violent only within the family; any history of legal issues is usually limited to actions related to his domestic violence. The family-only batterer tends to report the highest level of marital satisfaction and the most liberal attitudes toward women. As with the severity of his violence, the frequency with which he is violent is limited. He is the least likely batterer subtype to be psychologically abusive and generally reports low levels of anger, low incidences of jealousy, and little experience of depression. Approximately half of violence perpetrated by family-only batterers occurs following ingestion of drugs or alcohol. These batterers exhibit little psychopathology and do not generally suffer from personality disorders. When a personality disorder is present, it is typically a dependent personality disorder.

The second type of batterer identified by the researchers is the dysphoric/borderline batterer. In contrast to the family-only batterer, the dysphoric/borderline batterer engages in moderate to severe abuse, which can include both sexual and psychological abuse. These individuals are volatile; while their violence is primarily confined to the family, they may also exhibit violence toward those outside the family. As a result, they may have a history of non-domestic violence-related criminal behavior. Psychologically, these individuals may exhibit borderline or schizoid personality traits. The former is characterized by a pervasive pattern of instability in interpersonal relationships and self-image that vacillates between the extremes of idealization and devaluation, marked impulsivity, frantic efforts to avoid real or imaged abandonment, recurrent suicidal behavior ("If you leave, I'll kill myself"), or intense anger and difficulty controlling anger ("If you leave me, I will kill you"). The schizoid personality traits include detachment from social relationships except for relationships with first-degree relatives; the batterer views his family as responsible for meeting his needs for social interaction. These batterers may also have problems with drugs or alcohol. The dysphoric/borderline batterer is thought to constitute 25 percent of all batterers.

The final 25 percent of batterers fall into a category that the researchers labeled the generally violent/antisocial batterers. Like the dysphoric/borderline batterer, the generally violent/antisocial batterer engages in moderate to severe abuse, including sexual and psychological abuse. These batterers engage in both domestic and non-domestic violence and typically have a legal history related to non-domestic violence. They are likely to have problems with drugs or alcohol, and have antisocial personality disorder or psychopathy.

Subsequent research on the Holtzworth-Munroe and Stuart subtypes confirms that the family-only batterer is likely to engage in minimal acts of domestic violence on a sporadic and limited basis. Although indefensible, his violence is not likely to escalate and does not typically pose a severe threat to his partner or children.

Conversely, the borderline and generally violent batterer subtypes do tend to escalate. The former will likely engage in more severe violence in response to real or imagined acts of infidelity (consistent with the jealousy and abandonment fears exhibited by those suffering from borderline personality disorder). The latter will likely escalate in situations in which a partner attempts to make her own decisions; the perceived loss of power and control resulting from a partner's autonomy provokes a violent rage.

The Ramifications of DV Dynamics on Domestic Kidnapping Prevention

A woman who overcomes the practical and psychological barriers to leaving a domestic violence situation faces a potentially greater threat: the retaliation of an abuser whose jealousy or loss of control causes an escalation in violent behavior.

The U.S. Department of Justice estimates that women who separate from a relationship are three times more likely to be victims of violence by their former partner than women who are divorced, and 25 times more likely to be victimized than married women.

"Separation assault" can include the blatantly physical and sexual assaults perpetrated by Tidwell and Bowe, or the psychological terror inflicted by Raheman through his abduction of his children. It can also include spousal homicide, the likelihood of which increases by a factor of six in the aftermath of a separation.

Preventing violence by a dedicated perpetrator who targets a specific victim or victims is extremely challenging and requires the concerted effort of the potential victim, as well as social service and law enforcement personnel. The law enforcement or security professional supporting an individual who is attempting to separate from a violent intimate relationship should assist the victim to establish a safety plan. Typical plan components include

- Pre-identified escape routes (including windows and fire escapes) that provide a viable option for retreating from a potential assault;
- Packed bags in a non-predictable location and that include
  - A set of keys to the home, car, and workplace (or alternative location);
  - Money;
  - Clothes and toiletries;
  - Copies of important documents, including pay stubs, bank statements, utility bills, financial documents, Social Security card, passport, birth certificate;
  - Phone number of supportive friends, family members, or social service agencies;
  - Medications and prescriptions;
  - Directions to a predetermined destination deemed safe (including a nearby police or fire station).

Additionally, if children are involved, the safety plan should include pre-packed bags for the children as well as copies of custody agreements, birth certificates, Social Security cards, and school records.

During the turmoil of separation, victims typically assume one of two opposing—and counterproductive—approaches to dealing with an ex-partner. The victim may continue dialoging with the former partner, as the victims of Bowe and Raheman had done, hoping that the rationality not present in the relationship can grow outside it. In contrast, some victims shield themselves from past pain by ignoring any attempted contact by the ex-partner, especially when such contact is harassing or threatening.

The threats, phone taps, and surveillance employed by Raheman against his estranged wife in the months preceding his abduction of the couple's children are characteristic of the stalking behaviors that occur in 43 percent of formerly violent intimate partnerships.

As legally defined, stalking generally refers to the willful, malicious, and repeated following and harassing of another person in a manner which causes that person to fear for his or her safety.

Far too often, victims fail to recognize (or are unable to cope with) the risk stalking behaviors pose to their safety and the safety of their children, which is one of the factors that contributes to the underreporting of stalking crimes. A study of femicide cases in 10 American cities revealed that 76 percent of victims were stalked prior to their death, yet 42 percent did not report the stalking to police.

Assisting victims to recognize the possible link between stalking and violence following separation from a previously violent intimate relationship supports the interruption of post-relationship violence, including the domestic kidnapping.

Supporting victims to acknowledge and report stalking behaviors also improves the efficacy of law enforcement intervention. Unlike many crimes, both domestic violence and stalking represent a pattern of behavior rather than a discrete act. Victim documentation of the perpetrator's stalking behavior, including maintenance of a log that chronicles the harassment and tapes of harassing telephone messages, supports risk assessment and effective intervention. Additionally, victim actions that support prevention and interruption of escalation include carrying a pre-paid cell phone, screening calls, changing routines, and requesting employers or neighbors to call law enforcement if the perpetrator is sighted.

Securing a protection or stay-away order may also be indicated. Highly publicized cases of victims who have been severely injured following obtainment of a restraining order have caused some to question the wisdom of pursuing this course of action. In certain perpetrators, service of a restraining order poses an intolerable threat to their sense of control and does appear to precipitate an escalation of violence. As with any assessment of risk, past behavior is the best predictor of future action. Information regarding a perpetrator's past reaction to prior restraining orders or police intervention should be considered when suggesting that the victim pursue obtaining a protection order. Studies have found that civil protection orders are valuable for assisting victims attain a sense of well-being which, in turn, supports their active participation in deterring further violence. Additionally, when orders are properly crafted and vigorously enforced, they have been found to be an effective tool in stopping or reducing DV and stalking.

The involvement of children must also be considered. The heightened risk posed during separation coincides with the time when issues of custody or visitation are frequently decided. Surprisingly, research has demonstrated that the possession of a restraining order or a history of DV does not generally impact custody decisions, nor preempt the custody mediation process required by most states—despite the fact that mediation and the exchange of children for visitation offer the batterer the opportunity for further abuse. In instances in which the courts do not suspend visitation altogether, supervised visitation (preferably at a visitation center, if available, or with a trusted friend or relative) or a supervised exchange, such as at the police station, should be advocated.

Additional safeguards should be suggested for those who have cause to believe that the ex-partner will abduct children within or to another country.

Once a child is abducted to another country, the laws of that country determine whether and how the child will be returned. If the child is abducted to a county that abides by the Hague Convention on the Civil Aspects of International Child Abduction, the country may—but is not required to—restore the child to the custodial parent. It should be noted that a Hague Convention remedy is a civil action that is available only if the child is retained outside the "country of habitual residence" and if that country has determined that the child's removal was wrongful. As in the case of Raheman, many countries allow their courts to make custody decisions concerning the child, irrespective of custody orders made in this country and according to the cultural practices and priorities of the country.

Criminal charges can be brought under the International Parental Kidnapping Crime Act (IPKCA). IPKCA makes it a federal felony for anyone to remove, or attempt to remove, a child under age 16 from the United States or to retain a child (who has been in the United States) outside the United States with the intent to obstruct the lawful exercise of parental rights.

The Office of Juvenile Justice and Delinquency Prevention (OJJDP) notes that there are red flags that signify the risk of the domestic kidnapping to a foreign country. Specifically, risk increases if the domestic kidnapper has

1. Previously abducted or threatened to abduct the child.
2. Citizenship in another country and strong emotional or cultural ties to the country of origin.
3. Friends or family living in another country.
4. No strong ties to the child's home state.
5. A strong support network.
6. No financial reason to stay in the area (e.g., the parent is unemployed, able to work anywhere, or is financially independent).
7. Engaged in planning activities, such as quitting a job; selling a house; terminating a lease; closing a bank account or liquidating other assets; hiding or destroying documents; or securing a passport, a birth certificate, or school or medical records.
8. A history of marital instability, lack of cooperation with the other parent, domestic violence or child abuse.
9. A jealous reaction to the other parent's remarriage or new romantic involvement.
10. A criminal record.

If a potential for kidnapping to another country exists, law enforcement and security professionals should support the victim to consider one of the following:

- Including language expressly stating the child's place of residence in the custody order;

- Requesting that the State Department Office of Children's Issues enter the child's name into the Children's Passport Issuance Alert Program;
- Requesting that the State Department of Children's Issues deny issuance of a passport for the child without the court's consent;
- For minors under age 14, requiring that both parents sign the passport application.

Caution should be exercised to ensure that restrictions are not so severe as to give the perpetrator "nothing to lose" and actually trigger the kidnapping the restrictions are designed to prevent.

Implications for the Domestic Kidnapping Investigation

The challenge of intervention without escalating risk has particular relevance for the investigation of the domestic kidnapping. Whether motivated by jealousy or a need to control, the domestic kidnapper believes that he is entitled to the liberty of his victim(s). A direct challenge to this belief will not be tolerated, and can potentially result in escalated violence against the victim, or concealment to prevent recovery.

Conversely, the entitlement mind-set causes the kidnapper to refrain from hiding his victim from others; since he has done nothing wrong, why hide? Raheman took his children to his family's home in India. Tidwell took his victim to his cousin's home for a social visit. Bowe instructed his victim to phone both her family and her attorney.

The perpetrator's sense of entitlement, as well as his disclosure of his actions to others, can serve the investigator of the domestic kidnapping.

In domestic kidnappings, unlike other kidnappings, the use of the media at the initial stages may hinder apprehension and escalate violence. The kidnapper who believes he is acting within his rights will respond poorly to the public challenge of his perspective. The resulting sense of being misunderstood or isolated can prompt hiding behaviors or an attack against the victim(s).

In cases in which there is no known threat of imminent violence, the investigator should attempt to locate the victim through contact with the abductor's friends and family, the postal service (to obtain a forwarding address), telephone records, and bank and credit card transactions. If a child is abducted, OJJDP also recommends review of the child's school records to learn if the perpetrator requested information to facilitate enrollment in another school.

The domestic kidnapping of a child also requires the investigator to determine the custodial status of the reporting parent to ensure that law enforcement is not, in fact, being engaged by a would-be kidnapper with falsified documents. A review of court records or a background investigation on both parents ensures appropriate intervention.

Once it is determined that a child is a victim of a domestic kidnapping, the law enforcement or security professional can assist families to obtain a pick-up order, civil bench warrant, or arrest warrant.

When the location of the victim(s) has been ascertained, the delicate act of negotiating with the domestic kidnapper begins. The kidnapper's sense of entitlement renders it imperative that the investigator maintain a neutral tone that conveys respect for what the kidnapper believes is his right to control his victim(s). Empathizing with his perspective ("I understand how much you love your wife/child") and displaying interest in his goals ("What do you want to get out of this situation?") can establish the rapport necessary to offer alternatives to escalated violence.

The ever-present risk of escalation requires immediate action when the opportunity to recover the victim(s) arises. With adult victims, recovery is relatively straightforward given a secured environment. Additional factors must be considered when the domestic kidnapping involves a child victim whose relationship to the kidnapper is frequently more complex. In recovering the child victim of a domestic kidnapping, the OJJDP recommends the following whenever circumstances permit:

- Coordination with child protective service workers regarding the need for temporary shelter and/or foster care until any outstanding custody issues are determined, the left-behind parent/guardian or investigator arrives, and/or any outstanding criminal allegations are resolved;

- If an arrest of the abductor(s) is warranted, do so away from the child;

- Conduct a thorough interview of the child, abductor, left-behind parent/guardian, and any other appropriate persons involved in the situation. Document results of the interviews;

- Do not articulate an opinion related to custody issues;
- Enforce legal orders with the least amount of physical and emotional trauma to the child.

Additionally, law enforcement should coordinate with victim-witness advocates and mental health professionals as soon as feasible. The bond that forms during romantic and familial relationships does not break with the relationship's termination, even when the relationship was complicated by the dynamics of violence. Both adult and child victims may feel ambiguous about the prosecution of one with whom they were previously intimate. The adult may continue to blame herself for provoking the actions of her abductor. Children can suffer severe ambivalence or continued attachment to the abductor. This is particularly true if the abductor has convinced the child that the left-behind parent rejected him or her, that the left-behind parent is evil or criminal, or that the left-behind parent has died.

Both adult and child victims need to be supported to attribute the blame for the domestic kidnapping where such blame belongs: with the perpetrator of the traumatizing crime.

Kidnapping Investigations: Enhancing the Flow of Information

Undoubtedly one of the most traumatic experiences a family can face, a kidnapping also severely challenges the law enforcement agency responsible for successfully resolving the situation. In such difficult circumstances, however, agencies can turn to an effective aid—crisis negotiation teams. These teams fill a unique and effective role that ultimately benefits the on-scene commander, investigative personnel, and the victim's family. The true value of a crisis negotiation team's assistance, however, often does not become apparent until the kidnapping ends. The grandson of an 88-year-old victim shared his thoughts about how an FBI crisis negotiation team helped him endure his grandmother's kidnapping. He believed that the negotiators who remained with him during the 2-day ordeal were extremely valuable because of the information they provided, along with their experience, knowledge, and wisdom. He stated, "I had that [experience, knowledge, and wisdom] at my fingertips. I had answers to my questions in regard to how I might negotiate, how the transaction might happen, how the transfer might go down, what to say, how to personalize my messages, how to communicate effectively."

Continued...

One of the crisis negotiation team's primary responsibilities in any critical situation is to support the overall investigative effort. In the case of a kidnapping, the crisis negotiation team works closely with the victim family members. The team establishes a negotiation operations center, makes assessments of family members, and guides and supports them through what is likely their darkest hour. The team, using its negotiation training, develops strategies to reduce the subject's expectations, to respond to threats and demands, and, most important, to seek the safe return of the victim.

Establish Negotiation Operations Center

A crisis negotiation team typically sets up a negotiation operations center within the victim family's residence or place of business, whichever seems the most likely point of contact by the subjects. The team members immerse themselves with the family; in doing so, personnel can observe and converse with family members on a consistent basis, continually gleaning information regarding the victim, including past behaviors and routines, and the situation. This immersion with family members serves several more purposes. It limits the traffic in and around the victim family's residence; demonstrates the commitment and dedication to the safe recovery of their loved one; enables investigators to focus on investigative leads; and provides the on-scene commander and investigative personnel with real-time, accurate information. Negotiators can address questions from investigators or commanders immediately with the family. By the same token, if the family has questions about the investigation, negotiators can address these as well. This clearly becomes an effective and efficient means of obtaining and disseminating information pertinent to the kidnapping and takes full advantage of the capabilities of the negotiation team.

To successfully fill such an important role, the crisis negotiation team must be well trained, disciplined, and organized. The team, along with other investigators, should participate in the initial debriefing of the family members. Other members of the crisis negotiation team will begin equipment setup, designed to capture any future communication with the subjects.

In an effort to be the least intrusive, the crisis negotiation team should seek to establish the negotiation operations center in a suitable place within the residence or building where members can answer and discreetly monitor calls. The negotiation operations center also should have an area where the team can conduct private meetings, hold shift-change discussions, and conduct telephone conversations with investigators, yet offer sufficient privacy to the family. Team members and investigators should avoid conducting brainstorming or case discussions where family members inadvertently may overhear their remarks because the family may misinterpret such discussions as disagreements or inexperience.

Assess Family Members

Upon arrival at the residence, crisis negotiators immediately begin to assess family members to determine those best suited to serve as the spokespersons, usually referred to as third-party intermediaries (TPIs). The crisis negotiation team will select, coach, and role-play with the anticipated TPIs. The coaching and role-playing act is an invaluable exercise with the family members to help them become more comfortable with the conversations, threats, or demands they may encounter and to rehearse their responses. This practice also enables the negotiation team to observe and assess who is the most coachable, the most reliable, and the most able to handle the challenge of serving as the TPI, thereby following one of law enforcement's well-known theories—the manner in which officers train directly relates to the manner in which they perform.

Written by Toni Marie Chrabot and Winnie D. Miller for The FBI Law Enforcement Bulletin, *July 2004. Reprinted with permission.*

REFERENCES

Babcock, Julia C., Green, Charles E., Webb, Sarah A., and Yerington, Timothy P. (2005). Psychological Profiles of Batterers: Autonomic Emotional Reactivity as It Predicts the Antisocial Spectrum of Behavior Among Intimate Partner Abusers. *Journal of Abnormal Psychology, 114*(3), 444–455.

Berkowitz, Leonard, and Harmon-Jones, Eddie. (2004). Toward an Understanding of the Determinants of Anger. *Emotion, 4*(2), 107–130.

DeKeseredy, Walter S., Rogness, McKenzie, and Schwartz, Martin D. (2004). Separation/Divorce Sexual Assault: The Current State of Social Scientific Knowledge. *Aggression and Violent Behavior, 9,* 675–691.

Hammer, Heather, Finkelhor, David, and Sedlak, Andrea J. (2002, October). National Incidence Studies of Missing, Abducted, Runaway and Throwaway Children: Children Abducted by Family Members: National Estimates and Characteristics.

Hilton, N. Zoe, Harris, Grant T., Rice, Marnie E., Lang, Carol, Cormier, Catherine A., and Lines, Kathyrn J. (2004). A Brief Actuarial Assessment for the Prediction of Wife Assault Recidivism: The Ontario Domestic Assault Risk Assessment. *Psychological Assessment, 16*(3), 267–275.

Holtzworth-Munroe, and Stuart, Gregory L. (1994, November). Typologies of Male Batterers: Three Subtypes and the Differences Among Them. *Psychological Bulletin, 116*(3), 476–497.

Marvin, Douglas R. (1997, July). The Dynamics of Domestic Abuse. *Law Enforcement Bulletin.* Washington, D.C.

Murray, Sandra L., Holmes, John G., and Collins, Nancy L. (2006). Optimizing Assurance: The Risk Regulation System in Relationships. *Psychological Bulletin, 132*(5), 641–666.

Office of Juvenile Justice and Delinquency Prevention. (2007, January). *A Family Resource Guide on International Parental Kidnapping*. Washington, D.C.

Office of Juvenile Justice and Delinquency Prevention. (2006). *Missing and Abducted Children: A Law Enforcement Guide to Case Investigation and Program Management*, 3rd ed. Washington, D.C.

O'Sullivan, Chris S., King, Lori A., and Levin-Russell, Kyla. (2006, March). *Supervised and Unsupervised Parental Access in Domestic Violence Cases: Court Orders and Consequences*. The National Institute of Justice.

Renninson, Callie Marie, and Welchans, Sarah. (2002, January). *Intimate Partner Violence. Bureau of Justice Statistics: Special Report*.

Saccuzzzo, Dennis P., Johnson, Nancy E., and Koen, Wendy J. (2003, April). *Mandatory Custody Mediation: Empirical Evidence of Increased Risk for Domestic Violence Victims and Their Children*. National Institute of Justice.

Smith Slep, Amy M., and O'Leary, Susan G. (2005). Parent and Partner Violence in Families with Young Children: Rates, Patterns and Connections. *Journal of Consulting and Clinical Psychology*, 73(3), 435–444.

U.S. Department of Justice, Office of Justice Programs. *Domestic Violence and Stalking: The Second Annual Report to Congress under the Violence Against Women Act*. Washington, D.C., May 2001.

Chapter four

Predatory Kidnapping– Adult Victim

CHAPTER CONTENTS

WHAT DEFINES THE PREDATORY KIDNAPPING–ADULT VICTIM

The predatory kidnapping of the adult victim involves the sexually motivated abduction of individuals age 18 years and older.

The characteristics of the predatory kidnapping–adult victim are detailed in Table 4.1. The predatory kidnapping–adult victim is illustrated by the kidnappings perpetrated by David Watts, Richard Junior Frazier, and Victor T. Steele.

Table 4.1 Predatory Kidnapping-Adult Victim

Victimology & Offender Characteristics		
	1. The victim was under 18 years of age.	0%
	2. The victim and the offender were strangers to one another.	
	3. The victim and the offender had a relationship prior to the abduction.	56%
	4. The offender and the victim were of different genders.	39%
	5. The offender and the victim are of different ethnicities.	94%
	6. The victim was low risk, i.e., not likely to be immediately missed or reported as missing.	NA*
	7. The offender was unemployed at the time of the abduction.	11%
	8. The offender was employed at the time of the abduction.	NA*
		NA*
Abduction Site	1. The abduction occurred in a public place.	67%
	2. The victim was abducted from a private location (such as home, school, workplace).	33%
Modus Operandi	1. The abduction was perpetrated by more than one offender.	11%
	2. The victim was chosen randomly or opportunistically.	61%
	3. Physical force was used to abduct the victim.	56%
	4. The victim was abducted following verbal threats of harm to himself or herself and/or others.	17%
	5. The victim's abduction was the result of persuasion or deception.	39%
	6. The offender used a firearm to facilitate the abduction.	22%
	7. The offender used a knife to facilitate the abduction.	17%
	8. The offender used a weapon, other than a knife or a firearm, or did not use a weapon, to facilitate the abduction.	28%
	9. The offender sexually assaulted the victim during the abduction.	94%
	10. The offender physically assaulted the victim during the abduction in a manner that did result in death.	17%
	11. The offender physically assaulted the victim during the abduction in a manner that did not result in death.	56%
	12. The offender did not assault or physically harm the victim during the abduction (excludes sexual assault).	28%
	13. The offender transported the victim during the abduction.	78%
	14. The offender did not transport the victim during the abduction.	22%
	15. The offender exhibited obvious psychotic symptoms (delusions, hallucinations, etc.).	0%
	16. The offender held the victim captive for greater than 24 hours.	17%
	17. The offender held the victim captive for less than 24 hours.	83%
	18. The kidnapping occurred in the morning (midnight–8 a.m.).	28%
	19. The kidnapping occurred during the day (8 a.m.–4 p.m.).	6%

Continued...

Table 4.1 Predatory Kidnapping-Adult Victim—continued

	20. The kidnapping occurred in the evening/at night (4 p.m.– midnight).	50%
	21. More than one victim was abducted.	11%
Outcome	1. The abduction was witnessed.	39%
	2. The victim was released by the offender.	56%
	3. The victim escaped.	6%
	4. The victim was released following law enforcement intervention.	22%
	5. The victim was not found.	0%
	6. The victim was found dead.	17%
	7. The victim was discovered in a public place.	56%
	8. The victim was discovered in a private place (a home, school or workplace).	44%
	9. Witness testimony contributed to the offender's apprehension/conviction (not limited to event witnesses).	67%
	10. Physical evidence contributed to the offender's apprehension/conviction.	44%
	11. Accomplice statements contributed to the offender's apprehension/conviction.	0%
	12. Victim testimony contributed to the abductor's apprehension/conviction.	83%

NA-Insufficient data to render determination.

David Watts

On the night of January 20, 1996, David Watts pulled his truck into a parking space outside Wisconsin's Southridge shopping center. In the car beside him was the 19-year-old victim, Jennifer, who had just completed her shift working at one of the stores and was waiting for her car to warm up. She lit a cigarette, lowering her window a few inches to allow the smoke to escape. Watts exited his car, walked beside the victim's car, and reached through her window, pulling her hair. The victim mistakenly rolled her window down instead of up, allowing Watts to reach further into her car.

When the victim screamed, Watts hit her in the face and claimed that he had a gun. Once she was subdued, Watts reached further into the car, unbuttoned her blouse, and fondled her breasts. Thereafter, he pulled her into his truck and held her down as he drove to a small parking lot behind a gas station. During the drive, he asked her questions about her sexual history. After parking, he sexually assaulted her in numerous ways, including inserting his finger into her vagina, forcing her to touch his penis, and forcing her to perform fellatio on him. He masturbated himself to ejaculation, ordered the victim to get dressed, and told her to get out of his car.

Richard Junior Frazier

On the evening of October 31, 2000, an 18-year-old student stopped at a Georgia Wal-Mart store to check prices on Halloween candy. She exited the store and returned to her car. Before she could enter it, she was approached by Richard Junior Frazier, who wielded a knife, demanding, "Will you take me where I want to go?" The victim complied, allowing Frazier to enter the back seat of the car while the victim got behind the wheel.

Frazier initially told his victim that he wanted to visit his son in a neighboring county. He then directed her to drive onto a dirt road leading to a secluded, wooded area. He demanded that she turn off the engine. Knife in hand, he moved into the passenger seat. Frazier ordered his victim to remove her pants and underpants. He removed his own clothes and sexually assaulted the victim numerous times.

After the sexual assault, Frazier ordered the victim to dress. He took control of her car, forcing her to remain in the passenger seat. He stopped twice, once to buy gasoline and a second time to purchase cigarettes. At each stop, he made the victim accompany him, warning her not to do anything "stupid."

In the interim, the victim's fiancé and family grew alarmed at her absence. While her mother called 911, her father drove out to search for her. He sighted his daughter's car being driven by Frazier and followed it for several miles before pulling beside it. He saw his daughter in the passenger seat and motioned Frazier to stop. Instead, Frazier swerved into the victim's father's car, attempting to cut him off before leading him on a chase that reached speeds of up to 80 miles per hour. Though unable to stop Frazier, the victim's father drew the attention of a law enforcement officer who was driving in a marked police car. The officer made a U-turn and chased both vehicles, activating his flashing blue lights. Instead of pulling over, Frazier drove faster, increasing his speed to 100 miles per hour, while passing stop signs and running red lights. Several additional officers joined the pursuit. Frazier still refused to pull over and twice attempted to hit the cars of the officers who pursued him. Maintaining his 100-mile per hour speed, Frazier crossed state lines into North Carolina.

On the twisting and winding Route 28, Frazier lost control of the vehicle and crashed into a power pole. Neither Frazier nor his victim were seriously hurt in the crash. When asked why they fled the police, the victim reported that she had been kidnapped at knifepoint. A search of Frazier yielded two knives; one was found in his right hip pocket, its partially serrated blade locked in the open position.

Victor T. Steele

On the morning of June 25, 1998, Victor Steele knocked on the door of the victim's Indiana home. Steele was a member of the fitness center at which the victim, Anita, worked until the center closed in 1997. The two had never dated nor had a personal relationship, although the victim recognized Steele when she opened her front door. She allowed Steele to enter her home after he asked for a glass of water. Once inside, Steele subdued the victim by repeatedly shocking her with a stun gun.

Steele bound the victim's hands and feet with plastic ties and black electrical tape, disguised himself in women's clothing that he had brought in a backpack, and took the victim's car keys. He placed the victim in the trunk of her car and drove to another garage. Thereafter, Steele took his victim from the trunk and sexually assaulted her for the first time. When finished, he placed her in a cardboard box, which he took to his residence. There, he repeatedly sexually assaulted her. He placed her in his pickup truck and told her he was taking her to a building he rented in Wisconsin. When they arrived, he placed her in a large metal file cabinet, which he locked by placing a stick and butter knife through the door handles.

During the next 8 days, Steele frequently removed his victim from the cabinet to sexually assault her, returning her to her confinement when done.

Early in the investigation of Anita's disappearance, law enforcement dispatched an undercover officer to the Indiana residence that Steele shared with his mother. After initially denying knowledge of her son's whereabouts, Steele's mother gave the officer the address of the building that Steele rented. Based on this information, other law enforcement officers detained Steele when he exited the building. The officers entered the building and called to the victim, who did not answer. They discovered her in the metal cabinet that was held closed by the butter knife stuck between the cabinet's handles.

CHARACTERISTICS OF THE PREDATORY KIDNAPPING–ADULT VICTIM

Victimology

The victims of predatory kidnappings of adults are, by definition, over 18 years of age. Overwhelming, victims are females abducted by males (94 percent).

The majority of victims of the adult predatory kidnapping cases reviewed (56 percent) had no prior relationship to their abductors, as illustrated in the kidnappings perpetrated by David Watts and Richard Junior Frazier. In a minority of cases (39 percent), the victim and abductor had prior contact. As was true of the kidnapping perpetrated by Victor Steele, the offender often held a distorted and exaggerated perspective of the significance of the relationship. (In the balance of cases reviewed, the victim-offender relationship was not evident or disclosed.)

Abduction Site

The abduction sites chosen by David Watts and Richard Junior Frazier, each of whom kidnapped from shopping center parking lots, were consistent with those in many of the predatory kidnapping of adult cases reviewed. The vast majority of such abductions (67 percent) occurred in places with unrestricted public access.

Abductions such as the one perpetrated by Victor Steele, which began in the home of his victim, were far less common (33 percent).

The choice of site is consistent with the choice of victim: Those who had no prior relationship to their victim chose sites where the victim was selected at random. Those who had a prior relationship to the victim tended to target her home or workplace.

Modus Operandi

The approaches used by Watts, Frazier, and Steele to subdue their victims illustrate those frequently adopted by the predatory kidnapper of an adult. Predatory adult kidnappers rarely committed their crimes with an accomplice. Instead, they adopted one of two methods to subdue their victims: physical force (56 percent), as in the cases of Watts and Frazier, or persuasion or deception (39 percent). As in the case of Steele, a significant minority used deception in combination with physical force. Firearms were used in nearly a quarter of the predatory adult abductions reviewed (22 percent), while knives were used in less than a fifth (17 percent) of these abductions.

Predictably, predatory kidnappers of adults rarely abducted more than one victim at a time; multiple victims are more difficult to subdue, particularly when the goal of the abduction is sexual assault; the victim of the adult predatory kidnapping was sexually assaulted in the overwhelming majority (94 percent) of cases reviewed.

The majority of adult predatory kidnappers transported their victims during the abduction (78 percent). And as was true of the Watts and Frazier kidnappings, victims were generally held less than 24 hours (83 percent). Steele's 8-day abduction was the exception for adult predatory kidnappings. So too was the time at which Steele initiated his abduction: Only 6 percent of adult predatory kidnappings occurred during the day. The vast majority occurred at night (from 4 p.m. to midnight, 50 percent) and in the early morning hours (midnight to 8 a.m., 28 percent).

The sexual violence that was perpetrated by the adult predatory kidnapper is incomprehensible to normally adjusted individuals. Though this behavior is irrational, it is not rooted in psychosis or other forms of severe mental illness (known clinically as Axis I disorders). In the cases studied, none of the kidnappers exhibited obvious psychotic symptoms, such as delusions or hallucinations. Even when the kidnapping appeared to be spontaneous or opportunistic, and victim selection was random, the predatory adult kidnapper's efforts were organized and in service to his goal of abducting and sexually assaulting the victim.

Outcome

Despite the physical and sexual violence that was frequently present in adult predatory kidnappings, the majority of victims (83 percent) survived the abduction. Most (56 percent) are released by their abductors, as was true for the victim of David Watts. Successful intervention by law enforcement officials, as occurred in the Richard Frazier and David Steele kidnappings, was the second highest contributor to victim survival (22 percent).

While the survival rate for victims of predatory kidnappings is high, freedom is rarely achieved by the actions of the victim. Only 6 percent of victims who were not released by the kidnapper or rescued by law enforcement successfully escaped their captivity.

Unfortunately, victimization frequently did not end with release but continued as the kidnappers' prosecutions proceeded. The majority of adult predatory kidnappers defended themselves by offering a version of events that was quite disparate from actual circumstances and frequently disparaging to their victims.

David Watts claimed that after finishing work at a restaurant near the mall where the abduction took place, he bought and drank a case of beer before deciding that he could make money assisting motorists who were stranded in the snow. He claimed to have helped several motorists and to have purchased and consumed additional beers.

Watts reported that he was planning to return to his home when the victim approached him and asked for a ride to buy cigarettes. He saw the victim's car running, he said, and asked why she didn't drive herself. He stated that the victim told him that she was nervous because she sometimes had car trouble. Watts continued with a convoluted tale clearly designed to explain the presence of forensic evidence: The victim reached toward him with an object and stuck him in the finger, he said. He then claimed to have grabbed her by the shoulder, neck, and hair and demanded to know what was going on. Her assurances that "everything was fine" supposedly satisfied him, and he agreed to drive her, even after she opened the car door in such a way as to hit his leg. Once at the gas station, Watts claimed that the victim offered him sex for money. She also, he claimed, began to touch herself and act provocatively to entice him. Watts stated that he refused her sexual advances and ordered her out of his truck.

Like Watts, Richard Frazier would also claim to be the victim of his victim. Following his arrest, Frazier told an FBI agent that he was sitting on a bench outside the Wal-Mart where the abduction took place when he was approached by the victim. Throughout the day, Frazier said, he had been drinking beer and "had a good buzz on." When the victim approached him, he was wearing a cap that read "Official Booze Guzzling, Beer Chugging, Sud Sucking, Ass Kicking Party Cap." The victim, who Frazier admitted was a stranger, allegedly offered to give him a ride back to his residence.

Frazier says he accepted, and asked to be driven to his ex-girlfriend's home in North Carolina. He also said that the victim asked him to drive the car, even though he told her that he'd been drinking and that he did not have a valid driver's license. He said that he refused to stop for the victim's father and for law enforcement because the victim told him that if he did her father "would beat his ass."

Frazier denied any sexual contact with his victim.

Victor Steele's account of events was equally self-serving. His apprehension, he claimed, was the result of being framed by the police and the Indiana Department of Corrections in retaliation for a lawsuit he filed against the department. The physical evidence presented at trial, he declared, was planted by those out to get him.

Each of the offenders accurately deduced that physical evidence needed to be explained. Such evidence was equal to witness testimony in facilitating the apprehension and conviction of predatory adult kidnappers (44 percent).

Watts had explained his presence in the Wisconsin shopping center as an effort to earn money by assisting motorists stranded in snow. Meteorological records showed that no snow had fallen in the area on the night of the abduction and that the ground snow depth was zero.

In the case of Victor Steele, residue of black tape and red marks were found on the victim's wrists. Several sets of red dots that were the same distance apart as those that would be made by a stun gun were found on her stomach and back. The stun gun was found in Steele's truck, along with a backpack containing the wig and women's clothing that he wore from her home. The victim's address was found on a piece of paper in Steele's Indiana residence.

Witness testimony reinforced the improbable nature of the perpetrators' accounts and the validity of the physical evidence in pointing to their guilt.

After David Watts ordered his victim from the car, she ran to a nearby gas station and reported the assault to the clerk. The clerk would later testify that the victim was crying, and that she had a bloody nose and mussed hair. The clerk further reported that the victim was so upset that she was unable to write the license plate of her abductor, which she had seen as he was driving away; instead, the clerk recorded the plate number. The victim had also informed the clerk that her car was still running in the mall parking lot and that her purse was lying on the front seat.

Police would subsequently locate the car, still running, its driver's side door open, and the purse lying on the front seat.

Richard Frazier's conviction was also facilitated by the testimony of the law enforcement officers participating in the chase of the victim's fleeing vehicle, as well as the testimony of the sexual assault nurse examiner who treated the victim following the car crash.

While physical evidence and witness testimony were important, the testimony of victims was consistently found to be more compelling; victim testimony contributed to the apprehension and conviction of offenders in 83 percent of the adult predatory kidnapping cases reviewed.

IMPLICATIONS FOR PREVENTION AND INVESTIGATION

The victims of adult predatory kidnappers were overwhelming female and frequently did not have prior relationships with their abductors. The fact that they were often chosen randomly or opportunistically poses both an opportunity and a challenge for law enforcement and security professionals working to prevent the adult predatory kidnappings. Specifically, the opportunity that is presented is to assist women—the most likely potential victims—to improve their situational awareness and defensive tactics. The challenge is to overcome the denial that is so often the coping mechanism in matters of personal safety.

The U.S. Navy defines *situational awareness* as "the degree of accuracy by which one's perception of his current environment mirrors reality." To be aware, an individual must first perceive what is going on around her, i.e., process continuous and often competing sensations. She must then decide which stimuli are important to note and which can be ignored. All individuals have a limited capacity to attend to the stimuli that are present in any given moment; no one has the capacity to accurately process all the information with which she is confronted. Additionally, attentional capacity can be compromised by genetics, brain injury, arousal, and certain conditions such as depression or fatigue.

Fortunately, situational awareness is also influenced by two additional factors that are relevant to the prevention of crime in general, and the prevention of predatory adult kidnappings in particular: information and training.

Most sensory data enter neurobehavioral systems as perceptions already endowed with previously learned meanings. In other words, we tend to perceive what we've learned to expect.

The safety awareness classes and lectures conducted by the author include women who have not been victims of assault, and those who have and are determined to avoid revictimization. Each woman is aided to expand her expectation of human behavior to include actions that can be harmful or dangerous.

During these workshops, facts about violent crime are discussed, threat awareness is practiced, and response scenarios are rehearsed. In a safe and controlled environment, students expand situational awareness to encompass the possibility that those with whom they come in contact will not behave as they'd like or expect. Each participant mentally explores her "line in the sand," the action on the part of another that will catalyze her reaction. Based on past experience, training, and personality, she then identifies the most effective response for her. In formulating her response, she is asked to consider the relevant facts identified by various researchers.

For example, Brad Parker, director of Defend University and co-founder of the Rape Escape self-defense methodology, cites findings from his research that apply to the potential adult predatory kidnapping victim. In studying hundreds of attempted and actual sexual assaults, Parker found that women who are transported during an attack are more likely to be sexually assaulted than those who are not. As 78 percent of predatory adult kidnappers transport their victims, fighting against entering a car with a potential abductor may decrease the chances that such an assault occurs. Parker also cites studies that indicate that half of all attackers will break off their attack if the woman demonstrates that she is willing to resist. "Of course," he adds, "we need to deal with the other half that continues the attack, but Department of Justice studies show that women who resist are not injured anymore than women who don't resist."

The impossibility of predicting if one will be the victim of an adult predatory kidnapping or, if victimized, that the attacker will cease his attack if faced with resistance, necessitates the promotion of flexible coping strategies for potential victims.

The most commonly cited model of coping was developed by Lazarus et al., who divide coping into two components: problem-solving coping and emotional-focused coping.

Problem-solving coping is akin to situational awareness and defensive training. It is the moment-by-moment evaluation of a situation and the approach chosen to deal with it. Defensive training that supports a woman to identify and utilize different tactics depending on the immediate and most significant threat, as well as her own capabilities (as opposed to the "one tactic fits all" approach), will prove most effective when dealing with the opportunistic actions of the adult predatory kidnapper.

The efficacy of the use of defensive tactics is predicated on strengthening the second facet of Lazarus's coping process: emotional-focused coping. Most commonly, this involves regulating one of the greatest challenges to safety: the coping mechanism of denial.

In the individual, denial is the refusal to believe information that provokes anxiety. Denial can take many forms. It underlies the varied statements of even those who voluntarily seek safety training to overcome it:

> *"It can never happen to me."*
> *"If I focus on the bad things that can happen, they will happen."*
> *"If I focus on the bad things that can happen, I'll just become overwhelmed and paranoid."*
> *"I just refuse to believe that people are that bad."*

As security specialist Gavin de Becker notes, the efficacy of denial as a strategy is dubious:

> Denial is a save-now-pay-later scheme ... and it causes low-grade anxiety. Millions of people suffer that anxiety, and denial keeps them from taking action that could reduce the risks (and the worry).

Supporting individuals to replace denial of safety concerns with situational awareness and practical, personalized defensive skills can assist in the prevention of adult predatory kidnappings.

Unfortunately, denial can also extend beyond the individual and seep into the collective awareness. This is particularly true in crimes of sexual assault, which is a common element of adult predatory kidnappings.

Collective denial poses specific challenges for the investigation and prosecution of the adult predatory kidnapping. Despite rape shield laws that limit information to a victim's sexual history from being admitted at trial, a victim's character and intentions are consistently evaluated in cases of sexual assault. Judgments regarding the veracity of a sexual assault are based on such myriad factors as the victim's race and social class, the charges brought against the defendant, the defendant's use of a weapon, the extent of a victim's injuries, the clothes a victim wore, and even the tonal quality of a victim's voice. These judgments, collectively known as *rape myths*, represent a form of denial often referred to as *blaming the victim*.

Blaming the victim isolates the wounded, while providing those not directly involved with a crime with the illusion of control over threats to their own safety. It allows those who learn of such events to deny the possibility that similar circumstances can threaten them. This collective denial is evidenced in statements such as "It will never happen here: this is a safe neighborhood," or, more destructively, "she deserved it" for being in that place, at that time, wearing those clothes.

Unfortunately—as de Becker notes for the individual—the pseudo-protective mechanism of denial only heightens the trauma of community members when supposed protective risk factors such as a safe neighborhood, proper clothing, and "good" behavior prove inadequate.

Trauma and denial also complicate the efforts of law enforcement called to interview the victim of the predatory adult kidnapping.

Psychological studies reveal dynamics with which law enforcement experienced in dealing with victims of sexual assault and predatory adult kidnappings are all too familiar.

As with the majority of victims of severely traumatic events, the victim of the adult predatory kidnapping is likely to suffer from hypermnesia, i.e., improvement in the recall of the event following the passage of time. This phenomenon is the opposite of the one that occurs with memories of ordinary events, in which recall peaks immediately following the event and decays over time (a phenomenon referred to as the *Ebbinghaus decay curve*). Hypermnesia clashes with the civilian's belief that a delay in remembering the details of an attack compromises a victim's credibility.

As victim testimony is the greatest contributing factor to the apprehension and conviction of the adult predatory kidnapper, it is particularly important that a follow-up interview, conducted with the expectation that new information will be forthcoming, occurs. It may also be helpful to retain an expert witness in the field of trauma memory processing to educate jurors regarding the post-trauma recall process.

Investigative efforts may be further complicated by the possibility that the victim of the adult predatory kidnapping who has been sexually assaulted will delay reporting the crime against her.

A constellation of behavioral and psychological symptoms frequently occur in victims of sexual assault. Such symptoms can include somatic complaints, headaches, increased startle reactions, increased fear, decreased appetite, and self-blame. Commonly known as Rape Trauma Syndrome, this symptomology may also include dissociation from the event, which may explain why it is not unusual for victims of sexual assault to delay reporting the crime.

Again, given the civilian's association of report delay with compromised credibility, it may be helpful to retain an expert in Rape Trauma Syndrome to explain this phenomenon to jurors. (It should be noted that the admissibility of testimony by rape trauma experts has varied by state. Some jurisdictions have determined that Rape Trauma Syndrome has not met the scientific reliability of evidence required by the Frye standard. Others have objected when experts move beyond an explanation of the syndrome to opine that a particular victim suffers from its effects. Still other jurisdictions have allowed both testimony on the syndrome and opinions related to specific cases.)

Victim credibility is particularly important in relation to the adult predatory kidnapping in which physical evidence is absent, resulting in a "he said, she said" version of events. The fact that both kidnapping and sexual assault occur may help mitigate this challenge in terms of potential conviction, as civilians are more likely to credit a victim's account when a kidnapping has occurred than they are to credit the occurrence of sexual assault in which kidnapping is absent. Additionally, civilians are more apt to accept the veracity of a claim of sexual assault by a stranger, as occurs in 50 percent of adult predatory kidnappings.

Knowledge of the spectrum of the coping responses employed by both victims and civilians can support law enforcement and security professionals to prevent abductions whenever possible, and to successfully apprehend and convict the kidnapper.

Physical evidence is an important element in securing convictions in cases of sexual assault, including those that occur during the adult predatory kidnapping. Malinda Wheeler, Director of Forensic Nurse Specialists, Inc., recommends that the following be considered during the forensic evidentiary examination of victims:

It is vitally important to get any victim of sexual assault in to see an expert forensic examiner for evidence collection as soon as possible. However, with the rapid changes and improvements in DNA retrieval and analysis, DNA can be collected up to days later, even after bathing or showering. Sexual assault forensic evidence can include

- Clothing;
- Trace evidence from hair;
- Oral samples (both for victim reference DNA and potential semen);
- Nail scrapings or swabbings;
- Skin samples for any potential contact by the perpetrator (e.g., oral, semen, or "touch" as in scratches or strangulation);
- External genital samples, for potential saliva or semen;
- Internal genital samples (both vaginal and anal) for potential semen;
- Blood and urine samples for drug and alcohol analysis.

Situational awareness is one of the key elements in preventing victimization by the adult predatory kidnapper. Brad Parker, director of Defend University, a research and development group dedicated to the exploration of leading-edge techniques and strategies for self-defense, security, and defensive tactics, suggests that community-based safety efforts include the following five suggestions for avoiding abduction:

1. **Stay aware of people in your surroundings.** Not surprisingly, predatory criminals will exhibit certain behaviors in preparing to attack. They will try to pick a casual location to look for their prey. They will look at their intended victim far more and for longer periods of time than social norms. They will move when the prey moves. They will stop and look around for witnesses. They will often make several passes by the prey in a sort of "dry run," seeing if the victim will react or to get a sense of how the attack might work. Pay attention! Who is looking at you? Has the same person or car passed by you twice? Does someone appear to be moving with you?

2. **Stay vigilant in high-risk areas.** There are transitory areas which typically have a volume of vehicular and pedestrian traffic which offer cover for the predator while allowing him to scan for potential victims. In other words, a person would not look out of place in these areas as other people move in and through the same places. These include parking lots, parking garages, parks, running trails, and places like common laundry room areas.

Continued...

3. **Keep a barrier between you and the bad guy.** Use a barrier to block him. Keep your doors locked. Stay in your car. Force him to get through a barrier before he can get to you. Use a barrier of pepper spray. In a parking lot, don't walk directly to your car, but move through the rows of cars in a zig-zag fashion. The more difficult you make it, the greater chance the predator will search for a different victim.

4. **Recognize the interview.** Predators will use a pattern of questions to engage you in conversation while they assess your potential as a suitable victim and as a way to get close enough to attack. While the questions themselves can be mundane—"Do you have the time?" or "Got a light"— they typically come at a rapid-fire pace, and the predator will not take "no" for an answer. Recognize this kind of behavior and put your hands up to protect your face and head and move back to create distance.

5. **Develop a defensive mind-set.** Studies show that half of all predatory criminals will break off their attack if the victim even *indicates* she is willing to resist. Remember, hope is not a strategy. You must consider the consequences of acquiescing to the predator and resolve that you will do *whatever is necessary to come home to your family tonight.*

Parker recommends teaching the following interventions should an attack occur:

1. **Resist immediately.** Your chances of success are never better than in the first 20 seconds of the initial encounter. This is when the attacker is most vulnerable. The longer your contact with the attacker, the greater the control he exerts over you. Believing that he will not harm you or you are somehow going to find a time later when you can escape has proven to be a flawed strategy for many victims.

2. **Attract attention.** The first thing he will say to you is "Don't scream or I'll kill you." He's telling you exactly what will ruin his plan, which is to take you to somewhere private. Go ahead, ruin his plan—create a disturbance, scream, throw things, blow the horn. You can't count on others coming to your aid, but you want to appeal to his fear of getting caught and make him think that someone could hear you and be coming.

3. **Stay with people or go to people.** Do not ever let yourself be taken somewhere. Cops call it the "secondary crime scene," and most of the time it will be where your worst nightmare resides. If you are approached in a public place, do not get in a vehicle with him. Do not walk around the building to the alley—STAY where others can see you. His worst fear is the fear of getting caught, so you should drop to the ground if you need to in order to prevent him from carrying you away. On the other hand, if you are in a location that is private like a laundry room, you need to GO to people.

His worst fear is the fear of getting caught—run out the door into the street. Go to where other people can see you and hear you.

4. **Prepare to defend yourself from the hit.** It's common for an attacker to punch or slap the victim at the onset of the attack to coerce cooperation through fear. Protect your head and throat.

5. **Resist with your strongest weapons against his weakest targets.** His weakest targets are those that are most valuable yet, ironically, cannot be entirely strengthened. His eyes, throat, groin, and knees are your primary targets. Your secondary targets are his face and his abdomen. Strong weapons that you can employ are kicks using the bottom of your feet, your elbows, hammerfists, and palm heel strikes. An intended victim who resists completely destroys the abductor's plan.

Rape Trauma Syndrome

In 1974, Ann Wolbert Burgess and Lynda Lytle Holmstrom coined the term *Rape Trauma Syndrome* to describe the process that occurs to victims of forcible rape or attempted forcible rape. As the majority of predatory kidnappings of adult victims involve sexual assault, and as law enforcement professionals are frequently the first contact for victims, understanding Rape Trauma Syndrome can allow the responding officer to support the victim's recovery, as well as her ability to serve as an effective witness.

The syndrome includes an Acute Phase and a period of Long-Term Reorganization.

The Acute Phase of Disorganization refers to victims' responses in the immediate hours following the sexual or attempted sexual assault. Victims may present with

- An *Expressed Style*, including behaviors such as crying, sobbing, smiling, restlessness, tenseness, or joking;
- A *Controlled Style*, in which feelings are concealed behind a calm, composed, or subdued affect.

The victim can vacillate between the expressed and controlled style, and the interviewer must be prepared to work with either or both reactions. In the weeks immediately following the sexual assault trauma, victims may express a variety of somatic symptoms including a general feeling of soreness. Other symptoms can include

- Sleep pattern disturbances;
- Eating pattern disturbances;
- Physical symptoms, particularly in the areas of the body attacked by the assailant.

Continued...

Rape Trauma Syndrome—continued

Emotional reactions in the weeks following the assault can include feelings of guilt or shame, fear, humiliation, degradation, self-blame, anger, and a desire for revenge. Cognitively, the victim may experience obsessive thinking and intrusive imagery about the assault.

During the Long-Term Process of Reorganization, the victim may feel generalized anxiety or fear; continued eating, sleeping, or thought disturbances; relationship disturbances; impaired social functioning; and continued guilt for not preventing the assault.

The victim may also suddenly or unexpectedly change addresses or miss court appearances. It is particularly imperative that the investigator recognize the last response as normative; seeking the support of a victim advocate or mental health professional can assist in preventing victim flight prior to or during trial.

REFERENCES

Carver, Charles S., and Scheier, Michael F. (1994, January 1). Situational Coping and Coping Dispositions in a Stressful Transaction. *Journal of Personality and Social Psychology*, 66(1), 184–195.

David Watts v. Gary R. McCaughtry, 119 Fed. Appx. 830; 2005 U.S. App. Lexis 1358.

Finkel, N., and Groscup, J. (1976, April 21). Crime Prototypes, Objective Versus Subjective Culpability, and a Commonsense Balance. *Law and Human Behavior, 3*(2), 209–230.

Folkman, Susan, Lazarus, Richard S., Gruen, Rand J., and DeLongis, Anita. (1986, March 1). Appraisal, Coping, Health Status and Psychological Symptoms. *Journal of Personality and Social Psychology, 50*(3), 571–579.

Frazier, Patricia, and Borgida, Eugene. (1985, September 1). Rape Trauma Syndrome Evidence in Court. *American Psychologist, 40*(9), 984–993.

Hazelwood, Robert R., and Burgess, Ann Wolbert. (2001). *Practical Aspects of Rape Investigation: A Multidisciplinary Approach*, 3rd ed. New York: CRC Press.

Kalat, James W. (2002). *Introduction to Psychology*, 6th ed. Pacific Grove, CA: The Wadsworth Group.

Lezak, Muriel D., Howieson, Diane B., and Loring, David W. (2004). *Neuropsychological Assessment*, 4th ed. New York: Oxford University Press.

Mechanic, Mindy B., Resick, Patricia A., and Griffin, Michael G. (1998, January 1). A Comparison of Normal Forgetting, Psychopathology, and Information-Processing Models of Reported Amnesia for Recent Sexual Trauma. *Journal of Consulting and Clinical Psychology, 66*(6), 948–957.

McMahon, P., and Fehr, L. (1983, August). Methodological Problems in Mock Jury Research. *Journal of Social Psychology, 123*(2), 277–278.

Olsen-Fulero, Lynda, and Fulero, Solomon M. (1997, June 1). Commonsense Rape Judgements: An Empathy-Complexity Theory of Rape Juror Story Making. *Psychology, Public Policy and Law*, 3(2–3), 402–427.

U.S. v. Richard Junior Frazier, 387 F.3d 1244; 2004 U.S. App. Lexis 21503.

U.S. v. Victor T. Steele, 2000 U.S. App. Lexis 14097.

U.S. Navy, Naval Aviation Schools Command, Pensacola, Florida, 2006.

Chapter five

Predatory Kidnapping– Child Victim

CHAPTER CONTENTS

WHAT DEFINES THE PREDATORY KIDNAPPING–CHILD VICTIM?

As is true of the predatory kidnappings of adults, predatory kidnappings–child victims are sexually motivated acts perpetrated by offenders who purposefully or opportunistically abduct victims to

69

satiate their needs. By definition, these abductors prey on those who are under 18 years of age.

Table 5.1 summarizes the characteristics of the predatory kidnapping–child victim. This kidnapping subtype is also illustrated by the cases of Don Harris, John Whitehead, and Patrick Champion and Debra Williams.

Table 5.1 Elements of the Predatory Kidnapping–Child Victim

Victimology & Offender Characteristics	1. The victim was under 18 years of age.	100%
	2. The victim and the offender were strangers to one another.	57%
	3. The victim and the offender had a relationship prior to the abduction.	43%
	4. The offender and the victim were of different genders.	93%
	5. The offender and the victim are of different ethnicities.	NA*
	6. The victim was low risk, i.e., not likely to be immediately missed or reported as missing.	0%
	7. The offender was unemployed at the time of the abduction.	NA*
	8. The offender was employed at the time of the abduction.	NA*
Abduction Site	1. The abduction occurred in a public place.	64%
	2. The victim was abducted from a private location (such as home, school, workplace).	36%
Modus Operandi	1. The abduction was perpetrated by more than one offender.	36%
	2. The victim was chosen randomly or opportunistically.	60%
	3. Physical force was used to abduct the victim.	36%
	4. The victim was abducted following verbal threats of harm to himself or herself and/or others.	29%
	5. The victim's abduction was the result of persuasion or deception.	29%
	6. The offender used a firearm to facilitate the abduction.	21%
	7. The offender used a knife to facilitate the abduction.	14%
	8. The offender used a weapon, other than a knife or a firearm, or did not use a weapon, to facilitate the abduction.	36%
	9. The offender sexually assaulted the victim during the abduction.	93%
	10. The offender physically assaulted the victim during the abduction in a manner that did result in death.	36%
	11. The offender physically assaulted the victim during the abduction in a manner that did not result in death.	50%
	12. The offender did not assault or physically harm the victim during the abduction (excludes sexual assault).	14%
	13. The offender transported the victim during the abduction.	100%
	14. The offender did not transport the victim during the abduction.	0%

Continued...

Table 5.1 Elements of the Predatory Kidnapping–Child Victim—continued

	15. The offender exhibited obvious psychotic symptoms (delusions, hallucinations, etc.).	0%
	16. The offender held the victim captive for greater than 24 hours.	14%
	17. The offender held the victim captive for less than 24 hours.	79%
	18. The kidnapping occurred in the morning (midnight–8 a.m.).	0%
	19. The kidnapping occurred during the day (8 a.m.–4 p.m.).	29%
	20. The kidnapping occurred in the evening/at night (4 p.m.– midnight).	57%
	21. More than one victim was abducted.	14%
Outcome	1. The abduction was witnessed.	29%
	2. The victim was released by the offender.	29%
	3. The victim escaped.	14%
	4. The victim was released following law enforcement intervention.	14%
	5. The victim was not found.	0%
	6. The victim was found dead.	36%
	7. The victim was discovered in a public place.	57%
	8. The victim was discovered in a private place (a home, school, or workplace).	43%
	9. Witness testimony contributed to the offender's apprehension/ conviction (not limited to event witnesses).	71%
	10. Physical evidence contributed to the offender's apprehension/ conviction.	93%
	11. Accomplice statements contributed to the offender's apprehension/ conviction.	0%
	12. Victim testimony contributed to the abductor's apprehension/ conviction.	57%

*NA-Insufficient data to render determination.

Don Harris

On the morning of June 17, 1985, the 14-year-old female victim and her 4-year-old male cousin walked to the local store to buy milk. On their way home, the two were approached by Don Harris, with whom neither the victim nor her cousin had a prior relationship. Harris shoved a gun into the victim's side.

"Do you see this?" Harris reportedly demanded. He used the gun to force both children into his nearby car. Harris placed duct tape-covered glasses over the victim's eyes. He told her that she looked like a girl who had stabbed his sister. The victim denied knowledge of the stabbing. Harris demanded to know the victim's address and age. The victim lied, giving him a false address and stating that she was 12 instead of her actual age of 14.

Harris asked the victim if she was a virgin. The victim affirmed that she was. Harris drove to an alley and dragged the children from the car into a nearby garage. Once inside, he ordered the victim's 4-year-old cousin to sit on a couch and ordered the victim to lift her skirt and unbutton her shorts. Thereafter, he sexually assaulted the victim. Harris was unable to maintain his erection. He turned to the victim's cousin and said, "Thanks for ruining my fun" in response to the child's crying.

Harris ordered the victim to dress. He blindfolded her and drove her and her cousin to a location four blocks from where he had abducted them. He told his victim that he was glad that she had "cooperated" with him and that she was "the first one I didn't kill." He ordered the children to walk home and said that if they turned around, he would shoot them. He also told them that if they reported what had occurred, he would kill them.

When the victim returned home, she immediately told her aunt what had transpired. Her aunt called law enforcement, and the victim led officers to the garage where the assault occurred. She identified Harris's gray Riviera model automobile. A search of Harris's home yielded a shotgun, a Tek-9, and two handguns. The last were found in a brown paper bag in an oven; one was identified as the gun used to apprehend the victim and her cousin. A search of Harris's car yielded duct tape, and a search of the garage yielded the sunglasses that Harris had used to blindfold the victim. The victim subsequently identified Harris from a lineup.

John Whitehead

On the evening of August 9, 1982, the 5-year-old victim disappeared from her home in Joliet, Illinois. Her mother searched for the child at the house adjacent to her family's home. The victim's mother and her husband rented the house to a woman named Esther, Esther's daughter LeAllen and LeAllen's husband. The house was also shared by John Whitehead.

Esther told the victim's mother that she had not seen the victim. She did report, however, that both Whitehead and the car he would occasionally borrow from her were missing.

Shortly after midnight following the victim's disappearance, Whitehead telephoned Esther's home and reported his whereabouts. Esther's daughter told Whitehead to remain where he was. She then telephoned law enforcement.

Officers were dispatched to the reported location where they found Esther's car parked in front of the home and Whitehead seated in the living room. Whitehead admitted taking the car and was arrested for auto theft. He was questioned from 4:00 a.m. to 6:30 a.m., and was described as generally cooperative but unwilling to answer questions in relation to the victim or her whereabouts, responding "I can't" or "I can't tell you" in relation to inquiries. At 6:30 a.m., Whitehead asked for an attorney.

At approximately 7:30 a.m., railroad workers discovered a naked body floating in the Mazon River. The body was later identified as the victim's. Articles of the victim's clothing and a shirt later identified as that worn by Whitehead were found beside the river. Inside Whitehead's shirt pocket was a lottery ticket with writing later identified as his. Articles of the victim's clothing were also found in the front seat of the car that Whitehead stole from Esther, as was the cup that held a non-alcoholic "cocktail" that the victim was given at her parents' tavern.

Following the discovery of the victim's body, Whitehead made eight separate statements to law enforcement during which he admitted to forcing the victim to drink beer before sexually assaulting, strangling, and drowning her. Whitehead's account was consistent with the findings of the victim's autopsy.

Patrick Champion and Debra Williams

The 13-year-old victim met Patrick Champion and Debra Williams in an Internet chat room, where the two posed as a 19-year-old male. When the victim disclosed problems she was having with her parents, the 19-year-old persona of Champion and Williams suggested that the victim leave her Arizona home and join "him" at his house in Tennessee. The victim agreed to meet her Internet contact in Arizona.

When the victim arrived at the meeting place, she was greeted by Champion, who claimed to be the father of the 19-year-old the victim had met on the Internet.

The victim accompanied Champion to Tennessee, where she learned that the 19-year-old was actually the assumed identity of Champion and his girlfriend Debra Williams.

During her 3-day captivity, the victim was repeatedly sexually assaulted and photographed by both Champion and Williams.

On December 25, 1998, the victim was left alone in the abductors' home. She called 911 and law enforcement was dispatched to the home. Champion and Williams returned to the home while the victim was being interviewed. Upon questioning, the two admitted to abducting and sexually assaulting the victim. A search of the home yielded sexually explicit photographs of the victim, as well as various pornographic magazines, cameras, undeveloped film, computer floppy discs, and a notebook labeled "Internet." The last contained handwritten entries of the Internet addresses and e-mail contacts that Champion and Williams had acquired, including the contact information for the victim.

CHARACTERISTICS OF THE PREDATORY KIDNAPPING–CHILD VICTIM

Victimology

The victims of predatory kidnappings are children under the age of 18. With one exception, the victims of the cases reviewed were girls abducted by men. The exception occurred in the case of Harris, who also abducted the male cousin of his female victim.

Harris's case also illustrates the typical offender-victim relationship for this subtype: The majority of victims of child predatory kidnappings (57 percent) had no prior relationship to their abductors. In a significant minority of cases (43 percent), the victim and abductor were acquaintances. As in the case of Whitehead, the abductor was typically a familiar figure from school or a frequented play area, or had a relationship with the child's parent.

In several cases, the prior child/abductor relationship was forged via contact on the Internet, as in the abduction perpetrated by Patrick Champion and Debra Williams.

Abduction Site

Don Harris abducted his victims on a public street. Patrick Champion met his victim on a street in Arizona. John Whitehead took his victim from the street outside her family's tavern.

The choice of public places as abduction sites is consistent with the majority (64 percent) of predatory kidnappings of children. In public places, children are more likely to be unsupervised by parents or guardians, and are easier targets for the predatory kidnapper.

Modus Operandi

The approaches used by these abductors to subdue their victims reflect the spectrum of methods used by child predatory kidnappers. Use of force or verbal threats, as exhibited by Don Harris, occurred in 36 percent and 29 percent of cases, respectively. The deception perpetrated by Patrick Champion, and the persuasion most likely used by John Whitehead, was used in 29 percent of cases. Kidnapping by more than one offender, as occurred in the case of Champion and Williams, was consistent with slightly more than one-third of the cases reviewed (36 percent).

In every case reviewed (100 percent), the offender transported his victim, and in a majority of cases, he held her for less than 24 hours (79 percent). As in the case of Whitehead, the majority of abductions occurred between 4 p.m. and midnight (57 percent), hours when children have typically completed the school day.

The three cases presented are, tragically, also consistent in another respect to the majority of the predatory kidnapping–child victim cases reviewed: In the majority of cases reviewed (93 percent), the victim was sexually assaulted.

As with the sexual violence perpetrated by the adult predatory kidnapper, the sexual assault by the predatory kidnapper of the child is not the result of psychosis or other forms of severe mental illness (Axis I disorders). In the cases studied, none of the kidnappers exhibited obvious psychotic symptoms, such as delusions or hallucinations.

Victims of child predatory kidnappings survived their abduction in 64 percent of the cases reviewed; a significant minority (36%) did not. Additionally, and contrary to the myth that child predators are likely to gently "court" their victims, the majority of the child predatory kidnappers reviewed (86 percent) physically harmed their victims beyond the sexual assault.

Outcome

Harris's case illustrates the most common manner in which children survive the predatory kidnapper: release by the offender (29 percent of cases).

Children were equally likely to survive their abduction following law enforcement intervention (14 percent) as by facilitating their own escape (14 percent).

As in the kidnapping perpetrated by Harris, 93 percent of the child predatory kidnappers left significant physical evidence that contributed to their apprehension and convictions.

Victim testimony also played a crucial role in the offender's apprehension and conviction: 57 percent of the child victims who survived their ordeal provided critical testimony against their kidnappers.

Although the majority of child predatory kidnappings were unwitnessed, witnesses identified during the course of the investigation played a pivotal role in bringing the child predatory kidnapper to justice; witness testimony contributed to the offender's apprehension and conviction in 71 percent of the cases reviewed.

IMPLICATIONS FOR PREVENTION AND INVESTIGATION

The years known as childhood and adolescence are characterized by a significant number of physical, emotional, intellectual, and psychological changes. While there are individual differences in the rate and timing of development, the interplay of a child's genetic disposition and the environment generally results in a predictable trajectory of significant stages.

Knowledge of the developmental stages that typify the under-18-year-old can improve the effectiveness of the security or law enforcement professional engaged in the prevention and investigation of child predatory kidnappings.

In their landmark study on child abduction, Bourdreaux et al. (1999) found that risk factors for victimization varied according to the child's developmental stage. The researchers reviewed 550 Federal Bureau of Investigation cases and found that "victim age and gender have been shown to be critical variables in child victimization cases."

The Bourdreaux study subjects were divided into seven age categories: neonate (0–1 month); infant (1–12 months); toddler (13–36 months); preschool (3–5 years); elementary school (6–11 years); middle school (12–14 years); and high school (15–17 years). Consistent with the current research, the vast majority of abducted children age 6 and over were abducted by male offenders for sexually motivated reasons. (Neonates, infants, toddlers, and preschoolers were found to be equally likely to be abducted by males or females, and more likely to be abducted for what the researchers labeled "emotionally based" reasons or with the intent of keeping the child. The former is explored in Chapter 3, "Domestic Kidnapping," while the latter is discussed in Chapter 6, "Profit Kidnapping").

While the likely gender of both the victim and offender was found to remain consistent throughout childhood and adolescence, significant differences were found in the relationship between victim and offender. Children aged 6 through 11 and those aged 15 to 17 were more likely to be abducted by acquaintances than by strangers. Conversely, children aged 12 to 14 were more likely to be abducted by strangers than by acquaintances.

The differences in the offender-victim relationship is one of the many factors that is influenced by the child's developmental stage: Younger children are more likely to be supervised by consistent guardianship, while teens have generally affiliated with a consistent peer group; each environment is more difficult for the stranger to penetrate. Conversely, children aged 12 to 14 are typically in a period of identity confusion and are more likely to drift from one set of peers to another, rendering them more vulnerable to approach by a stranger.

Several additional developmental factors, including the child's cognitive characteristics and learning abilities, also suggest safety promotion approaches that can be incorporated into community education efforts and maximize the available resources of local law enforcement and security professionals.

Factors Related to the 6- to 10-Year-Old

Between the ages of 6 and 11, the child's world expands. Her social sphere grows beyond her immediate family to include relationships with friends, teachers, coaches, and others. Through these interactions, the child realizes that she is not the center of the universe. She becomes acquainted with new rules and codes of conduct. As she negotiates this previously unfamiliar territory, she typically obeys the directions of the adults around her.

She also seeks approval for her efforts in the eyes of adults other than her parents or guardians. During this time, children are prone to "hero worship." In contrast to the preschool years, when children are more likely to idolize popular fictional characters, it is not unusual for elementary school children to speak frequently of an adult and to behave in a manner that pleases him or her.

These normal developments have implications for the prevention of child predatory kidnappings: As children obey and seek to please adults who they perceive to be in positions of authority, they are vulnerable to manipulation by those with malintent.

Prior to age 10, the child is typically unaware of the potential for individuals to manipulate their presentation. Children tend to be very concrete and believe that "what you see is what you get." They also tend to believe they "know" someone based on the briefest of encounters and to decide they like someone based on that individual's most recent behavior. "Mr. B. is my friend because he let me play with his dog," the elementary schoolchild will think. The child's willingness to orient his relationships based on limited experience of others is partially why experts have abandoned "stranger danger" prevention curriculum. "Never talk to strangers" is not effective when the child believes that anyone who is nice is a friend. "Children do not have the same understanding of 'strangers' as adults," cautions the National Center for Missing and Exploited Children.

In the cases reviewed, 29 percent of child predatory kidnappers used persuasion or deception as a means to approach their victims; these perpetrators took advantage of the child's vulnerability to manipulation.

Advising parents and guardians to carefully attend to the content of the child's discussions about the new "heroes" and "friends" in her world can serve as an important tool in preventing harm, including that perpetrated by the child predatory kidnapper.

Additional prevention efforts can include the use of "what if" scenarios. Children at this stage generally have the language skills and cognitive ability to tell a story from beginning to end. This ability, coupled with their developing problem-solving skills, allows them to participate in "what if" safety narratives. (For example, "What if one of the adults at school offers to drive you home?" "What if your friend's older brother wants you to take a walk with him?") As noted earlier, children's thinking at this stage is concrete; "what if" scenarios should be likewise and should include examples from as many typical experiences in the child's life as possible. At this stage of development, children may not be able to abstract the lesson from one "what if" scenario to a different (albeit similar) situation. Additionally, children at this stage learn more effectively through active learning. Studies related to traffic safety curriculum, for example, reveal that children are more likely to engage in safe behaviors—such as looking both ways before crossing the street, not running in a crowded parking lot—when the lesson is taught amidst real or play cars. The same is true with the "what if" safety lessons: Conducting these lessons *in vivo* (outside the school when discussing school-based scenarios, outside a library when "what if" scenarios involve that location) can facilitate the child's integration of safety lessons.

Factors That Affect the 11- to 13-Year-Old

Age 11 for girls, and a year later for boys, typically heralds the beginning of puberty. While the cognitive abilities that the child has attained prior to this time remain intact, the physical, hormonal, and sexual changes challenge her emotional balance. This disequilibrium is often reflected in—and imposed upon—her outer world.

The child's emotional volatility corresponds with her attempts to establish autonomy while negotiating relationships with both caregivers and peers. She regresses to a self-centeredness not seen since preschool as she attempts to understand and define herself. These attempts frequently include "trying out" different social circles, which help her identify her interests and values. As noted earlier, her shifting allegiances may render her more vulnerable to abduction by a stranger than when she was younger, or than when she matures and her peer group becomes more stable. Additionally, the pre-teen's vulnerability stems from the further expansion of her world. She may venture further from her immediate community to meet with her new friends. She may engage in after-school activities that involve less direct supervision.

The pre-teen has the capacity to evaluate the trustworthiness of others and is no longer easily manipulated by their initial presentation. She also strives to present herself in a manner that is socially desirable. She may find herself behaving in ways or participating in activities that she finds uncomfortable in an effort to "fit in."

During this developmental stage, the child tends to vacillate between rebellion and dependence as she struggles to be appropriately assertive, i.e., to actively defend and pursue her own interests. Mastery of this critical developmental milestone has been linked to classroom participation and educational success, positive relationships with parents and peers, and the ability to sustain healthy relationships throughout adulthood. It has also been linked to the prevention of victimization. Lack of success in developing assertiveness has been implicated in the development of depression, anxiety, social phobias, and increased risk of victimization.

The law enforcement or security professional who participates in community-based safety education efforts with children at this developmental stage should consider the use of "what if" scenarios that allow the child to verbally and physically defend herself (such as via scenarios through which she can envision herself saying "no," raising her voice, or walking away). The scenarios can support the child to effectively self-advocate, when appropriate, and self-defend, when necessary.

Engaging the child in "what if" scenarios during the pre-teen years may be more challenging than during previous stages. The emotionality and rebelliousness displayed by the pre-teen gives the impression that she is no longer willing to take direction or advice from adults. Eye rolling and giggling are typical behaviors of the pre-teen. Nonetheless, the professional who asserts control over the group will have an impact. The pre-teen's values and worldview continue to be primarily influenced by adults during this stage.

Factors That Affect the 14- to 17-Year-Old

During the teen years, the child's social sphere stabilizes once again. As she draws conclusions about her interests and values, she tends to affiliate with a peer group that shares both. Developmentally, the typical adolescent has the cognitive, physical, and psychological capacities of the adult she is becoming. The teenager will frequently sound—and may even look—older than her years.

Her maturity, however, is untempered by experience, and she may overestimate her ability to negotiate challenging situations. Often this is reflected in the excessiveness—driving too fast, drinking too much, dressing too provocatively—that has been associated with the adolescent's seeming sense of immortality. Her opportunity for risk-taking behaviors increases as she spends greater time in peer-only interactions outside the supervision of adults, and as she learns to drive, which grants her greater freedom to explore unfamiliar geographic and social territory.

Increasingly, adolescents are also traveling the vast expanse of cyberspace. In 2002, the U.S. Department of Justice estimated that 30 million children under the age of 18 go online each year. Youth ages 12 to 17 were estimated to spend up to 15 hours per week "surfing," e-mailing, or doing homework online. Use of the Internet by adolescents has been found to fall into three major categories: (1) cognitive development and academic achievement, in which the Internet is used as a tool in completing school-related projects; (2) access to sensitive subjects, such as health-related sites that offer information on safe sex practices and sexually transmitted diseases that the adolescent may be embarrassed to discuss in person; and (3) communication with others, frequently through "bulletin boards," chat rooms, and social networking sites such as My Space.

The last offers the adolescent an easy, fast way to communicate with friends and family (such as via instant messages), as well as a means to interact with youth from across the county and around the world.

This type of Internet use also poses potential challenges to the adolescent's safety (as illustrated by the kidnapping perpetrated by Champion and Williams, discussed previously). The milieu of the Internet allows individuals to share deeply personal information at any hour of the day, creating a false sense of intimacy. This intimacy is exploited by online sexual predators, who frequently masquerade as adolescents with similar interests, values, and needs. In recent years, the stigma of meeting the individual with whom one has developed a relationship online has eased, with the unintended consequence of allowing sexual predators greater access to the youth with whom they communicate. Research conducted by the University of New Hampshire and the National Center for Missing and Exploited Children found that one in five children aged 10 to 17 received a sexual solicitation over the Internet during the previous year.

To mitigate the potential risk posed by the Internet, community safety efforts with this age group should incorporate Federal Bureau of Investigation guidelines, including

- Communicating with the child about sexual victimization and potential online dangers;
- Identifying and evaluating teens' favorite online destinations;
- Recommending that computers be kept in a common room;
- Recommending that parents and educators utilize parental controls and/or blocking software;

- Recommending that parents and guardians maintain access to the child's online account and randomly check his or her e-mail;
- Teaching children the responsible use of resources online;
- Instructing teens
  - To never arrange a face-to-face meeting with someone they meet online;
  - To never upload (post) pictures of themselves onto the Internet or online service to people they don't personally know;
  - To never give out identifying information such as their name, home, address, school name, or telephone number;
  - To never download pictures from an unknown source;
  - To never respond to messages or bulletin board postings that are suggestive, obscene, belligerent, or harassing;
  - That whatever they are told online may or may not be true.

The adolescent actively seeks the respect of the adults with whom she interacts and wants to "practice" her new capacities by participating in decision making. Engaging adolescents in the creation of rules to which they would be willing to commit will enhance the likelihood of compliance and of effectively supporting safety offline and online.

The Predatory Kidnapping–Child Victim Investigation

Despite community-based prevention efforts by law enforcement and numerous laws enacted during the past several decades, nearly 60,000 children are abducted by non-family members each year.

As was true in the cases reviewed for this research, the Office of Juvenile Justice and Delinquency Prevention (OJJDP) reports that the majority of children abducted by strangers or acquaintances are reunited with their families. The Office notes, however, the first few hours following the abduction of a child "are critical."

Law enforcement personnel must immediately determine the type of case being reported, i.e., whether the child has been abducted, is lost, or is a runaway. The resources needed to investigate, including social service support, must also be determined. In the past several decades, many police departments, working in conjunction with the OJJDP and the National Center for Missing and Exploited Children (NCMEC), have adopted operational procedures that help guide the officer's decision making. The OJJDP/NCMEC Model Policy suggests that the law enforcement officer who receives a missing child report respond as if the child is at risk, particularly if the report involves a child who is

- Under 13 years of age;
- Believed to be out of the zone which is considered safe for his or her age, developmental stage, or physical condition;
- Mentally diminished;
- Drug-dependent;
- A potential victim of foul play or sexual exploitation (as suggested by the abduction site);
- In a life-threatening situation;
- Missing for more than 24 hours;
- Believed to be with others who could endanger his or her welfare;
- Is absent under circumstances inconsistent with established patterns of behavior.

After the law enforcement officer takes the missing child report, the National Child Search Assistance Act of 1990 mandates that descriptive information about the child be entered into the Federal Bureau of Investigation's National Crime Information Center (NCIC) Missing Persons File. Thereafter, the law enforcement can

- Issue alerts and bulletins, including a Be On the Lookout (BOLO) alert to other law enforcement agencies;

- Activate the America's Missing: Broadcasting Emergency Response (AMBERT Alert), through which details of the abduction are disseminated to media and transportation agencies that, in turn, issue bulletins about the child's disappearance. AMBER Alerts are typically used when it appears an abduction involves a child who is 17 or younger who is feared to be in imminent danger of serious bodily harm or death. For an AMBER Alert to be issued, there must also be enough information to believe that the broadcast will be helpful;

- Administer polygraph tests to rule out immediate family members;

- Establish a command post to coordinate searches, interviews, and potential media communication.

Given the proliferation of online predators and the increasing number of children who are exposed to offenders online, law enforcement should also consider removing the child's or family's computer for potential evidence. The computer should be turned off and evaluated by an individual skilled in doing so to ensure that any evidence is preserved.

Additionally, law enforcement confronted with the potential predatory kidnapping of the child can access the Sex Offender Registration list.

With the passage of the Jacob Wetterling Crimes Against Children and Sexually Violent Offender Registration Program in 1994, each state is required to establish a sex offender registration and community notification program or lose a percentage of federal law enforcement funds. The registration lists, which are now widely accessible on the Internet, typically include the convicted sex offender's current address, telephone number, Social Security number, and employment information. In 2006, Congress took steps to improve offender registration compliance via the passage of the Adam Walsh Child Protection and Safety Act. Through this act, the NCMEC and the United States Marshall Services join to apprehend non-compliant offenders.

Sex offender registration laws are designed to meet two purposes: to deter sex offenders from recidivism and to assist law enforcement in investigating known sex offenders in an area where a sex crime is committed. Current research shows little evidence that the registration lists are effective in either regard. A study of the Washington State notification law, the oldest such law in the nation, concluded that there is no significant difference in the recidivism rate for registered and non-registered offenders. Additional research has also led to the conclusion that the lists do not facilitate law enforcement in their investigations.

Despite prevailing research, law enforcement personnel report that they believe registration lists assist in crime investigation. Additionally, there are anecdotal accounts of the successful use of registration lists in preventing re-offense and facilitating apprehension of recidivists.

Given the sexual motivation that underlies the predatory kidnapping of a child, the Sex Offender Registry is an appropriate investigatory tool.

In addition to identifying information, the offender registry typically includes information on the offense for which the offender was convicted, such as lewd and lascivious behavior with a child, forcible rape, indecent exposure, etc.

These distinctions may not be as relevant as once believed. In the past, it was generally accepted that offenders tend to group by victim selection, i.e., that offenders who violate children only violate children; those who violate strangers do not violate acquaintances or family members; those who offend in non-contact ways, such as "peeping" or exhibitionism, do not perpetrate acts involving physical contact. More recent analysis reveals that sex offenders frequently exhibit more than one category of sexually deviant behavior. The exception is the offender diagnosed with the Pedophilia-Exclusive Type. As with all pedophiles, these individuals exhibit a minimum 6-month history of intensely sexually arousing fantasies, sexual urges, or behaviors involving sexual activity with a prepubescent child or children who are generally age 13 or younger. By clinical definition, these individuals are at least 16 years of age and at least 5 years older than their victims. The Pedophile-Exclusive Type focuses solely on children to derive sexual satisfaction. The majority of pedophiles, however, are non-exclusive and also engage in age-appropriate sexual relationships.

The likelihood that sex offenders who recidivate defy single offense categories supports the allocation of resources to interview all offenders within a given area, regardless of the controlling offense for which the offender is registered.

An additional factor that has been linked to an offender's likelihood to recidivate is an antisocial lifestyle. From a clinical perspective, antisocial traits include a failure to conform to social norms with respect to lawful behaviors; deceitfulness; impulsivity or failure to plan ahead; irritability and aggressiveness; reckless disregard for the safety of self or others; consistent irresponsibility; and lack of remorse. These traits may manifest as an inability to sustain relationships or employment, or belligerence in interactions with the offender's parole agent or other law enforcement official.

In this author's experience, paroled sex offenders fall into three broad categories:

1. Those who committed their offense while under the influence of drugs and alcohol, have no prior or only substance-related prior offenses, and typically commit statutory or partner rape.

2. Those who are convicted under aggressive sex offender prosecutions. These individuals, while representing a very

small minority of offenders, typically commit non-contact crimes, have no prior offense history, and are convicted under ambiguous circumstances. (One offender with whom the author worked, for example, was convicted of exhibitionism after an adult female witnessed his urinating behind a tree in a public park after dark.)

3. Those who exhibit the antisocial traits that place them at higher recidivism risk.

The last category is, in the author's experience, by far the most prevalent. These offenders commit crimes against children, adults, or both and have prior offense histories that may include sexual offenses and typically include non-sex offenses. They tend to rationalize or deny their crimes. In part this is a habituated response. Sex offenders are at higher risk of prison violence and, as a result, spend their incarcerated time denying their offense; by the time of release (which averages 6 years following conviction in state court and 8 years when convicted in federal court), they believe their own lies. These offenders frequently take no personal responsibility for any significant aspect of their lives. They claim that their convictions are the products of an unjust judicial system or an incompetent defense attorney or a political conspiracy. They see themselves as the victims, particularly when subject to parole conditions that limit their freedom (such as those that prohibit drinking alcohol or Internet use) and state regulations that limit the locations in which they can live.

A number of the child molesters with whom the author has worked blamed a "sexually repressed" American society for their crimes, claiming that sex with minors was an acceptable practice in other cultures and should be so in the United States. Some cited biblical references to justify their sexual assaults. A significant number also blamed the child victim; it is not uncommon to hear claims that the child "seduced" or somehow invited the offender's advances.

In short, a significant number of sex offenders express justification for their actions and may not be diligent in concealing their activities to the interrogator who appears sympathetic to their deviance.

While a potential aid to the investigator, the offender's proclivity for blaming his victim collides with the child's own tendency to blame herself for the trauma inflicted upon her and is, therefore, also a factor that the investigator should consider when interviewing the child victim.

The initial meeting between the child and her family plays a significant role in the child's recovery and in her ability to report the circumstances of her abduction. Investigators should arrange for an initial meeting that is limited to the child, her immediate family, and the lead investigator.

Following the initial reunification, the investigator must proceed with the delicate task of interviewing the child victim. As the testimony of victims contributed to the apprehension and conviction of abductors in 57 percent of the cases reviewed, the ability to successfully interview children has particular relevance to the child predatory kidnapping.

The investigator must be prepared for the potential spectrum of the child's post-trauma reactions, which can range from being highly emotive to being non-responsive or "numb." Investigators should also recognize that children can be vulnerable to cognitive distortions about the events that occurred and be highly susceptible to suggestibility, i.e., the tendency to incorporate outside influences or others' biases into their accounts. Each of these challenges can be mitigated by the investigator's knowledge of and sensitivity to the child's developmental stage.

Younger children, for example, are more vulnerable to suggestion than adolescents and adults. Young children's memory processing (encoding, storage, and retrieval) is not as advanced as adults. They are more likely to make source attributions and have a greater tendency to blame themselves for the trauma they experience. They are more likely to provide the "right answer" (i.e., the answer they perceive their interviewer wants to hear) upon repeated questioning.

Both young children and adolescents differ from adults in their judgment. Youth are more likely to provide answers that they believe offer short-term gain—such as stopping a painful interview. Additionally, and as is true for adults, fatigue and sleep deprivation (a common occurrence following involvement in a traumatic episode) can increase the likelihood of suggestibility during the interview process.

The skilled interviewer will consider these factors when interviewing the child victim of the predatory kidnapper. "Despite frequent claims that children are uniquely susceptible to external influence, it is clear that when children are encouraged to describe their experience without manipulation by interviewers, their accounts can be extremely informative and accurate," concluded a group of 22 international scholars who convened in Sweden in 1993 to evaluate child testimony. The group also made the following recommendations for the interviewer:

1. Interviews should be conducted as soon after the event as possible.
2. Multiple interviews should be discouraged, since frequent questioning by different interviewers can distort memory and lead to confusion.
3. Leading questions should be avoided.
4. With older children, open-ended questions (e.g., "Tell me everything you remember about what happened") designed to elicit free narrative accounts should be used.
5. With children younger than 6, direct questions using developmentally appropriate vocabulary can be used.

Researchers Ceci and Bruck add that the following acts by interviewers can adversely impact the credibility of the child's testimony:

1. Neglecting to ask questions that might provide alternate explanations than what the interviewer believes occurred;
2. Neglecting to inquire about events that are consistent with the investigator's hypothesis;
3. Neglecting to challenge the authenticity of the report when it confirms the investigator's hypothesis;
4. Ignoring inconsistent and bizarre evidence.

The international group also found that anatomical dolls can be useful early in the interviewing process to understand the child's labels for various body parts and to help with the reenactment of events that are beyond the child's vocabulary. Consistent with developmental stages, younger children do appear to use the dolls for language substitution, while children age 12 and over tend to use dolls for memory retrieval. Several studies have cautioned, however, that the use of dolls can produce information that is more fantasy or fear-based than reality-based. This is especially true of the young child, whose concrete thinking and inability to abstract may prevent her from seeing the doll as a self-representation, rather than as a separate object. Overall, anatomical dolls should be used with extreme caution.

A final recommendation made by the international group has been consistently endorsed: All interviews with children should be videotaped.

Videotaping preempts the need for multiple interviews and interviews by different individuals involved in the investigation, each of which tax limited resources, create unnecessary stress for the child, and expose interviewers to accusations of coaching or leading. In some jurisdictions and under certain circumstances, the use of videotape may be an acceptable substitute for the child testifying in the intimidating atmosphere of the courtroom. (It should be noted that many courts require children to testify in person to protect the accused kidnappers' Sixth Amendment right to confront witnesses.)

In relation to suspect identification, children as young as 5 years have been found to be as accurate as adults in making correct identifications from lineups and "six packs" when the offender is present. However, they do not perform as well as adults when the offender is absent. Cautioning the child that the offender (or his picture) may or may not be present has been shown to increase identification accuracy.

In the emotionally charged period following the recovery of child kidnapping victims, it is not unusual for parents to turn to law enforcement when the slow pace of the justice system seems to interfere with the child's emotional healing process. While every child responds differently to a traumatic event, children generally have a more difficult time "turning off" memories of these events, particularly in the immediate aftermath. The trial, which typically occurs months after the incident, can re-activate memories at a time when they no longer dominate the youth's consciousness. In cases in which the child is required to testify, law enforcement should consider the use of "court schools," which can help minimize the risk of re-traumatization. Allowing the child to become familiar with the courtroom prior to the trial, clearly explaining what the child can expect in language she can understand, listening to and answering any questions she may have, and allowing a trusted adult to remain in the courtroom during trial can support the child to be a more credible witness, as well as provide her with a much needed sense of control. For some children, the trial experience can actually help restore their sense of power.

Other child victims may exhibit intense anxiety, depression, and/or anger. Depending on the child's age, the last may manifest in play with other children, in which the child emulates the aggressor and may "bully" playmates. This is of particular concern with male victims; there is some evidence that males who are sexually exploited as children are more likely to become abusers as adults.

The trauma of the child predatory kidnapping is also frequently felt throughout the community and can have a "contagion" effect upon a community's youth, causing an increase in acting-out behaviors, including delinquency.

The investigator involved in the child predatory kidnapping investigation should consider engaging mental health professionals, facilitating the establishment of peer support groups, and involving trained professionals, such as those affiliated with the National Center for Missing and Exploited Children, to ensure that the child predatory kidnapper does not continue to trail victims in his wake.

THE McMARTIN PRESCHOOL TRIAL

In April 1983, 28-year-old Ray Buckley, his mother Peggy, his sister Peggy Ann, his grandmother Virginia, and three female teachers (each of whom was over 50 years of age) were imprisoned on charges stemming from 360 alleged cases of sexual abuse against the children of their Manhattan Beach, California, preschool. The McMartin Preschool trial became one of the longest court cases—and one of the greatest travesties of justice—in modern history. Passion, politics, and fear overruled evidence. Children were all but coerced into accusing the McMartin staff of abusing them. To prepare for trial, the Los Angeles District Attorney's Office involved an unlicensed social worker from the Children's Institute International at the University of California Los Angeles. By trial's end, it would become apparent that the social worker's interview strategies—which included suggesting abuse narratives to the children instead of allowing spontaneous disclosure; repeatedly asking the same question until receiving a desired response; using anatomically explicit dolls to determine that sexual assault had, in fact, occurred; and informing children who denied victimization that their friends said they were lying—resulted in predictably fabricated incidents. The resulting accounts were at times improbable (that Ray took the children to a ranch and a hotel) and at times bizarre (that Ray chopped off a baby's head and forced a child to drink the blood). Despite consistent judicial rulings that placed the defendants at extreme disadvantage, the jury of six ultimately acquitted all defendants save Ray Buckley, on whose charges they hung. He was subsequently acquitted during a second trial.

Promoting Community-Based Internet Safety

The National Center for Missing and Exploited Children estimates that one in five children aged 10 to 17 receive a sexual solicitation over the Internet during a 1-year period. Increasingly, child sexual predators utilize the Internet to connect with potential victims. Law enforcement personnel and security professionals can offer parents and guardians sample contracts, such as the following, to support the prevention of predatory kidnappings.

Parent-Child Contract for Internet Safety

I ——, have read this contract with my mom/dad/legal guardian —— and I understand the rules of Internet use in my home. I will keep this contract clearly posted by my computer. If I should run into any problems while surfing the Internet or while in a chat room, I will contact my parents and abide by the rules listed in this contract.

Child's Responsibilities:

1. I will never give out my home telephone number or address over the Internet.
2. I will not give out any information about my family, such as where my parents work and the names of my brothers or sisters.
3. I will not use my real name in chat rooms and will always use a "nickname."
4. I will not tell a stranger on the Internet where I go to school.
5. I will never meet someone I have talked to on the Internet unless my parents approve and come with me to the meeting.
6. I will never send pictures of my family or me over the Internet without my parent's permission.
7. I will not talk to anyone over the Internet who makes me feel uncomfortable; I will tell my parents right away when this happens.
8. I will tell my parents if anyone is threatening me or using bad language.
9. I will always keep in mind while talking to people on the Internet that they are strangers and some strangers can be bad.
10. I will obey my parents' rules about being on the Internet, including obtaining their permission to sign on and download material.

Parent's Responsibilities:

I ——, will supervise my children while they are on the Internet to ensure they are using this tool responsibly and not endangering themselves by communicating inappropriately with strangers they may meet over the Internet.

1. I will not use this contact as a way to control every action taken by my child on the Internet.
2. I will respect my child's need for a degree of privacy while speaking to friends on the Internet.

Continued...

3. I will spend time with my child and learn about what interests him or her on the Internet.

4. I will be aware of the procedure for contacting my online provider for advice should someone appear to be bothering my child. I will also contact the Cyber Tip Line at 800-843-5678 or http://www.cybertipline.com if I suspect someone has been soliciting my child for sex or sending pornographic material to my child.

5. I will teach my child to use judgment while online, and I will ensure that my child is educated about the hazards of Internet use and how to safely use the Internet.

Parent's Signature:

Child's Signature:

Date:

Reprinted with permission.

REFERENCES

Allen, Joseph P., Porter, Maryfrances R., Land, Debbie, Insabella, Glenda, Smith, Felicia D., and Phillips, Nicole. (2006). A Social-Interactional Model of the Development of Depressive Symptoms in Adolescence. *Journal of Consulting Psychology, 74*(1), 55–65.

Becker, Judith V. (1994, Summer/Fall). Offenders: Characteristics and Treatment. *The Future of Children, Sexual Abuse of Children, 4*(2), 176–197.

Beresford, Jayne, and Blades, Mark. (2006). Children's Identification of Faces from Lineups: The Effects of Lineup Presentation and Instructions on Accuracy. *Journal of Applied Psychology, 91*(5), 1102–1113.

Beuscher, Eva, and Roebers, Claudia M. (2005). Does a Warning Help Children to More Accurately Remember an Event, to Resist Misleading Questions, and to Identify Unanswerable Questions. *Experimental Psychology, 52*(3), 232–241.

Bourdreaux, Monique C., Lord, Wayne D., and Dutra, Robin L. (1999). Child Abduction: Age-Based Analyses of Offender, Victim and Offense Characteristics in 550 Cases of Alleged Child Disappearance. *Journal of Forensic Science, 44*(3), 539–553.

Briere, John N., and Elliott, Diana M. (1994, Summer/Fall). Immediate and Long-Term Impacts of Child Sexual Abuse. *The Future of Children, Sexual Abuse of Children, 4*(2), 54–59.

Daro, Deborah A. (1994, Summer/Fall). Prevention of Child Sexual Abuse. *The Future of Children, Sexual Abuse of Children, 4*(2), 198–223.

Dombrowski, Stefan C., LeMasney, John W., Ahia, C. Emmanuel, and Dickson, Shannon A. (2004). Protecting Children from Online Sexual Predators: Technological, Psychoeducational, and Legal Considerations. *Professional Psychology: Research and Practice, 35*(1), 65–73.

Don Harris v. Charles Hinsley, 2004 U.S. Dist. Lexis 16053.

Garaigordobil, Maite. (2004). Effects of a Psychological Intervention on Factors of Emotional Development During Adolescence. *European Journal of Psychological Assessment, 20*(1), 66–80.

Gardner, Margo, and Steinberg, Laurence. (2005). Peer Influence on Risk Taking, Risk Preference, and Risky Decision Making in Adolescence and Adulthood: An Experimental Study. *Developmental Psychology, 41*(4), 625–635.

Gilstrap, Livia, L. (2004). A Missing Link in Suggestibility Research: What Is Known About the Behavior of Field Interviewers in Unstructured Interviews with Young Children? *Journal of Experimental Psychology: Applied, 10*(1), 13–24.

Greenfield, Patricia, and Yan, Zheng. (2006). Children, Adolescents, and the Internet: A New Field of Inquiry in Development Psychology. *Developmental Psychology, 42*(3), 391–394.

Hanson, R. Karl, and Morton-Bourgon, Kelly E. (2005). The Characteristics of Persistent Sexual Offenders: A Meta-Analysis of Recidivism Studies. *Journal of Consulting and Clinical Psychology, 73*(6), 1154–1163.

Heyman, Gail D., and Legare, Christine H. (2005). Children's Evaluation of Sources of Information About Traits. *Development Psychology, 41*(4), 636–647.

John Whitehead v. Roger D. Cowan, 263 F.3d 708, 2001 U.S. App. Lexis 19259.

LaFond, John Q. (2005). *Preventing Sexual Violence: How Society Should Cope with Sex Offenders.* Washington, D.C.: American Psychological Association.

London, Kamala, Bruck, Maggie, Ceci, Stephen J., and Shuman, Daniel W. (2005). Disclosure of Child Sexual Abuse: What Does Research Tell Us About the Ways Children Tell? *Psychology, Public Policy and Law, 11*(1), 194–226.

Medaris, Michael, and Girouard, Cathy. (2002, January). Protecting Children in Cyberspace: The ICAC Task Force Program. *Juvenile Justice Bulletin,* 1–8.

Miller, Lawrence. *Law Enforcement Traumatic Stress: Clinical Syndromes and Intervention Strategies.* Commack, New York: The American Academy of Experts in Traumatic Stress.

Monahon, Cynthia. (1993). *Children and Trauma: A Guide for Parents and Professionals.* San Francisco: John Wiley & Sons, Inc.

Myers, John E. B. (1994, Summer/Fall). Adjudication of Child Abuse Cases. *The Future of Children, Sexual Abuse of Children, 4*(2), 84–101.

National Center for Missing and Exploited Children, Office of Juvenile Justice and Delinquency Prevention. (2006). *Missing and Abducted Children: A Law Enforcement Guide to Case Investigation and Program Management.*

Office of Juvenile Justice and Delinquency Prevention. (2004, May). *When Your Child Is Missing: A Family Survival Guide*.

Owen-Kostelnik, N., Reppucci, N. Dickon, and Meyer, Jessica R. (2006). Testimony and Interrogation of Minors: Assumptions About Maturity and Morality. *American Psychologist, 61*(4), 286–304.

Pence, Donna M., and Wilson, Charles A. (1994, Summer/Fall). Reporting and Investigating Child Sexual Abuse. *The Future of Children, Sexual Abuse of Children, 4*(2), 70–83.

Thierry, Karen L., Lamb, Michael E., Orbach, Yael, and Pipe, Margaret-Ellen. (2005). Developmental Differences in the Function and Use of Anatomical Dolls During Interviews with Alleged Sexual Abuse Victims. *Journal of Consulting and Clinical Psychology, 73*(6), 1125–1134.

Tsethlikai, Monica, and Greenhoot, Andrea F. (2006). The Influence of Another's Perspective on Children's Recall of Previously Misconstrued Events. *Developmental Psychology, 42*(4), 732–745.

Chapter six

Profit Kidnapping

CHAPTER CONTENTS

WHAT DEFINES THE PROFIT KIDNAPPING

The profit kidnapping is motivated by the tangible gain that the abductor believes will be realized by stealing the liberty of another. The gain need not be monetary, although this is typically the case.

The profit kidnapping is illustrated by the cases of Jean Ferreira, Pedro Caraballo-Martinez, and Edwin Martinez; Robert Leroy Bryan; and Joseph Kindler. The characteristics of the profit kidnapping are included in Table 6.1.

Table 6.1 Elements of the Profit Kidnapping

Victimology & Offender Characteristics		
	1. The victim was under 18 years of age.	16%
	2. The victim and the offender were strangers to one another.	57%
	3. The victim and the offender had a relationship prior to the abduction.	41%
	4. The offender and the victim were of different genders.	38%
	5. The offender and the victim are of different ethnicities.	NA*
	6. The victim was low risk, i.e., not likely to be immediately missed or reported as missing.	13%
	7. The offender was unemployed at the time of the abduction.	NA*
	8. The offender was employed at the time of the abduction.	NA*
Abduction Site	1. The abduction occurred in a public place.	16%
	2. The victim was abducted from a private location (such as home, school, workplace).	78%
Modus Operandi	1. The abduction was perpetrated by more than one offender.	88%
	2. The victim was chosen randomly or opportunistically.	34%
	3. Physical force was used to abduct the victim.	72%
	4. The victim was abducted following verbal threats of harm to himself or herself and/or others.	41%
	5. The victim's abduction was the result of persuasion or deception.	9%
	6. The offender used a firearm to facilitate the abduction.	63%
	7. The offender used a knife to facilitate the abduction.	6%
	8. The offender used a weapon, other than a knife or a firearm, or did not use a weapon, to facilitate the abduction.	22%
	9. The offender sexually assaulted the victim during the abduction.	13%
	10. The offender physically assaulted the victim during the abduction in a manner that did result in death.	53%
	11. The offender physically assaulted the victim during the abduction in a manner that did not result in death.	25%
	12. The offender did not assault or physically harm the victim during the abduction.	22%
	13. The offender transported the victim during the abduction.	88%
	14. The offender did not transport the victim during the abduction.	12%
	15. The offender exhibited obvious psychotic symptoms (delusions, hallucinations, etc.).	0%
	16. The offender held the victim captive for greater than 24 hours.	31%
	17. The offender held the victim captive for less than 24 hours.	63%
	18. The kidnapping occurred in the morning (midnight–8 a.m.).	25%
	19. The kidnapping occurred during the day (8 a.m.–4 p.m.).	9%
	20. The kidnapping occurred in the evening/at night (4 p.m.–midnight).	22%
	21. More than one victim was abducted.	41%

Continued...

Table 6.1 Elements of the Profit Kidnapping—continued

Outcome		
	1. The abduction was witnessed.	38%
	2. The victim was released by the offender.	19%
	3. The victim escaped.	3%
	4. The victim was released following law enforcement intervention.	25%
	5. The victim was not found.	0%
	6. The victim was found dead.	53%
	7. The victim was discovered in a public place.	47%
	8. The victim was discovered in a private place (a home, school, or workplace).	53%
	9. Witness testimony contributed to the offender's apprehension/conviction.	53%
	10. Physical evidence contributed to the offender's apprehension/conviction.	63%
	11. Accomplice statements contributed to the offender's apprehension/conviction.	56%
	12. Victim testimony contributed to the abductor's apprehension/conviction.	47%

NA-Insufficient data to render determination.

Jean Ferreira, Pedro Caraballo-Martinez, and Edwin Martinez

On December 13, 1999, Jean Carlo Ferreira, Pedro Rafael Caraballo-Martinez, and Edwin Oscar Martinez accosted the victim, Christina, and her two sons, aged 9 and 1, in the parking garage near the family's North Miami condominium. The victim was the wife of a successful North Miami businessman. The perpetrators repeatedly shocked the victim with a stun gun, causing her to drop her infant to the floor of the garage. They also stun-gunned the victim's 9-year-old son when he attempted to flee.

Following the assault, the perpetrators forced the family into their Lincoln Navigator SUV and transported them to a house located approximately 15 minutes away. Once inside, the kidnappers tied the victim's hands and legs to a chair and placed her in a closet. They similarly tied her 9-year-old son and placed him in another closet. They kept the infant in a separate room.

On the second day of their captivity, the victim and her older son were removed from the closets and placed in shuttered rooms. At nightfall, the 9-year-old was forced to sleep in his underwear in a bed with Martinez.

During the 4½ days of the family's abduction, the kidnappers ordered the victim to use her cellular phone to call her husband and arrange a meeting with Martinez. When the calls did not result in a meeting, the perpetrators forced the victim to type a letter stating that if the husband did not "turn over all his money," the family would be murdered.

The victim's husband refused to meet with his family's kidnappers. He contacted the Federal Bureau of Investigation. Federal investigators traced one of the calls that the kidnappers had the victim place on her cellular phone and located the house in which the family was being held.

On the morning of December 18, 1999, law enforcement recovered the victims and arrested Ferreira, Martinez, and Caraballo-Martinez. An investigation of the house in which the victims were held yielded a torn paper version of the letter that had been sent to the victim's husband and an electronic version on Martinez's laptop.

At trial, the victim and her 9-year-old son identified Martinez and Caraballo-Martinez as two of the three men who kidnapped them. The third abductor was later identified as Ferreira, who had worked as a parking attendant at the family's garage. The victim's son testified that Ferreira had asked him about the family's plans for the night of the abduction. A cellular phone registered to Ferreira had made 22 calls to a cellular phone registered to Martinez, which was found in the house in which the victims were held.

On June 2, 2000, a jury found each man guilty of hostage taking, carjacking, and using a firearm during a crime of violence.

Robert Leroy Bryan

On Saturday, September 11, 1993, a neighbor reported that the victim, Inabel, was missing from her home. Tire skid marks were found in the victim's front- and backyards. A fresh potted plant purchased for the victim by her nephew, Robert Leroy Bryan, was found in the victim's home.

During the investigation, law enforcement discovered that Bryan had been arrested several years earlier for soliciting an undercover police officer to kidnap and kill a local banker. Bryan's plan had been to force the banker to sign a number of promissory notes, which Bryan intended to endorse following the banker's death. It was also discovered that on September 8, the Wednesday prior to the victim's disappearance, Bryan rented a 1986 Lincoln from a local car dealership after requesting a car with a "large trunk." He had returned the vehicle on Monday, September 13, at which time he was unable to pay for the rental but showed the owner a check signed by the victim. Bryan promised to return to the dealership after cashing the check.

Based on this information, law enforcement searched the rural property belonging to Bryan's parents, which included the house in which Bryan resided. The property was the location where Bryan suggested the undercover officer leave the body of the banker in his failed contract kidnapping of years before.

On September 16, the victim's body was found on the property, approximately one-quarter mile from the home in which Bryan lived with his parents. The victim died from a gunshot wound to the forehead. She had a pillowcase duct-taped over her head. Tire tracks belonging to a single vehicle were found in the field by the body.

A search of Bryan's bedroom yielded several handwritten promissory notes purportedly between the victim and Bryan. The notes stated that the victim owed Bryan millions of dollars as a result of her investment in his failed business. Several checks signed by the victim and made payable to Bryan were also found. A roll of duct tape was also found inside Bryan's bedroom. A partially burned checkbook was found in a can of ashes outside Bryan's home.

A search of the rented vehicle revealed the presence of fibers consistent with those found on the victim's clothes and the tape found on and near the victim's body. Hair consistent with that of the victim was also found in the vehicle's trunk. Grass and vegetation, similar to that found on the rural property, were discovered throughout the car's undercarriage.

The jury trial that resulted in Bryan's conviction included expert testimony confirming that the edges of the duct tape found in Bryan's room were consistent with those found on the victim. A handwriting expert testified that the promissory notes and signatures on several checks found in Bryan's room were forged by Bryan. The tire mark found by the body of the victim was consistent with the rented Lincoln. Evidence was also presented that indicated the victim was killed with a .22 caliber bullet, consistent with the .22 caliber rifle and ammunition found in one of the bedrooms of Bryan's home.

Bryan was sentenced to death for first degree malice murder.

Joseph Kindler

On April 2, 1982, a Sound Odyssey store in Bucks County was burglarized. A patrol officer noticed a vehicle pull out of the cul-de-sac behind the store. The vehicle was traveling at a high rate of speed and had its lights off. The officer pursued and stopped the vehicle, at which time the driver fled. The two remaining passengers, the 22-year-old victim and a 16-year-old named Scott were arrested for the burglary of the store.

While being detained, the victim reported that the burglary was the idea of the driver, Joseph Kindler. The victim stated that he was willing to testify against both Scott and Kindler. Law enforcement secured a warrant for Kindler's arrest, which was executed by officers of the city in which Kindler resided. A brief struggle ensued between Kindler and the officers. After subduing Kindler, officers presented him with the arrest warrant, which clearly listed the victim as an informant.

Kindler was charged with the burglary, along with several unrelated thefts, and scheduled to appear at a preliminary hearing on July 23, 1982. Kindler failed to appear. During the hearing, the victim was granted immunity in return for trial testimony against Kindler. The trial was set for August 17, 1982.

Allegedly fearing Kindler would attempt to prevent him from testifying, the victim planned to move from his apartment to his parents' home for the duration of the trial.

In the interim, Kindler contacted the second offender in the burglary, Scott, and Scott's girlfriend, and arranged to secure a car from the girlfriend. On July 24, 1982, Kindler met with Scott and the girlfriend, and the three drove to within a block of the victim's apartment. The girlfriend placed a call to the victim, confirming his presence at the apartment. At between 2:30 and 2:45 a.m. on July 25, 1982, the girlfriend rang the victim's doorbell and persuaded him to exit the apartment. Kindler and Scott, who were hiding in an alleyway adjacent to the apartment building, emerged with a baseball bat and an electric prod. Kindler beat the victim over the head approximately 20 times, while Scott electrically prodded him five times in the ribs.

The attack rendered the victim immobile. Kindler and Scott dragged the victim to the girlfriend's waiting vehicle and threw him into the trunk. The three drove the victim, who was still alive,

7 miles to the Delaware River. Thereafter, Kindler and Scott removed the victim from the trunk and attempted to throw him into the river. When the victim's body would not sink, they tied a cinder block around it to weigh it down.

Kindler instructed the girlfriend to drive to Philadelphia and to stop at various sewer inlets along Grant Avenue so he could discard the baseball bat, clothes, and shoes he and Scott used during the murder. Once at Kindler's home, Kindler and Scott attempted to wash the bloodstains from the car, using a Styrofoam ice chest. They threw the chest and the car's trunk mat into another sewer inlet.

The victim's girlfriend, who was in his apartment during his abduction, and a neighbor, who had heard the victim being beaten, telephoned police. Based on their accounts, and a trail of blood found at the scene, law enforcement intercepted Scott's girlfriend at her home, seizing the blood-soaked car. The girlfriend confessed and implicated Scott and Kindler. Thereafter, she led police to the various sewer inlets in which the three had discarded the clothing, baseball bat, and Styrofoam chest, which were recovered.

At approximately 7:30 p.m. on July 26, 1982, the victim's body surfaced in the Delaware River. The body had a cinder block tied around the neck.

On November 15, 1983, Kindler was convicted of first degree murder, kidnapping, and criminal conspiracy. During the trial, evidence recovered from the sewer inlets, as well as the testimony of Scott's girlfriend, the victim's girlfriend, and the victim's neighbor was presented.

CHARACTERISTICS OF THE PROFIT KIDNAPPING
Victimology

The victims of profit kidnappings are chosen for the real or perceived benefit they afford the abductor. As illustrated by the cases of Jean Carlo Ferreira, Pedro Rafael Caraballo-Martinez, and Edwin Oscar Martinez and Robert Leroy Bryan, the anticipated gain can be monetary. As illustrated by the kidnapping perpetrated by Joseph Kindler, the gain can also be non-monetary but of significant value to the offender. In 41 percent of the profit kidnappings reviewed, the victim and offender had a prior relationship. In the majority of cases, however, no direct prior relationship existed; the offender was nonetheless familiar with the victim's potential worth.

Abduction Site

The profit kidnapper was familiar with his victim even in cases in which no prior relationship existed. Consistent with this familiarity, the vast majority of profit kidnappings occurred at private locations (78 percent), such as the victim's home or workplace.

Modus Operandi

The physical force used against the victims of Jean Carlo Ferreira, Pedro Rafael Caraballo-Martinez, and Edwin Oscar Martinez and against the victim of Joseph Kindler was consistent with the majority of profit kidnapping cases reviewed (72 percent). Abductions frequently involved the use of a firearm (63 percent) or some other weapon (22 percent), such as the stun gun used by Ferreira, Caraballo-Martinez, and Martinez and the electric prod used by Kindler. Physical force resulted in harm to the victim in 78 percent of the cases reviewed. In an additional 13 percent of cases reviewed, the victim was sexually assaulted.

The majority of profit kidnapping victims were transported during the abduction (88 percent), which most frequently occurred between midnight and 8:00 a.m. (25 percent). Once abducted, the victim was held for greater than 24 hours in 31 percent of cases, which is second only to domestic kidnappings in terms of crime duration and likely reflective of the offender(s)' need for time to negotiate for the object of the abduction.

Profit kidnappers were also more likely to work in tandem with others than in any other subtype; 88 percent of profit kidnappings reviewed were perpetrated by more than one offender.

Outcome

The majority of victims of profit kidnappings did not survive their abductions (53 percent). Survival most often resulted from law enforcement intervention (25 percent) or release by the offender (19 percent). In a small number of cases (3 percent), the victim escaped his or her abductor.

The surviving victim contributed to the investigation and conviction of the kidnapper in 47 percent of the cases reviewed. In these cases, as well as in cases in which the victim did not survive, witness testimony also contributed to the kidnapper's apprehension and conviction (53 percent).

The profit kidnapper's decision to engage an accomplice to commit his crime is also a frequent source of his demise; accomplice testimony was second only to physical evidence in supporting the apprehension and conviction of the profit kidnapper (56 percent and 63 percent, respectively).

IMPLICATIONS FOR PREVENTION AND INVESTIGATION

Victims of the profit kidnapping are chosen for their perceived worth to their abductor. In many instances, the potential target clearly has the financial resources or influential power that would be coveted by others. Prevention efforts related to these individuals should include an assessment of the physical security of environments frequented by the target, including the workplace and residence, and an analysis of the protocols and practices designed to limit target access. A security survey, inclusive of an analysis of thefts and other non-kidnapping related crimes, can provide information on areas of vulnerability.

As illustrated by the kidnapping perpetrated by Ferreira, Caraballo-Martinez, and Martinez, prevention efforts must also engage the spouse and children of the potential victim, when appropriate. Unfortunately, many potential victims, particularly those new to positions of wealth or influence, resist engagement of family members in safety efforts. It is not uncommon for potential targets to mistakenly believe that shielding family members from the realities of the dangers they face offers an "emotional protection" that is worth the risk of exposure. This form of denial must be countered with palatable and age-appropriate alternatives. Spouses and adult children will often respond to a rational and neutral vulnerability assessment, and will acknowledge the need to be cautious when dealing with unknown individuals and environments. The law enforcement or security professional may consider assisting families to protect personal information, remain aware of surroundings, and rehearse response options should a threat be suspected or identified. Doing so supports the family member to have greater situational awareness and to replace denial with a sense of control. Doing so can also "emotionally redirect" the family member who experiences resentment against the primary target for heightening his safety risk, helping to avert rebellion behaviors that increase vulnerability.

Child protection efforts should also include the use of neutral statements of risk using age-appropriate language and role-playing of potential scenarios in which the child may be vulnerable. (See Chapter 5, "Predatory Kidnapping–Child Victim," for additional information on developmental considerations when working with children.)

As with all prevention efforts, those directed at the potential profit kidnapping victim minimize but do not eliminate risk; in some instances the kidnapper(s)' determination to abduct the victim or sophistication of approach thwart the security measures employed. Alternatively, the monetary or influential value of the victim may only be known to or envisioned by the offender, as was the case in Robert Bryan's kidnapping of his aunt. Such cases typically do not come to the attention of law enforcement or security professionals until after the act.

The investigation of the profit kidnapping begins with the determination that an abduction has, in fact, occurred; the possibility that the victim has not voluntarily disappeared, or been the subject of a different crime or accident must be ruled out. The investigation of the profit kidnapping will typically reveal evidence of a disruption of mundane, daily activities, such as an uneaten meal, laundry left unfolded, or a television that remains switched on. As the majority of profit kidnappings are perpetrated by more than one offender, there may also be evidence of multiple individuals at the victim's last known location. Witnesses may describe the victim following an individual into a car driven by another. A home or workspace may include evidence of an unusual level of disturbance or multiple forensic traces.

A victim profile and timeline of victim actions during the hours preceding the abduction are particularly critical in aiding the investigation of the profit kidnapping, as the timeline will likely reveal times of victim vulnerability, as well as possible offender-victim connections.

When the motive for the profit kidnapping is monetary, the abductor will seek to realize his goal either directly through the victim or indirectly through a third party. A review of any actions on the part of the victim, such as removal of resources from bank accounts or safety deposit boxes immediately before or immediately after the kidnapping, should be conducted. As in the kidnapping perpetrated by Ferreira, Caraballo-Martinez, and Martinez, the offenders may seek more "traditional" means of attaining their end through the use of ransom communications, such as letters, e-mails, and telephone calls. Each of these demand options offers information that can potentially reveal the identity of the abductor or the location of the victim.

Professional staff who routinely accept and open packages or answer telephone calls should be trained in advance to handle threatening or demand communications. Letters and envelopes should be protected from unnecessary fingerprints to allow for fingerprint analysis and handwriting or printer analysis.

Telephone communication can reveal voice characteristics and ambient noises that may aid in offender identification and identification of victim location. As many staff members will panic when accepting a threatening call—regardless of training—ensuring availability of a call checklist for recording observations and details can assist staff to remain calm and focused.

Once the demand is made, the law enforcement or security professional can assist the victim's colleagues and family to evaluate the risks of acceding to the kidnapper's demands based on an analysis of any known behavioral characteristics of the offender and the likelihood of successful recovery.

When the investigation yields information pertaining to a specific suspect, the advantage gained by the kidnapper in working with an accomplice quickly becomes a liability. Eighty-eight percent of the profit kidnapping cases reviewed involved an accomplice. In 56 percent of cases, the accomplice's testimony was a significant contributor to the apprehension and conviction of the offender. Many accomplices will confess their involvement and implicate the offender in return for the mere suggestion of leniency. While courts have generally held that a confession based on the promise of leniency is inadmissible, a confession obtained by the suggestion that the accomplice may be treated more leniently is typically admissible. Tactics such as telling an accomplice that others have received reduced sentences for their cooperation in similar crimes or that others have received counseling or other forms of assistance for their confessions have all been deemed admissible by courts. Given the probative value of confessions during trial, the use of such strategies ensures that those who perpetrate the profit kidnappings are brought to justice for their actions.

THE PRISONER'S DILEMMA

In 56 percent of the profit kidnappings reviewed, accomplice testimony contributed to the apprehension and conviction of the kidnapper. In general, accomplice testimony is secured by the mere suggestion that admission of guilt will be accompanied by leniency.

Why would an offender willingly risk the freedom that might follow maintaining silence about his crime in exchange for certain punishment in which leniency is not guaranteed?

In 1950, researchers Merrill Floor and Melvin Dresher explored this dynamic in what would later be named the *Prisoner's Dilemma*. The following is the classic Prisoner's Dilemma scenario:

Two suspects, A and B, are arrested. The police have insufficient evidence for conviction. They separate the prisoners and offer each the same deal: Testify against the other and, if the other remains silent, the betrayer goes free and the silent offender receives a full 10-year sentence. If both stay silent, both prisoners are sentenced to only 6 months in jail for a minor charge. If each betrays the other, each receives a 5-year sentence.

The most beneficial course of action would be for both prisoners to remain silent, which would pose the best chance for a favorable outcome for each. The irony of the prisoner's dilemma is that the most beneficial cause of action is not the most rational for the individual. In self-interested rational decision making, an individual makes the decision best for him, regardless of the decisions made by another. The most rational choice, therefore, is for each prisoner to forgo the cooperation demonstrated during the commission of the crime and "defect" against his cohort.

Fortunately, such defection is the norm among the accomplices of profit kidnappings.

Threat Assessment Checklist

In profit kidnappings, staff are frequently the first to receive a kidnappers' demand. The following is a suggested checklist to assist staff to remain calm and focused in the event that they receive a threatening communication.

1. Was the threat communicated over the telephone, via e-mail, or through a delivery?
   ❑ E-mail   ❑ Telephone   ❑ Delivery   Date:_____

Note: If the threat is received through e-mail, call security immediately. DO NOT TOUCH OR ALLOW OTHERS TO TOUCH THE COMPUTER UNTIL SECURITY ARRIVES.

Questions to ask and actions to take if the threat is received by telephone:

1. If the threat is received over the telephone, attempt to write down as much information WORD FOR WORD as you can. Maintain as calm and cooperative a tone as possible.

2. Has [NAME OF VICTIM] been harmed in anyway?_____
   _____
   _____
   _____
   _____
   _____

3. We receive many prank calls here. So I am sure that this is not a prank, can you tell me what [NAME OF VICTIM] is wearing?
   _____
   _____
   _____
   _____
   _____
   _____

4. Can I speak with [NAME OF VICTIM]?
   _____
   _____
   _____
   _____
   _____
   _____

5. What is it you want?_____
   _____
   _____
   _____
   _____
   _____
   _____
   _____

   a. If money:_____ How much/what currency?_____
   _____

6. Where do you want the demand delivered?_____
   _____

Continued...

7. I will give this information to my supervisor immediately. How can we communicate with you?

_____

_____

_____

_____

Please indicate the following:

Gender of the caller:_____ Race of the caller:_____ Age of the caller:_____

Time call received:_____ Length of call:_____

Caller's Voice (Mark all that apply)

❑ Calm   ❑ Agitated/Excited   ❑ Soft   ❑ Loud
❑ Stutter   ❑ Lisp   ❑ Crying   ❑ Deep
❑ High   ❑ Rapid   ❑ Slurred   ❑ Whispered
❑ Accent   ❑ Disguised   ❑ Taped   ❑ Foul/Cursing
❑ Educated/Well Spoken

Was the voice familiar?   ❑ Yes   ❑ No

Background Noises

❑ Street Noises   ❑ Machine Noises   ❑ Animal Noises
❑ Voices   ❑ PA System   ❑ Motor/Car Noises
❑ Static   ❑ Other:_____

Questions to ask and actions to take if the threat is received by delivery:

1. Do not touch the package more than necessary, nor allow others to touch the package. Contact security immediately.

2. What time was the package delivered?_____

3. Did you notice the delivery person or notice anyone who may have delivered the package?
❑ Yes   ❑ No

If yes:

Gender:_____ Race:_____ Height:_____

Age:_____ Hair Color:_____ Eye Color:_____

Distinguishing Marks/Tattoos:_____

Clothing:_____

Mannerisms/Demeanor: ❑ Calm   ❑ Agitated/Excited   ❑ Other:_____

How did individual enter the area:_____

How did individual exit the area:_____

Kidnapping Motherhood

In the current study, the profit kidnapping included abductions motivated by monetary as well as non-monetary gain. The motivation shared by the perpetrator of these crimes was the attainment of something he or she deemed to be of value. Within this subset falls the non-traditional kidnappings of infants by non-family members.

The U.S. Department of Justice estimates that 217 infants were abducted by non-family members between 1983 and 2002. Although rare, the infant abduction has a significant emotional impact on family members and caregivers, as well as a significant impact on the resources of law enforcement and security professionals engaged in investigation and recovery efforts. Because more than two-thirds of infant abductions occur at healthcare facilities, these incidents also significantly impact the security professional working within this setting.

An analysis of infant abductions conducted for the U.S. Department of Justice by the National Center for Missing and Exploited Children, the FBI, and the University of Pennsylvania School of Nursing found that the infant abductors

- Are typically females of childbearing age (12 to 50);
- Are often overweight;
- Are most likely compulsive and reliant on manipulation, lying, and deception;
- Are likely to indicate that she has lost a baby or is incapable of having one;
- Are often married or cohabitating;
- Usually live within the community where the abduction occurs;
- Frequently visit nursery and maternity units at more than one healthcare facility prior to the abduction, asking detailed questions about floor plans and fire exits;
- Usually plan the abduction but do not necessarily target a specific infant;
- Frequently impersonate nurses or other healthcare workers;
- Frequently develop a familiarity with healthcare staff, staff work routines, and victim parents;
- Demonstrate the capacity to provide "good" care to the baby post-abduction.

The researchers also found that infant abductions by non-family members frequently occur in four stages:

Stage One: Setting the Stage and Feigning a Pregnancy. During this stage, the perpetrator speaks of the pregnancy or life circumstance that will explain the legitimate presence of an infant in her life.

Stage Two: Planning the Abduction. During the second stage, the abductor methodically plans the elements of the abduction. She identifies the location

Continued...

from which she will take the infant and may target a particular mother. She also identifies the false identity she will assume, such as a healthcare worker, social worker, or babysitter, that will provide her with access to the infant.

Stage Three: Abduction. During stage three, the perpetrator realizes her plan. She acts on the deception she has planned and escapes to a pre-designated location. She also spends time explaining the presence of the infant to others.

Stage Four: Post Abduction. In stage four, the perpetrator continues efforts to conceal her crime. This phase challenges the success of the perpetrator's effort during stage one; despite careful planning, it is usually someone in the perpetrator's social circle who will alert authorities of her actions.

The interruption of stage two of the infant abduction will significantly support the prevention of this crime. The NCMEC and Joint Commission Accreditation Hospital Organization recommend that healthcare facilities train staff to

- Recognize and report unusual behaviors, including those by individuals who
    - Visit repeatedly or frequently request to hold infants;
    - Ask detailed questions about hospital procedures or floor plans;
    - Leave the hospital on foot with an infant, instead of in a wheelchair;
    - Remove large packages from the maternity ward;
    - Take hospital uniforms or other identification.
- Utilize appropriate codes, such as Code Pink, to immediately alert hospital personnel if an abduction is suspected;
- Immediately notify security and law enforcement;
- Search the unit;
- Protect the crime scene;
- Notify other local healthcare facilities;
- Hold the shift if the incident occurs during shift changes;
- Care for the parents;
- Care for workers who may experience acute or post-traumatic stress responses.

In addition, recommended physical security measures include

- Attaching matching identification bands to the infant, mother, and father or significant other;
- Taking footprints, color photographs, and a full physical assessment of the infant within 2 hours after birth;

- Using distinctive photo identification badges and uniforms in maternity, nursery, neonatal intensive care, and pediatric units;
- Keeping infants in line-of-sight supervision at all times;
- Transporting infants by authorized staff in a bassinet only;
- Verifying that the persons leaving the hospital with an infant are wearing matching identification bands;
- Maintaining the confidentiality of the mother's and infant's full names, address, and telephone number.

At times the security measures prove inadequate to prevent the infant abduction, or the abduction occurs at a private location, such as the infant's home. In these instances, immediate mobilization of law enforcement is critical.

In the sample cases reviewed in the Justice Department Study, more than 92 percent of abducted infants were successfully recovered. In most cases, infants were found within 25 miles of the abduction site and within 5 days of the crime.

Early and immediate media involvement was critical to victim recovery. Widely televised accounts, inclusive of photos of the infant, greatly enhanced the likelihood that a member of the perpetrator's social circle would become aware of, and report, the presence of the newborn. Avoiding derogatory or threatening remarks in media coverage, such as substituting the word *missing* for kidnapped or abducted, is important in the prevention of concealment or harmful behaviors on the part of the perpetrator.

In pursuing tips received from potential witnesses, law enforcement should pay particular attention to suspects who have worked in or nearby the healthcare facility where the abduction took place, or who recently had a miscarriage or still birth. In the cases studied, forensic traces also frequently included the absence of forced entry at a private residence or the presence of unexplained items such as discarded clothing or wigs at a healthcare facility.

REFERENCES

Burgess, Ann Wolbert, and Lanning, Kenneth V. (2003). *An Analysis of Infant Abductions*. Office of Juvenile Justice and Delinquency Prevention.

Joseph J. Kindler v. Martin Horn, 291 F. Supp. 2d 323; 2003 U.S. Dist. Lexis 16897.

Robert Leroy Bryan v. Gary Gibson, 276 F.3d 1163; 2001 U.S. App. Lexis 27249.

United States of America v. Jean Carlo Ferreira, Pedro Rafael Caraballo-Martinez, et al., 275 F.3d 1020; 2001 U.S. App. Lexis 26374; 15 Fla. L. Weekly Fed. C. 134.

U.S. Army Center for Health Promotion and Preventive Medicine, Industrial Hygiene and Medical Safety Management Program, *Just the Facts: Hospital Safety and Security Infant Abduction*, 59-021-0402.

Chapter | seven

Revenge Kidnapping

CHAPTER CONTENTS

WHAT DEFINES THE REVENGE KIDNAPPING

The revenge kidnapping is about retaliation. The kidnapper abducts his victim as a form of punishment for a real or perceived insult or event.

The diversity of circumstances that provoke the revenge kidnapping are illustrated by the cases of William Young, Robert Zane Bogle, Jose Lopez, and Dustin John Higgs. The characteristics of the revenge kidnapping are included in Table 7.1.

Table 7.1 Elements of the Revenge Kidnapping

Victimology & Offender Characteristics	1. The victim was under 18 years of age.	22%
	2. The victim and the offender were strangers to one another.	11%
	3. The victim and the offender had a relationship prior to the abduction.	89%
	4. The offender and the victim were of different genders.	50%
	5. The offender and the victim are of different ethnicities.	NA*
	6. The victim was low risk, i.e., not likely to be immediately missed or reported as missing.	13%
	7. The offender was unemployed at the time of the abduction.	NA*
	8. The offender was employed at the time of the abduction.	NA*
Abduction Site	1. The abduction occurred in a public place.	33%
	2. The victim was abducted from a private location (such as home, school, workplace).	61%
Modus Operandi	1. The abduction was perpetrated by more than one offender.	72%
	2. The victim was chosen randomly or opportunistically.	34%
	3. Physical force was used to abduct the victim.	61%
	4. The victim was abducted following verbal threats of harm to himself or herself and/or others.	11%
	5. The victim's abduction was the result of persuasion or deception.	39%
	6. The offender used a firearm to facilitate the abduction.	28%
	7. The offender used a knife to facilitate the abduction.	17%
	8. The offender used a weapon, other than a knife or a firearm, or did not use a weapon, to facilitate the abduction.	44%
	9. The offender sexually assaulted the victim during the abduction.	22%
	10. The offender physically assaulted the victim during the abduction in a manner that did result in death.	78%
	11. The offender physically assaulted the victim during the abduction in a manner that did not result in death.	17%
	12. The offender did not assault or physically harm the victim during the abduction (excludes sexual assault).	5%
	13. The offender transported the victim during the abduction.	72%
	14. The offender did not transport the victim during the abduction.	28%
	15. The offender exhibited obvious psychotic symptoms (delusions, hallucinations, etc.).	17%

Continued...

Table 7.1 Elements of the Revenge Kidnapping—continued

	16. The offender held the victim captive for greater than 24 hours.	11%
	17. The offender held the victim captive for less than 24 hours.	83%
	18. The kidnapping occurred in the morning (midnight–8 a.m.).	28%
	19. The kidnapping occurred during the day (8 a.m.–4 p.m.).	0%
	20. The kidnapping occurred in the evening/at night (4 p.m.–midnight).	44%
	21. More than one victim was abducted.	28%
Outcome	1. The abduction was witnessed.	67%
	2. The victim was released by the offender.	11%
	3. The victim escaped.	5%
	4. The victim was released following law enforcement intervention.	5%
	5. The victim was not found.	0%
	6. The victim was found dead.	78%
	7. The victim was discovered in a public place.	61%
	8. The victim was discovered in a private place (a home, school, or workplace).	39%
	9. Witness testimony contributed to the offender's apprehension/conviction (not limited to event witnesses).	89%
	10. Physical evidence contributed to the offender's apprehension/conviction.	67%
	11. Accomplice statements contributed to the offender's apprehension/conviction.	44%
	12. Victim testimony contributed to the abductor's apprehension/conviction.	22%

*NA-Insufficient data to render determination.

William Young

In the winter of 1998, retired police officer William Young placed an order for approximately 200,000 T-shirts from Henry, the victim. Young intended to resell the shirts. He paid the victim $2,100 in shipping costs. When Young did not receive the ordered shirts, he contacted former law enforcement colleagues to ascertain additional information regarding the victim and the victim's whereabouts.

Through his sources, Young learned that the victim had a criminal history and was living in Florida with a girlfriend. Young telephoned the victim's girlfriend several times. During their conversations, the girlfriend told Young that the victim had sodomized her 2-year-old son, a claim she later retracted. During a subsequent conversation, the girlfriend informed Young that she and the victim would be traveling to the area where Young resided. Young informed the girlfriend that he would stage an arrest of the victim at the Hampton Inn at which the two would be staying. The victim's girlfriend mailed pictures of herself and the victim to Young to assist him to identify the victim.

Young contacted an employee of a New Jersey warehouse where he conducted business, requesting assistance to "unload [a] trailer." Young and the employee arranged to meet at the warehouse at 10:00 a.m. on May 24, 1998. When Young arrived, he informed the warehouse employee that the individual who had cheated him of $2,100 had also sexually assaulted a 2-year-old. He stated that "the mother [of the molested boy] was begging for help." Young offered the warehouse employee $200 to assist him in "scaring" the victim.

The warehouse employee accepted Young's offer, and the two men equipped themselves with the police hats, badges, and firearms that Young had brought with him. Thereafter, they drove to the Hampton Inn. Shortly after their arrival, Young noticed the victim and his girlfriend exit the Inn. He approached the victim, told him he was under arrest, and placed him in the back seat of his car. The three men crossed state lines into New Jersey and exited at the warehouse. Young wrapped the victim in duct tape from head to foot, leaving his nose uncovered to allow him to breathe. He tied the victim to a forklift. He and the warehouse employee then left the warehouse.

Within an hour, Young returned to the scene, where he found the victim with law enforcement personnel who had responded to reports of screams emanating from the warehouse. Young fled the scene.

On July 1, 1998, law enforcement arrested Young. After a 5-day jury trial, he was convicted of kidnapping.

Robert Zane Bogle

On July 1, 1993, Robert Zane Bogle and his brother visited the home of the victim and the woman with whom he lived. Bogle was allegedly angry with the victim for a business deal that the two men had previously discussed, but that had not been executed. The victim allowed Bogle and his brother entrance into the house. Shortly thereafter, Bogle's brother hit the victim with a handgun and shot at the victim's stereo. Bogle handcuffed the victim's roommate and tied up the victim with an extension cord. Thereafter, Bogle took $500 from the roommate's wallet, and the two men beat both the roommate and the victim with the handgun. Bogle demanded that the victim sign over the title to his motor home, beating him unconscious when he refused. Bogle then demanded the keys to the roommate's car, which she surrendered.

Bogle stabbed at the victim's feet with a butcher knife and ordered the victim's roommate to straddle the victim and have sexual relations with him. When neither the roommate nor Bogle could revive the victim, Bogle's brother ordered the roommate to the bedroom, where he forced her to perform oral sex on him, after which Bogle tied and gagged her. The roommate feigned loss of consciousness, an act which she continued even when Bogle threatened to "blow off [her] kneecap." The men left the home and escaped in the roommate's car. They were apprehended when their car broke down in California.

During a joint trial with his brother, Bogle was convicted of charges including burglary in the first degree, robbery in the first degree, and kidnapping in the first degree.

Dustin John Higgs

On the evening of January 26, 1996, Dustin John Higgs and two friends drove from Higgs's Maryland home to Washington, D.C. There, the three men picked up the three victims, Higgs's friend and two of her girlfriends. The six traveled to a liquor store before returning to Higgs's apartment to drink and listen to music. Later in the evening, Higgs and one of the victims argued. The victim retrieved a knife from the kitchen and brandished it at Higgs. One of Higgs's friends broke up the fight and took the knife from the victim, who was allegedly still angry. The victim walked to the door of the home, verbally threatening to have Higgs "all f****d up or robbed."

The victim and her two friends left the apartment. Higgs reportedly watched the victim stop behind his Mazda MPV van and record the plate number. Higgs complained to his friends that the victim was "writing down [his] s***." Reportedly, Higgs said, "F*** that," before grabbing his jacket and a .38 caliber firearm, and ordering his friends to follow. The three men entered Higgs's van and drove to the roadside where the three victims were walking. Higgs stopped the van and told one of his friends to get the victims into the back of the van. The friend exited the vehicle, spoke to the victims, and the four re-entered the van. The victims reportedly believed that Higgs was driving them to the victim's Washington, D.C., home.

Instead of exiting at Baltimore-Washington, Higgs drove to the Patuxent National Wildlife Refuge, where he pulled to a secluded location. One of the victims allegedly asked if Higgs was "going to make us walk from here?" Higgs replied, "Something like that," and made the victims exit the van.

Higgs handed his firearm to one of his friends. He and the second man remained in the car, while the friend with the gun exited the vehicle and followed the victims.

It was reported that Higgs watched in the vehicle's rearview mirror as his friend shot one of the victims in the chest. Several more gunshots sounded before Higgs's friend returned to the van, and Higgs drove from the scene. The men drove to the Anacostia River, where they disposed of the gun before returning to Higgs's home.

Once at the home, the men proceeded to wipe down any surface that the victims might have touched and to discard any items that could be linked to them. Higgs and the shooter drove the third man to a fast-food restaurant, warning him to "keep [his mouth] shut" before driving off.

At approximately 4:30 a.m. on January 27, a motorist found the bodies of the three victims strewn across the roadway and contacted law enforcement. Two of the victims had died from gunshot wounds to the chest and back. The third victim had been shot once in the back of the head.

Police recovered one of the victim's day planners, which included Higgs's phone number, address and the tag number for his Mazda van. A .38 caliber wadcutter was also found at the scene.

Higgs was interviewed and told law enforcement that he knew one of the victims but that she had never been to his apartment. Higgs claimed that he had been attending a party at the home of his girlfriend on the night of the kidnappings. The girlfriend confirmed his alibi.

Shortly after the interview, police arrested Higgs on suspicion of involvement in an unrelated crime. A search warrant related to this arrest yielded cash, crack cocaine, a .380 semiautomatic firearm, and boxes of ammunition for .380, .45, and .38 caliber weapons.

Higgs pled guilty to federal drug charges a little more than a year after the kidnapping and murder. Thereafter, Higgs's girlfriend recanted her alibi for the night of the kidnapping.

Law enforcement received information from another girlfriend of Higgs, whom he apparently had contacted following the kidnappings in an attempt to convince her that he was with her during the night of the crime, thereby creating a second alibi. When this girlfriend refused to comply, Higgs apparently admitted that he was present when the women were shot. He stated that the victim had been at his house because she had been "snitching" on his friend, a circumstance which led to her murder.

Further investigation revealed that Higgs had also been involved in two additional shootings involving a .38 caliber weapon. In the first, which occurred approximately 2 months prior to the kidnapping, Higgs got into an argument outside a D.C. nightclub and shot out the window of a vehicle. Police searched the vehicle and recovered a .38 caliber bullet. The man with Higgs at the time of the shooting testified that he later threw the gun out the window of Higgs's Mazda, but that the two returned to retrieve it at Higgs's insistence.

Approximately a month later, Higgs used the .38 caliber handgun in a shootout with a romantic rival of one of his friends. The groove pattern created by the barrel of the .38 in this shooting was consistent with the pattern of the bullets fired at the nightclub shooting and with the bullets found at the kidnapping/homicide scene in Patuxent National Wildlife Refuge.

On October 11, 2000, a jury found Higgs guilty of crimes including kidnapping. On October 26, he was sentenced to death.

Jose Lopez

In July 1993, Jose Lopez moved into a home shared by the victim, the victim's mother, and the victim's brother. Within a year, the relationship between Lopez and the victim's mother deteriorated, and Lopez threatened to "take the kids away [and] hide them." The victim's mother obtained an order of protection against Lopez but would let him return to sleep on her couch several nights each week. The two co-existed in this manner for several months. On June 28, 1994, the victim's mother entered a sham marriage with another man, earning $1,000 for helping the man obtain U.S. citizenship. The marriage precipitated an argument between the victim's mother and Lopez and resulted in Lopez leaving the home. In the early morning of June 29, Lopez returned to the home, banged on the door, and was admitted by the victim's mother. Lopez slept on the couch for the remainder of the night.

At approximately 4 p.m. on June 29, the victim's mother left Lopez in the living room watching television. Lopez allegedly agreed to baby-sit the victim, who was playing at a neighbor's home. Shortly after the victim's mother departed, Lopez went to the neighbor's apartment and offered the victim $5 to help him fix a window in his mother's home. Witnesses reported seeing the victim get into Lopez's truck and the two driving away.

Lopez returned to the home of the victim's mother later in the evening of June 29 without the victim. Lopez reportedly told the victim's mother that he paid the victim money to assist with the window but denied leaving with the victim in his truck. Lopez and the victim's mother went to the local precinct to report the victim as missing.

In his statement to law enforcement, Lopez again denied taking the victim into his truck. Instead, Lopez claimed that at approximately 4:30 p.m., he went to the neighbor's home and offered the victim money to assist with closing a window. After the victim had done so, Lopez claimed that the victim stated that he was going to return to the neighbor's home. Thereafter, Lopez claimed to walk to a friend's home, where he retrieved his truck before returning to the victim's house at approximately 5:00 p.m. At this time, Lopez claimed to have parked his truck in the victim's driveway. Lopez stated that it appeared that no one was at the home, so he ran an errand before visiting another friend at whose apartment he stored clothes in exchange for $50 per month. He claimed to have changed out of the dirty clothes he was wearing and returned to the victim's mother's home.

On the basis of Lopez's statements, written consent was obtained to search his pickup truck and to retrieve the dirty clothing from his friend's apartment. Law enforcement subsequently recovered wet, black pants from the apartment and a number of items from the truck, including a length of rope. Lopez was arrested for kidnapping. His truck was impounded for forensic examination.

On July 8, 1994, 9 days after the victim's disappearance, workers at a salvage yard discovered the victim's body in the trunk of a white Chrysler Cordoba marked to be destroyed by a "crusher." The body was weighted down by a 100-pound transmission, and a rope was looped around the neck and tied to the trunk hinges.

Further investigation into the victim's disappearance yielded additional evidence against Lopez. Law enforcement interviewed witnesses who placed Lopez at the salvage yard approximately one and one-half weeks prior to the day the victim was found. Lopez had been looking for a transmission and had been directed to an area of the yard where the victim's body was found. Paint smears taken from a screwdriver found in Lopez's truck matched the paint of the automobile in which the victim's body was found. Fibers consistent with those from the victim's multicolored shorts were found in Lopez's truck, while black fibers consistent with the truck's carpet were found in the victim's sandals. The black pants recovered from Lopez's friend's home were covered with iron and rust and with red fibers consistent with those from the victim's hooded shirt.

At trial, the prosecution presented the testimony of Lopez's cellmate, who reported that Lopez told him that he had offered the victim $10, driven him to a junkyard, strangled him with a brown towel, and placed him inside the trunk of a car marked "to be crushed." The prosecution also presented the testimony of a friend of Lopez who stated that Lopez had told her that if the victim's mother left him, he'd "hurt [her] where it hurts the most." The friend also related a story told to her by Lopez: A man and a woman were having problems so the man took the woman's children away, returning them safely only after the couple reunited.

Lopez was convicted following a jury trial.

THE CHARACTERISTICS OF THE REVENGE KIDNAPPING

Victimology

The victims of revenge kidnappings unwittingly or intentionally behaved in a manner that offended the abductor(s) at some point during the offender/victim relationship. In the majority of the cases reviewed (89 percent), such as in the kidnapping perpetrated by William Young, the kidnapper retaliated by kidnapping the individual whom he believed directly responsible for the insult. In many of these cases, including those of Dustin Higgs and Robert Bogle, the kidnapper also abducted those who happened to be present during the time of the offense. In a minority of cases (11 percent), such as in the kidnapping perpetrated by Jose Lopez, the kidnapper purposely selected a victim who was important to the offending individual.

Abduction Site

The choice of abduction sites in revenge kidnappings tended to reflect the nature of the offender/victim relationship. Bogle and Lopez, who had extensive prior dealings with their victims, perpetrated their offenses at private residences; private residences were the abduction site of choice in 61 percent of the revenge kidnapping cases reviewed. In contrast, Young and Higgs had more limited relationships to their victims. As in 33 percent of the revenge kidnappings reviewed, their abductions were perpetrated in publicly accessible locations.

Modus Operandi

As was true in the kidnappings perpetrated by Young, Bogle, and Higgs, the majority of revenge kidnappers (72 percent) enlisted an accomplice and utilized physical force to abduct their victims (61 percent). A minority of revenge kidnappers also used persuasion or deception instead of or in addition to physical force (39 percent). Young pretended to be an active law enforcement officer; Bogle persuaded his victim to permit him to enter his home; Lopez pretended to require assistance closing a window. Bogle's use of a knife during the abduction was consistent with 17 percent of the revenge kidnapping cases reviewed, while his use of a firearm was consistent with 28 percent of these cases.

In a minority of cases (22 percent), including that of Bogle, a victim was sexually assaulted during the abduction. Victims were typically held less than 24 hours (83 percent).

Outcome

The victim of William Young was one of a minority of victims who survived the revenge kidnapping. As in 5 percent of the cases reviewed, Young's victim was released following law enforcement intervention. An additional 5 percent of victims escaped, while another 11 percent were released by the offender. The vast majority of revenge kidnapping victims (78 percent) did not survive the abduction.

Victim survivors contributed to the apprehension and conviction of their offenders in each case reviewed. Apprehension and conviction were also aided by the testimony of witnesses (89 percent) and accomplices (44 percent). Physical evidence also played a significant role in offender apprehension and conviction (67 percent).

IMPLICATIONS FOR PREVENTION AND INVESTIGATION

"Mankind," Martin Luther King, Jr. pronounced, "must evolve for all human conflict a method that rejects revenge, aggression and retaliation."

Absent such an evolution, a subset of humanity will continue to engage in revenge behaviors and pose a significant challenge for law enforcement and security professionals charged with preventing the potential revenge kidnapping.

In many cases, such as in the kidnapping perpetrated by Dustin Higgs, the offender will immediately and brutally act to secure retribution, precluding preventive intervention. Precursors, when extant, tend to take the form of verbal or written threats, such as the threatening story relayed by Jose Lopez prior to his abduction of the son of his love interest, or the threats most likely made by Robert Bogle before his kidnapping of his would-be business associate. As in any assessment of risk, verbal and written threats must be considered in the context of other factors; verbally threatening another is such a common human behavior that it offers little predictive value when considered in isolation. Specificity, context, repetition, and the ability of threatening party to act on the threat (e.g., "I'm going to introduce him to my shotgun and leave his body in the scorching desert," by an individual known to own a shotgun and frequent the desert) should be considered.

The dynamics of revenge offer additional factors that can be used to determine the likelihood that an individual will, in fact, retaliate against another.

A person who suffers a real or perceived insult or injury typically believes that the offender "owes" him and demands repayment of the "debt" in a manner that restores balance to the relationship. The method the individual utilizes to cancel the debt is influenced by both the nature of the injury and the personality of the offended individual.

On the most basic level, the debt can be canceled by terminating future interpersonal contact or cognitively minimizing the severity of the impact of the offense. For some would-be offenders, interventions that restore a sense of worth ("You don't need him anyway. There's got to be even better investors who will support your idea.")

or minimize the magnitude of the offense or offender ("This guy just isn't worth it.") will support the injured party to "forgive" the debt.

Further strategies that can support offended individuals to substitute retaliation with a more neutral behavioral response include facilitating a formal apology by the offending individual, regardless of whether the offense occurred solely in the mind of the offended. For certain individuals, the mere validation that they suffered, coupled with another's willingness to admit wrongdoing, provides an emotional cover, a "face-saving" option that diffuses the need for further action.

Depending on the nature of the actual or perceived offense, negotiating restitution offers an additional option for averting an attack by the party who believes he or she has been offended. Such restitution requires the injury to be quantified in a manner that can be repaid, either monetarily or through other means, such as through the provision of services or items.

Research has identified two additional factors that support an offended individual to forgive another: the nature of the relationship between the two parties and the religiosity of the offended. The former is useful if the parties are colleagues or family members whose relationship is unlikely to terminate as a result of the precipitating event: The fact that the individuals will have a continued association can be a powerful motivator for both parties to identify a non-violent solution. In the case of religiosity, the law enforcement or security professional may be able to appeal to the offended party's character, allowing him to claim the "moral high ground" as restitution for the offense.

In addition to factors that can support non-violent reconciliation, a specific personality trait, narcissistic entitlement, has been found to significantly increase the likelihood that an individual will believe himself to be aggrieved and significantly decrease the likelihood that he will accept reasonable amends.

Clinically, narcissism is reflected by a persistent and enduring pattern of grandiosity, need for admiration, and lack of empathy. Narcissistic traits can include self-importance, a preoccupation with fantasies of unlimited success or power, a belief that one is "special" and can only be understood by those who are unique, a need for excessive admiration, a tendency to be exploitive in interpersonal relationships, a tendency to be envious or to believe that he or she is the object of others' envy, and arrogance. Additionally, many narcissists exhibit a sense of entitlement and expect special treatment or automatic compliance with their wishes.

Narcissistic entitlement causes an individual to demand that his desires be met. Unfortunately, the narcissist's desires are often distorted and unrealistic. Consequently, he is easily frustrated and more prone to feel slighted by another; i.e., more likely to believe another "owes" him. Just as his perception of the magnitude of the offense against him is inflated, so too will his demand for restitution be unreasonable and frequently unattainable. As others will not be able to meet these unreasonable demands, the narcissist becomes inconsolable: The narcissist comes to believe that revenge is the only option for balancing the interpersonal scale.

Interviews with family, friends, and colleagues can assist the law enforcement or security professional determine if he or she is dealing with an individual with narcissistic entitlement. Those with this character trait will behave consistently, regardless of environment or context. Associates will likely describe such an individual as arrogant, rigid, conceited, or quick to anger when crossed. Given that narcissistic entitlement remains consistent over time, these individuals may also have a history of interpersonal altercations that can further assist in assessing risk for revenge behaviors.

If an individual is deemed high risk, potential victims should be supported to adopt standard safety precautions, including heightened situational awareness, varied routines, installation or upgrading of security systems, verification of security protocol and procedure integrity, and increased presence of security personnel. Additional precautions, such as obtaining a restraining order, should also be considered.

Depending on the dynamics and actions of the potential offender, as well as the jurisdiction in which the situation occurs, criminal charges may be brought prior to an escalation in violence. In most jurisdictions, verbal threats of sufficient severity constitute a crime. In California, for example, Section 422 of the Penal Code describes the crime of terrorist threats as

> Any person who willfully threatens to commit a crime which will result in death or great bodily injury to another person, with the specific intent that the statement, made verbally, in writing, or by means of an electronic communication device, is to be taken as a threat, even if there is no intent of actually carrying it out, which, on its face and under the

circumstances in which it is made, is so unequivocal, unconditional, immediate, and specific as to convey to the person threatened, a gravity of purpose and an immediate prospect of execution of the threat, and thereby causes that person reasonably to be in sustained fear for his or her own safety or for his or her immediate family's safety, shall be punished by imprisonment in the county jail not to exceed one year, or by imprisonment in the state prison.

As in any risk assessment, the value of pressing charges against the potential offender must be weighed against the risk that such actions will precipitate the very act the charges are designed to avert.

In many cases, law enforcement and security professionals are not engaged until after the revenge kidnapping has occurred. The offender may immediately act on his need for retaliation or not exhibit any warning signs signaling his intentions regarding his actions. Conversely, the victim may not recognize the threat posed by the potential abductor until the kidnapping has occurred.

Victim survivors are clearly the greatest aid to the investigation of the revenge kidnapping. The interpersonal relationship between abductor and victim generally allows for immediate suspect identification. The victim's prior relationship to the offender may also yield details about the offender's habits and routines that can assist in apprehension. As was true in each of the cases reviewed in which the victim survived the abduction, victim testimony plays a critical role, particularly because the revenge kidnapper will likely continue to justify his actions following apprehension.

Because a significant number of victims do not survive the revenge kidnapping, crime scene analysis is an important investigative avenue. In each of the revenge kidnapping cases reviewed, the crime included elements of "overkill" typically associated with crimes of passion, i.e., crimes in which the offender acts from a heightened emotional state. Bogle stabbed the feet of his victim. Lopez left his victim to be crushed. Young wrapped his victim almost entirely in duct tape. Higgs's victims were shot multiple times and left on a public road. These behaviors are consistent with expressive rather than instrumental behaviors, i.e., emotional acts in which the offender's motive is expressing rage at the victim (in contrast to instrumental crimes in which harm to the victim is incidental to the offender's objective). Expressive criminals typically engage in more personal attacks, including the stabbing, beating, and headshots employed by the offenders in the review cases. Because the offender approaches the victim intending a violent confrontation, he will typically bring his weapon to the crime scene.

Expressive criminal behavior is also associated with mental instability. This is not inconsistent with the revenge kidnapping; this subtype was one of two in which certain offenders displayed obvious psychotic symptoms, such as delusions or hallucinations, during the crime.

The Limited Predictive Power of the Verbal and Written Threat

Many revenge kidnappings are preceded by verbal threats against the victim. However, threats are of dubious value as an element of a risk assessment. Research related to the likelihood that a threat will lead to violence has consistently found a weak link between verbalizing a behavior and action.

In the Exceptional Case Study Project conducted on behalf of the U.S. Secret Service, psychologist Robert Fein and Special Agent-in-Charge Bryan Vossekuil studied the behaviors of individuals who approach or attack prominent individuals. In relation to communicated threats, the researchers found that

> None of the 43 assassins and attackers studied communicated a direct threat to the target before their attack;
> Fewer than one-tenth of all 83 attackers and near-lethal approachers studied communicated a direct threat to the target or to a law enforcement agency.

The researchers' findings mirror those of forensic psychologist J. Reid Meloy in his analysis of the relationship between communicated threats and violence toward both public and private individuals. As in the Fein/Vossekuil research, Meloy found that public targets are unlikely to receive a direct threat by those who subsequently attack or attempt an attack. Conversely, threatening communications were correlated with increased risk of violence against private individuals. As Reid points out, however, such threats are "so common that they have little predictive value."

Both Fein/Vossekuil and Meloy concluded that while threatening communications should not be ignored, they need to be assessed in relation to additional risk factors.

REFERENCES

American Psychiatric Association. (1994). *Diagnostic and Statistical Manual of Mental Disorders*, 4th ed., Washington D.C.

Aquino, Karl, Martinko, Mark J., and Douglas, Scott. (2004). Overt Anger in Response to Victimization: Attributional Style and Organizational Norms as Moderators. *Journal of Occupational Health Psychology, 9*(2), 154–164.

Barclay, Laurie J., Skarlicki, Daniel P., and Pugh, S. Douglas. (2005). Exploring the Role of Emotions in Injustice Perceptions and Retaliation. *Journal of Abnormal Psychology, 90*(4), 629–643.

Exline, Julie J., Bushman, Brad J., Finkel, Eli J., Baumeister, Roy F., and Campbell, W. Keith. (2004). Too Proud to Let Go: Narcissistic Entitlement as a Barrier to Forgiveness. *Journal of Personality and Social Psychology, 87*(6), 894–912.

Fein, Robert A., and Vossekuil, Bryan. (1998, July). *Protective Intelligence and Threat Assessment Investigations: A Guide for State and Local Law Enforcement Officials*. Washington, D.C.: National Institute of Justice.

Jose Lopez v. Commonwealth of Massachusetts, 349 F. Supp. 2d 109; 2004 U.S. Dist. Lexis 24847.

Meloy, J. Reid. (2001). Communicated Threats and Violence Toward Public and Private Targets: Discerning Differences Among Those Who Stalk and Attack. *Journal of Forensic Sciences, 46*(5), 1211–1213.

Palermo, George B., and Kocsis, Richard N. (2005). *Offender Profiling: An Introduction to the Sociopsychological Analysis of Violent Crime*. Springfield, IL: Charles C Thomas Publisher LTD.

Robert Zane Bogle v. Stan Czerniak, 2004 U.S. Dist. Lexis 8385.

United States of America v. Dustin John Higgs, 353 F.2d 281; 2003 U.S. App. Lexis 25904.

United States of America v. William E. Young, Sr., 2000 U.S. App. Lexis 11916.

Wade, Nathaniel G., and Worthington, Everett L. Jr. (2005). In Search of a Common Core: A Content Analysis of Interventions to Promote Forgiveness. *Psychotherapy: Research, Practice and Training, 42*(2), 160–177.

Chapter eight

Staged Kidnapping

CHAPTER CONTENTS

WHAT DEFINES THE STAGED KIDNAPPING

The staged kidnapping creates the appearance that a kidnapping has occurred when it has not. The purpose of falsifying the kidnapping is to conceal an event or crime that the perpetrator deems detrimental or to further an end the perpetrator deems beneficial. Staged kidnappings are typically prosecuted for the crime they conceal. As a result, staged kidnappings are underrepresented in the review process ($n = 3$). While the staged kidnapping is not often prosecuted as such in the courts, these crimes are closely followed by the media. Aspects of the highly publicized staged kidnapping offer further insight into the dynamics of this crime. Consequently, the staged kidnapping perpetrated by Susan Smith is included in the case illustrations.

The characteristics of the staged kidnapping are included in Table 8.1. In addition to the Susan Smith case, staged kidnappings perpetrated by Michael Gianakos and Jamie Dennis and by Edward Hughes are provided as illustrations of this crime.

Table 8.1 Elements of the Staged Kidnapping

Victimology & Offender Characteristics	1. The victim was under 18 years of age.	0%
	2. The victim and the offender were strangers to one another.	0%
	3. The victim and the offender had a relationship prior to the abduction.	100%
	4. The offender and the victim were of different genders.	67%
	5. The offender and the victim are of different ethnicities.	NA*
	6. The victim was low risk, i.e., not likely to be immediately missed or reported as missing.	0%
	7. The offender was unemployed at the time of the abduction.	NA*
	8. The offender was employed at the time of the abduction.	NA*
Abduction Site	1. The abduction occurred in a public place.	33%
	2. The victim was abducted from a private location (such as home, school, workplace).	67%
Modus Operandi	1. The abduction was perpetrated by more than one offender.	33%
	2. The victim was chosen randomly or opportunistically.	0%
	3. Physical force was used to abduct the victim.	33%
	4. The victim was abducted following verbal threats of harm to himself or herself and/or others.	33%
	5. The victim's abduction was the result of persuasion or deception.	67%
	6. The offender used a firearm to facilitate the abduction.	67%
	7. The offender used a knife to facilitate the abduction.	0%
	8. The offender used a weapon, other than a knife or a firearm, or did not use a weapon, to facilitate the abduction.	0%
	9. The offender sexually assaulted the victim during the abduction.	0%
	10. The offender physically assaulted the victim during the abduction in a manner that did result in death.	100%
	11. The offender physically assaulted the victim during the abduction in a manner that did not result in death.	0%
	12. The offender did not assault or physically harm the victim during the abduction.	0%
	13. The offender transported the victim during the abduction.	67%

Continued...

Table 8.1 Elements of the Staged Kidnapping—continued

	14. The offender did not transport the victim during the abduction.	33%
	15. The offender exhibited obvious psychotic symptoms (delusions, hallucinations, etc.).	0%
	16. The offender held the victim captive for greater than 24 hours.	0%
	17. The offender held the victim captive for less than 24 hours.	100%
	18. The kidnapping occurred in the morning (midnight–8 a.m.).	0%
	19. The kidnapping occurred during the day (8 a.m.–4 p.m.).	0%
	20. The kidnapping occurred in the evening/at night (4 p.m.–midnight).	100%
	21. More than one victim was abducted.	0%
Outcome	1. The abduction was witnessed.	33%
	2. The victim was released by the offender.	0%
	3. The victim escaped.	0%
	4. The victim was released following law enforcement intervention.	0%
	5. The victim was not found.	0%
	6. The victim was found dead.	100%
	7. The victim was discovered in a public place.	33%
	8. The victim was discovered in a private place (a home, school, or workplace).	67%
	9. Witness testimony contributed to the offender's apprehension/conviction.	67%
	10. Physical evidence contributed to the offender's apprehension/conviction.	67%
	11. Accomplice statements contributed to the offender's apprehension/conviction.	33%
	12. Victim testimony contributed to the abductor's apprehension/conviction.	0%

*NA-Insufficient data to render determination.

Michael Gianakos and Jamie Dennis

In April 1997, Michael Gianakos and Jamie Dennis robbed the motel at which Gianakos worked. The couple returned to their home where the victim, Anne Marie, was babysitting their children. The victim regularly babysat the children and had served as Dennis's maid of honor when the couple was married on Valentine's Day in 1997.

Days after the robbery, the victim was interviewed by law enforcement. She stated that, on the night of the robbery, she witnessed Dennis with a bag of money and was with the couple when they ordered a "celebratory" pizza.

On May 1, 1997, the victim's mother called law enforcement after the victim was uncharacteristically absent from a church service.

Several days later, the victim's body was found near a rural farmhouse outside her hometown of Moorhead. She had been shot in the head, and her throat was cut. One latex glove was found at the scene, and a purse was found approximately a mile away.

On May 9, 1997, Gianakos pled guilty to the motel robbery. Dennis was subsequently convicted following a jury trial.

A year after the victim's unsolved homicide, Gianakos's mother phoned police, claiming to have information regarding the murder. Gianakos's mother reported that her son had telephoned her and told her that he had found details of the victim's murder in a diary kept by Dennis. The diary allegedly revealed that the offender used latex gloves, that the victim had been shot, and that her throat had been cut. The diary also allegedly indicated that the victim was given sleeping pills prior to her death.

As part of their investigation, law enforcement had withheld the details of the victim's injuries from the media. Investigators were unaware of the presence of sleeping pills in the victim's system.

With the information provided by Gianakos's mother, law enforcement obtained a warrant for Gianakos's home. The search yielded several journals and notebooks in which Dennis had written. None of the writings detailed the murder.

Shortly after the search, Dennis's cellmate contacted the Clay County sheriff's office, claiming she had information about the murder. According to the cellmate, on the day of the victim's murder, Gianakos purchased a shotgun, ammunition, gin, and a package of wine coolers from a liquor store proximate to where the homicide occurred. Dennis allegedly reported that she believed Gianakos would use his purchases to frighten the victim and prevent her from testifying about the couple's actions following the motel robbery. Gianakos, Dennis, and the couple's children met the victim at her home and asked her to accompany them to a farmhouse they feigned interest in purchasing.

During the drive to the farmhouse, Dennis gave the victim a wine cooler contaminated with a toxic level of sleeping pills. When the group arrived at the farmhouse, everyone but Gianakos exited the car. Shortly thereafter, Dennis claimed that one of the children was "irritated," and she took all of the children back to the car. Dennis told her cellmate that when she retuned to the car, the trunk of the car was open and Gianakos was absent. Dennis claimed that she turned to look for Gianakos and witnessed him shoot the victim in the back of the head. She claimed that Gianakos then instructed her to assist him to drag the victim's body to the farmhouse, and told her to retrieve the victim's house and car keys from her pocket. Thereafter, Gianakos and Dennis placed the victim face up behind the house, and Gianakos shot her in the face to obscure her identity. Gianakos also reportedly cut the victim's throat.

Dennis claimed that Gianakos ordered her back to the car, while he destroyed the shotgun by cutting it into small pieces. The two returned the children to their home. Dennis then went to the victim's home and retrieved the victim's purse. Gianakos took the purse and the victim's keys back to the farmhouse in an apparent attempt to imply that the victim had been abducted to the farmhouse.

A jury convicted Gianakos of kidnapping resulting in death. For her cooperation and testimony against her husband, Dennis was allowed to plead guilty to second-degree murder.

Edward Hughes

Edward Hughes was the co-founder and vice president of a major software company when the victim, Brian, was promoted to a position above him. Hughes, who reportedly had greater technical qualifications and corporate experience, resigned his vice presidency but continued working half time at the company for two-thirds of his original salary. Hughes maintained a residence in Rhode Island and purchased a home in Mexico, where he spent the majority of his time installing and servicing computer software for the company's Mexican clientele. Hughes allegedly complained, often before clients, about the direction the victim was taking the company.

When the victim learned of Hughes's complaints, he convened the company's board of directors, informing them that he was going to terminate Hughes's contract. The board approved his decision.

The victim planned a trip to Mexico to visit other corporate executives and clients and to conduct a final interview with Hughes.

Upon learning of the victim's impending arrival, Hughes arranged to meet the victim at the Mexico City airport and drive him to San Luis Potosi, 4 hours northeast. Hughes's colleague warned him about the lack of security along his chosen route. The colleague also offered to undertake the drive with Hughes and the victim. Hughes insisted upon driving alone with the victim.

On Sunday, February 6, 1994, the victim celebrated his daughter's 10th birthday before boarding a plane to Mexico City. He was met by Hughes at 10:30 p.m. The two left the airport and drove northwest to the city of Queretaro, halfway between Mexico City and San Luis Potosi.

On February 7, 1994, Hughes boarded the 5:15 p.m. flight from Mexico City to New York. The following morning, he telephoned the computer company's controller and reported the following:

- He had stopped en route to San Louis Potosi so the victim could relieve himself on a roadside.
- While stopped, he was attacked by three men who threw him into the backseat of his rental car.
- He was ordered to keep his head down.
- The assailants drove the car for an unknown distance before stopping at a house.
- Once inside the house, Hughes overheard his assailants speak of the victim in the present tense. He, therefore, believed that the victim was still alive.
- The assailants drove Hughes to the airport, where they returned his credit cards and passport, and ordered him to return to the United States to obtain one million pesos (approximately $325,000) within 48 hours.
- The assailants threatened to kill the victim if Hughes did not return with the money as instructed.

After obtaining Hughes's statement, the controller contacted the corporation's insurance company and was connected to the Miami-based Ackerman Group. The firm devised a plan that included sending Hughes and a company vice president to Mexico. Once there, the firm would wire ransom money with which the two could make an exchange for the victim. Hughes responded with an alternative plan whereby the company would give him the money and he would fly to Mexico to make the exchange alone. On Ackerman's advice, company executives declined Hughes's offer.

Hughes returned to his home to shower. From his residence, he telephoned company executives, informing them that he would not return to Mexico. At the executives' insistence, Hughes reluctantly agreed to fly to Ackerman's Miami offices for consultation with the firm.

In the interim, Mexican authorities found a partially buried body alongside the Queretaro bypass highway. The body was that of a man who had been shot five times. In his shirt pocket was a parking ticket that was traced to the victim's company car. Mexican officials also recovered shell cases from the bullets that killed the victim. FBI officials recovered matching cartridge casings on Hughes's Rhode Island property. Ballistics experts testified that only one gun could have produced the signature markings shared by the casings: the SIG Sauer 9-mm pistol purchased by Hughes in September 1993.

Hughes was convicted and sentenced to 20 years' imprisonment and 3 years' supervised release. At the time of his trial, Hughes was a fugitive from the Mexican judicial system, where he was convicted of murder.

Susan Smith

At approximately 9:00 p.m. on Tuesday, October 25, 1997, Susan Smith knocked on the door to a home in Monarch Mills, South Carolina, where she reportedly told the occupant that "he got my kids." Smith, whom the homeowner described as "hysterical," stated that she was stopped at a traffic light when a man jumped into her car's passenger seat. Smith said the man was Black, in his late twenties or early thirties; 5 feet 9 inches to 6 feet tall; and wore a dark blue ski cap, blue jeans, and a blue jacket. She reported that the man warned her to "shut up and drive or I'll kill you."

After driving approximately 10 miles, the man allegedly demanded that Smith stop and vacate the car. She reportedly begged to take her 3-year-old and 14-month-old sons with her. The sons were in the car's back seat. The man allegedly stated that he didn't "have time." In several subsequent interviews, Smith reported that the man told her "I'm not going to hurt them" or "I'll take care of them."

More than 100 local law enforcement and Federal Bureau of Investigation officials searched for the two missing children. Four days following the alleged abduction, investigators had not located the car or the children, nor had they identified a suspect.

Smith and her ex-husband were interviewed and polygraphed. Smith's responses indicated a possible deception.

A background investigation of Smith revealed that she was born on September 26, 1971, and that her parents divorced in 1977. Smith's biological father committed suicide when Smith was 7 years old.

The following year, her mother remarried to the son of a prominent local family. Smith attempted to overdose on aspirin when she was 13, after which her family, rejecting professional advice, did not hospitalize her. When Smith was 16, her stepfather was charged with molesting her. Her stepfather signed a court order in which he admitted that the molestation had occurred. He wasn't charged and the family was ordered into therapy. Smith attempted suicide a second time when she was 18. She was hospitalized 5 months later after a third attempt to overdose on aspirin. She gave birth to her first child at age 19, married, and was separated 2 days after her first wedding anniversary. She and her estranged husband attempted reunification and had a second child before separating once more.

The investigation also revealed that Smith had been romantically involved with the community's wealthiest bachelor, who ended the relationship on October 16. In a note written to Smith on October 18, Smith's ex-boyfriend stated, "I could really fall for you. But like I have told you before, there are some things about you that aren't suited for me and, yes, I am speaking about your children.... The fact is, I just don't want children."

In addition to the motive offered in the note written by her ex-lover, Smith's own account of the kidnapping included several inconsistencies. Smith said the carjacking happened while she was stopped at a traffic light with no other cars around, yet another car's presence was required to make the light turn red. Smith also stated that she had been at a Wal-Mart in the hours prior to the abduction and then changed her story to say she was driving around, on her way to meet a friend.

Investigators confronted Smith regarding the inconsistencies and improbabilities in her statements. Thereafter, Smith changed her narrative to include details that were harder to verify.

Nine days after her sons' disappearance, Smith told news reporters, "I don't think that any parent could love my children more than I do, and I would never even think about doing anything that would harm them. I did not have anything to do with the abduction of my children."

Hours later, Smith confessed to drowning her sons in the murky waters of the John D. Long Lake, near where Smith told police that she had been forced from her car. In her written confession, Smith stated:

Because of my romantic and financial situation, I've never been so low.... I felt I couldn't be a good mom anymore, but I didn't want my children to grow up without a mom. I wanted to end my life so bad and was in my car, ready to go down that ramp into the water and I did go part way, but I stopped. I went again, and I stopped. Then I got out of the car a nervous wreck. I dropped to the lowest when I allowed my children to go down that ramp into the water without me. I took off running and screaming "Oh God, oh God no. What have I done?"

The investigation and autopsy revealed that Smith put the car in drive and let her children, who were still alive, roll into the water. The car flipped before landing in the water, drowning her sons.

CHARACTERISTICS OF THE STAGED KIDNAPPING

Victimology

As with all the staged kidnappings reviewed, those perpetrated by Gianakos and Dennis, Hughes, and Smith were a means to conceal another event that had occurred earlier in the offender/victim relationship; 100 percent of victims in the staged kidnappings reviewed had a prior relationship to the offender. At some point in the relationship, the victim was deemed to be a threat to the offender's objectives. Gianakos's and Dennis's victim knew too much about a motel robbery. Hughes's victim was going to force his separation from the company he founded. Smith needed to be childless to further a relationship with her former boyfriend.

Abduction Site

Staged kidnappings can originate in public or private locations (33 and 67 percent, respectively), depending on the scenario being played out by the perpetrator and the offender/victim relationship. Gianakos's and Dennis's personal relationship with the victim allowed them to lure her from her home, while the professional relationship between Hughes and his victim resulted in an abduction from the more impersonal location of an airport. Smith's victims were her children, her scenario an abduction by a stranger; she claimed the kidnapping occurred in the privacy of her car on a public street.

Modus Operandi

As was true in the abductions staged by Gianakos and Dennis and Hughes, the staged kidnapping is generally perpetrated via persuasion and deception (67 percent). One-third of all offenders (33 percent) also used verbal threats and physical force. A firearm was used in 67 percent of the staged kidnappings that were reviewed.

In each of the staged kidnappings reviewed (100 percent), force was sufficient to cause the death of the victim. (It should be noted that there is a subset of staged kidnappings that are victim-perpetrated and rarely result in death. See "Marriage and the Staged Kidnapping" and "Holding Truth Hostage: The Staged Kidnapping for False Justice.")

A majority of staged kidnapping victims (67 percent) were transported during the abduction. All the victims (100 percent) were held less than 24 hours.

Outcome

After their convictions for the motel robbery, Gianakos and Dennis sought to implicate each other in the staged kidnapping. Gianakos did so through his parents. Dennis did so through her cellmate. The testimony of these witnesses, as with the testimony of witnesses in 67 percent of staged kidnappings reviewed, contributed to Gianakos's and Dennis's apprehension and convictions.

The apprehension and convictions of the majority of the staged kidnappings reviewed (67 percent) were also facilitated by physical evidence. The evidence at Anne Marie's murder scene was consistent with Dennis's account. It would contribute to Gianakos's conviction and Dennis's own conviction of murder in the second degree. The parking ticket found in the pocket of Hughes's victim, as well as a ballistics match between shell casings at the scene and a firearm owned by Hughes, contributed to his apprehension and conviction.

IMPLICATIONS FOR PREVENTION AND INVESTIGATION

It is unlikely that the victim of Gianakos and Dennis suspected that the couple at whose wedding she stood witness and for whom she babysat would kill her and stage a kidnapping to avoid incarceration for a motel robbery. Similarly, Hughes's victim did not likely suspect that his colleague, a man with an impressive reputation within the computer industry and no criminal history, would stage his abduction to conceal a murder over a denied promotion. The children of Susan Smith were too young to comprehend, much less consider, the possibility that their mother would drown them, leaving them submerged at the bottom of a local lake while she claimed they were in the hands of a nefarious stranger.

The challenge for law enforcement and security professionals in preventing the staged kidnapping is that the precursors are often too well hidden—if extant—to provide warning to the potential victim. For the rational individual, the motivations of the offenders—avoiding apprehension for robbery, a denied promotion, a failed relationship—are too minor to justify the staging of a kidnapping. This incomprehension renders it difficult, if not impossible, for the typical individual to anticipate or interrupt victimization by the offender intent on staging a kidnapping and equally difficult for law enforcement to intervene until after the crime is reported. Any resources allocated toward prevention must, therefore, focus on general safety and situational awareness training.

As was true in the kidnappings staged by Gianakos and Dennis, Hughes, and Smith, law enforcement must often reconstruct events to determine the crime veiled by the alleged kidnapping. As in any staged crime, doing so requires identification of inconsistencies at the crime scene and deceptions by alleged witnesses and potential suspects.

Detecting Crime Scene Inconsistencies

In general, the staged crime is defined as an attempt to redirect the investigation away from the perpetrator and his or her actions. Such staging can include removing items from the scene to suggest theft as a motive, or arranging the victim or victim's clothing in a manner suggestive of sexual assault. Staging can also include placing items at the scene to obscure the victim's pre-crime activities; Gianakos placed his victim's purse and keys proximate to her body, for example, in an attempt to imply that she was either alone or with an unfamiliar individual when she went to the farmhouse where he murdered her.

In Douglas et al.'s *Crime Classification Manual*, John Douglas and Corinne Munn (1992) suggest that the following questions be raised to identify the staged scene:

1. Were inappropriate items taken from the scene if burglary appears to be the motive?
2. Does the point of entry make sense?
3. Did the perpetration of this crime pose a high risk to the offender?

4. Did the offender first target the person posing the greatest threat, or did the person who posed the greatest threat suffer the least amount of injury?
5. Do the injuries fit the crime?
6. Is the victim (not money or goods) the primary focus of the offender?

Possible explanations for inconsistent crime scene characteristics should be identified, and the most plausible explanation pursued. In the staged kidnapping perpetrated by Susan Smith, a second vehicle would have been required to trigger the red light at which she claimed she was stopped when a stranger carjacked her and abducted her children. The light could possibly have been triggered by a second vehicle driven by an accomplice of the alleged kidnapper or by a witness. Neither accomplice nor witness came forward following the publicity surrounding the alleged crime, nor did Smith report the presence of an additional party during the carjacking. The most plausible explanation, therefore, was that she was not stopped at a red light as she claimed. Confronting her with this inconsistency contributed to her confession of staging the kidnapping of her children to conceal her murder of them.

Palermo and Kocsis (2005) offer several additional investigative suggestions for identifying a staged scene:

1. Conduct a comprehensive and thorough review of the documented scene, giving little thought to the time involved.
2. Study and take account of the victim (i.e., victimology).
3. Identify and document all indicators of staging.
4. Identify and document possible motives for the original act and for the staging of the crime.
5. Determine who would have benefited from the original act and the staging of the crime scene. Keep in mind that the responsible person may be the victim even in death-related cases.

Those suspected of perpetrating the staged kidnapping, as well as alleged witnesses or survivors, offer additional avenues for investigation: inconsistent or improbable testimony.

Detecting Testimonial Inconsistencies

There is no single physical response, statement, or gesture that separates the liar from the truth teller, nor does a specific combination of words or behaviors indicate deception. Nonetheless, one of the investigator's best opportunities to solve the staged kidnapping comes from the lies the suspect offers to obscure his crime. Psychological science offers three main techniques for discriminating between truthful and deceptive statements: psychophysiological response measurement, verbal response analysis, and paraverbal response analysis. While none of these techniques offers a foolproof formula for discerning truth from lies, each offers the trained practitioner the potential to increase his or her discernment ability beyond the 50 percent accuracy that would occur by chance.

The most common psychophysiological response measurement tool is the polygraph, a combination of medical devices that measure an individual's heart rate, blood pressure, respiratory rate, and electro-dermal activity (such as sweat), and monitor changes from an established baseline. In North America, the typical polygraph examination includes a pre-test interview during which the examiner or forensic psychophysiologist explains the polygraph procedure and gains preliminary information that will be used as the basis for the Control Question Test. During the testing phase, the examiner asks control questions (e.g., "Is your name John Smith?" "Are you 45 years of age?") to which most individuals will respond honestly. The responses to these questions are used to establish an individual baseline. Fluctuations from the baseline when questions related to a crime or incident are posed ("Did you murder the victim?" "Did you hide evidence of your crime?") reflect a stress reaction that may signify deception. During the third, post-test phase of the examination, the examiner interprets the results to determine if the interviewee has been deceptive. (It should be noted that an alternative approach to the Controlled Question Test, known as the Concealed Information Test or Guilty Knowledge Test has been used extensively in Japan, and has been shown to improve interpretive accuracy. Instead of the yes-no response format of the Controlled Question Test, the CIT contains a series of multiple-choice questions, each having one relevant alternative to the crime and several neutral alternatives. Physiological responses to crime alternatives are consistently higher than those to neutral alternatives in deceitful subjects.)

Several factors compromise the reliability of the polygraph. Stress responses, for example, can result from a variety of emotions; a fluctuation may signify anger, anxiety, or fear rather than deception, rendering a false positive result (i.e., the response of a truthful person is determined to be deceptive). Poorly crafted control questions can also influence reliability. For example, questions such as "Have you ever been in trouble with the law?" or "Have you ever hit your daughter?" can result in false positives when dealing with an individual who has a stress response to the question content, or false negatives in individuals who do not consider traffic violations unlawful or spanking a form of hitting. Suspects can also attempt countermeasures, such as the use of sedatives or the application of antiperspirant to the fingertips to relax or interrupt a sweat response. Suspects have also placed sharp objects in a shoe or bitten their tongues, lips, or cheeks in an attempt to distract from stressful questions or to ensure that reactions to all questions evoke identical physiological responses. Research also suggests that certain test subjects, such as psychopaths, do not exhibit an arousal response to stress and would therefore result in false negative responses to the examination.

According to the National Research Council, the polygraph "can discriminate lying from truth telling at rates well above chance, though well below perfection." Across studies, the polygraph has been found to have between an 80 and 90 percent accuracy rate when administered by a skilled examiner. The subjectivity involved in interpreting exam results, coupled with the less than 90 percent accuracy rate, renders the polygraph generally inadmissible in court (save in cases in which both parties agree or the presiding judge allows admission). The polygraph has, however, proven effective as a tool in narrowing and focusing the investigation.

As in the case of Susan Smith, a polygraph examination that suggests deception will invariably be followed by an interview or interrogation by the investigator. To further determine whether the suspect is lying, the trained investigator relies on analysis of verbal and non-verbal communication. Notable techniques that improve discernment of falsehood via verbal communication include the Criteria-Based Content Analysis (CBCA) and the reality monitoring (RM) technique.

Criteria-Based Content Analysis was originally developed to evaluate children's statements in sexual abuse cases but has also been utilized as a tool to identify deception by adults. CBCA is based on the premise that only a person who has actually experienced an event will be able to produce a statement with the characteristics that are described in the CBCA criteria. Specifically, these criteria include general characteristics (i.e., the narrative of an actual event will be logical and coherent, the interviewee will digress or shift focus at points, and the narrative will be significantly detailed). Truthful statements must also meet a substantial number of specific content criteria (contextual embedding, interactions, reproduction of speech, unexpected complications, unusual details, superfluous details, accurately reported details misunderstood, related external associations, subjective experience, attribution of the accused's mental state) and motivation-related criteria (spontaneous corrections or additions, admitting lack of memory or knowledge, raising doubts about one's own testimony, self-deprecation, and pardoning the accused). Accuracy rates of discerning truth from falsehood when utilizing CBCA have ranged from 65 to 80 percent.

Additional research has suggested that several features, including those identified in the CBCA, reliably distinguish truth from falsehood. In one study, interviewees who gave a truthful account of an episode (a) expressed more insecurities regarding their descriptions, (b) more often admitted that they could not remember a particular element of the incident, (c) used a more issue-related as opposed to a long-winded reporting style, (d) provided structured accounts, (e) described more details, (f) more often explained why they were unable to provide a more detailed description, and (g) used fewer clichés but, contrary to expectations, repeated descriptions more frequently than did fabricating interviewees.

A second notable technique used in verbal analysis of lie detection is the reality monitoring technique. RM is based on the premise that memories based on experienced events differ in quality from memories of fabricated events. Real experiences are perceived through the five senses of sight, hearing, smell, taste, and touch. Memories of real experiences, therefore, are more likely to contain perceptual information, such as details related to smell ("He had a very noticeable body odor"), taste ("He gagged me with a rag that tasted like cologne"), touch ("The ground beneath me was rough and uneven"), as well as specific visual and auditory details ("There was light from a nearby streetlamp" and "I could hear a toilet flush somewhere in the house"). Experienced memories also tend to include contextual information, such as spatial and temporal details ("He stood right next to me, leaning into my shoulder" and "He stopped the car, then yanked the door open, then grabbed my arm"). Accounts of imagined events, in contrast, are the result of internal reasoning and are more likely to include cognitive statements such as "He must have had a knife because I was stabbed" or "I know he took my purse because it was gone when he left." Consistent with accuracy rates of CBCA, research has found RM to be accurate between 65 and 80 percent of the time.

There is no documented facial expression that correlates with guilt. In the analysis of non-verbal or paraverbal communications, however, investigators observe a person's behavior to infer whether he or she is lying. The analysis of non-verbal communication is based on the premise that because lying is cognitively more complex than telling the truth, those who are being deceptive will have uncontrolled behaviors as they focus on fabricating their narrative. In other words, the liar is so busy constructing his lie that he doesn't have the resources to control his mannerisms. Researcher Paul Ekman indicates that behavioral cues indicative of deception include higher, faster, and louder speech; greater pupil dilation; and fewer hand movements to accompany and illustrate speech. Liars who have not carefully prepared their narratives, and need to think carefully about their lies as they tell them, may speak more slowly than truth tellers.

The ability to detect deception through non-verbal communication is also influenced by the relationship between the liar and the interviewer, the interviewer's degree of familiarity with the liar's normal behavior, the interviewer's familiarity with the situation, the number of times the liar is interviewed, the liar's motivation to lie, and the interviewer's expectations. The last is particularly influential. Psychological research has consistently demonstrated that individuals "see what they believe." With this phenomenon, known as the *self-fulfilling prophecy* or *confirmation bias*, investigators who begin with the theory that a suspect is guilty may unconsciously seek, interpret, and even create behavioral data to support their hypothesis.

Researchers Inbau, Reid, Buckley, and Jayne (2005), creators of "The Reid Technique" on which many law enforcement officers are trained, clearly caution against the guilt bias when evaluating a suspect's behavior:

> Although behavior symptoms can be very helpful in differentiating truth from deception, they may not be considered determinative of the issue....

To be meaningfully interpreted, a subject's behavior must be considered along with the investigative findings and the subject's background, personality, and attitudes.

Absent new developments that definitively allow discernment between truth and falsehood, a combination of crime scene analysis and physiological, verbal, and paraverbal analysis strategies is the most efficacious approach to solving the staged kidnapping.

George Palermo and Richard Kocsis (2005) suggest three specific areas of inconsistencies that the investigator of the potentially staged crime should focus on: Victim-Centered Inconsistencies, Inconsistencies at the Immediate Location, and Inconsistencies at Distant Locations. They offer the following examples:

Victim-Centered Inconsistencies

1. A murder victim was known to be an aggressive and assertive person. She suffered four stab wounds to the chest, but there were no defense wounds. Why not?
2. The position of a murder victim's body and the arrangement of her clothing suggest a sexual assault, but there is no evidence of penetration. Why not?
3. A murder victim's slacks and panties were lowered to expose her pubic region, but they were not sufficiently low to permit penetration. Why bother lowering the clothing?
4. A murder victim was bound, but the bindings were too loose to actually restrain him. Why would a killer tie him so loosely?
5. A woman alleging rape suffered numerous scratches on her chest and lower abdomen, but none impacted on the sensitive areas (nipples, vaginal lips, etc.) of the body. Would an offender have been so careful?
6. A husband of a murder victim suffered minor wounds to his hands and a blunt force to his head, yet his wife was stabbed 52 times. Why wasn't the husband more seriously injured?
7. An apparent suicide victim died of a gunshot wound to the head, but there was no stippling on the head and no gunshot residue on the hands. Why not?

Continued...

Inconsistencies at the Immediate Location

1. An elderly woman was murdered in her residence, and the scene indicates that robbery was the motive. However, only credit cards were taken even though money and jewelry were present and obvious. Why kill and not take the more valuable and least traceable items?

2. An alleged victim of rape reports extensive damage of a crystal glass collection, but it is determined that only inexpensive items were destroyed. Why weren't the more valuable items destroyed as well?

3. The residence of a homicide victim had elaborate intruder-detection devices, and the scene suggests an interrupted burglary occurred. There are signs of forced entry, yet the alarm was not activated. Why wasn't the alarm activated?

4. The homicide scene of an elderly victim consisted of a small disturbed area with magazines strewn about haphazardly. Also lying across the wooden floor were several pieces of expensive and undamaged china. Why weren't any of the plates broken?

5. Police responding to an automobile fire in the desert at 2 a.m. find an injured woman. She alleged she had been kidnapped almost 12 hours earlier, physically assaulted, and then managed to hide from her attackers in the desert. She alleged that the offenders became frustrated and set fire to her car before leaving. Why would assailants set the car on fire when it would attract immediate attention to the location of the victim?

Inconsistence at Distant Locations

1. In an apparent robbery-homicide, several pieces of expensive diamond jewelry were taken. The jewelry pieces are later found in a garbage bin located some miles from the homicide scene. Why kill to obtain the valuable pieces and then throw them away?

2. A person was shot in the head during an apparent carjacking. The vehicle was discovered a short distance from the victim's body in an upper-middle class neighborhood. Why murder to obtain a car and then abandon it within a short distance?

3. A woman was murdered and her credit cards were taken. The unused cards were found at a bus stop in a high crime area approximately 20 miles from the murder scene. Why kill for credit cards, not use them, and dispose of them in an area where they are highly likely to be found and used?

4. A married woman and her expensive 3-month-old luxury automobile are reported missing. Within hours, the car was found in the short-term parking lot of a nearby airport and the victim's body in the trunk. The windows and door were locked, and the key was in the ignition. Why would the killer lock the windows and doors and leave the key in the ignition?

5. A woman alleged abduction and rape. Her clothing was torn and had grass stains. She directed police to a wooded area approximately 35 miles from the abduction site. The type of vegetation in that area was inconsistent with the stains on her clothing. Why?

Marriage and the Staged Kidnapping

In recent decades, a bizarre subset of the staged kidnappings has emerged: the staging of kidnappings to avoid and end marriages. As the cases of Jennifer Wilbanks and Mark Hacking illustrate, these cases invariably tax the financial resources of the communities in which they occur and the emotional resources of the family and community members they affect. Case resolution is often the result of law enforcement investigation of the alleged crime scene and evaluation of the verbal inconsistencies and non-verbal cues provided by the alleged victims.

On April 26, 2005, Georgia resident John Mason called law enforcement after his fiancée, Jennifer Carol Wilbanks, failed to return home from her evening jog. Three days after her disappearance, and a day following the involvement of the Federal Bureau of Investigation, Wilbanks telephoned Mason and law enforcement from a pay phone, reporting that she had been kidnapped and sexually assaulted by a Hispanic man and a Caucasian woman. The two were in their forties, Wilbanks reported, and were driving a blue van. Her captors had freed her, she said, but she did not know where she was. Her calls were traced to a 7-Eleven convenience store in Albuquerque, New Mexico.

In her statement to law enforcement, Wilbanks reported that on the evening of Tuesday, April 26, she was jogging when she was grabbed by two individuals, a Hispanic man and a White female. The two threw her in the back of the van. Her hands were tied with rope and the individuals placed her on the right side of the floor and made her face the back door. The male then began driving, while the woman remained in the back. They drove approximately 30 minutes before the male pulled to the side of the rode and turned off the vehicle. Wilbanks claimed that during this time she was sexually assaulted by both her female and male abductors. After dressing themselves and Wilbanks, the male returned to the driver's seat and resumed driving.

Continued...

Law enforcement questioned Wilbanks about several aspects of her story. She had stated, for example, that she could not see within the van, yet she knew that her abductors were fully undressed. She was unable to state whether the Hispanic man wore a condom when he assaulted her. She also stated that she was unable to see anything but the sky from the back of the van, although the van's windows were not obstructed.

Eventually, investigators told Wilbanks that her statement did not seem credible and that they believed she left Georgia on her own to escape her wedding. The wedding had been scheduled for April 30, the day on which she was being interviewed. Wilbanks admitted that she had lied about the kidnapping and sexual assault.

The investigation into Wilbanks's staged kidnapping cost an estimated $40,000–50,000.

On May 17, "The Runaway Bride" officially canceled her engagement. A week later, she was charged with making false statements. In a plea agreement with the city of Duluth, Georgia, Wilbanks agreed to 2 years' probation, community service, and a restitution payment to offset a portion of the cost associated with the search into her disappearance.

Nine months prior to Wilbanks's staged abduction, another woman was reported missing after she did not return from jogging. Mark Douglas Hacking, age 28, telephoned Salt Lake City police at 10:07 a.m. when he learned that his pregnant wife, Lori, did not arrive at her job at the local Wells Fargo bank. Law enforcement found Lori's car outside the park at which she jogged, its driver seat adjusted for someone significantly taller than Lori's 5-foot, 4-inch frame. A search of the couple's apartment yielded a receipt for a new mattress and bedding and a bloody knife. The search also yielded keys to Lori's car, which would have been in her possession or in the vehicle had she driven herself to the park. During the investigation, law enforcement also learned that between 9:45 and 10:23 a.m., when Hacking was allegedly searching for his wife, he was actually purchasing a new mattress.

Hacking was identified as a person of interest.

The following day, Lori's family held a press conference, urging anyone with information about their daughter to come forward. Twelve hundred volunteers began a community search.

As law enforcement continued its investigation, Hacking was institutionalized after police found him wandering around a Salt Lake City motel, naked except for a pair of sandals. Hacking was apparently experiencing a mental breakdown.

The continuing investigation revealed that Hacking had lied to his wife and her family, claiming that he had graduated with honors in psychology from the University of Utah, and had been accepted to the University of North Carolina's medical school, an event that resulted in the couple's planned relocation to that state. Hacking had never graduated from college.

On July 25, Hacking's brothers telephoned law enforcement, stating that during their visit to the hospital in which Hacking was institutionalized, Hacking confessed to Lori's murder. Specifically, it was reported that, on July 16, Lori had telephoned the University of North Carolina medical school to obtain information regarding financial aid and was informed that her husband was not enrolled in the school. Lori apparently left work to confront Hacking, and he told her that the school was experiencing a computer malfunction. Two days later, he admitted his lie. The two argued and Lori went to sleep, while Hacking stayed awake and played video games and packed several boxes. Sometime during these activities, Hacking found a .22 caliber rifle. At approximately 1 a.m., he went into the bedroom where Lori was sleeping and shot her in the head. He cut away a portion of the mattress which was bloodied and wrapped it and Lori's body in some garbage bags. He disposed of the body in a dumpster. Hacking allegedly disposed of the bloodied mattress in a church trash bin and the gun in another unidentified dumpster.

On August 2, 2004, Hacking was arrested and charged with first-degree murder.

Two months later, on October 1, 2004, Lori's remains were found in the Salt Lake County Landfill. On October 30, 2004, despite the evidence against him, Hacking entered a plea of not guilty in the murder of his wife. On April 15, 2005, Hacking changed his plea to guilty. He was sentenced to 6 years to life in prison, the maximum sentence allowed under Utah law. One month later, the Utah Board of Prisons determined that Hacking's first parole hearing would not occur until August 2034.

The Reid Technique, one of the most widely used methods of deception detection by law enforcement, suggests the following key points when attempting to detect deception:

- It is important to establish a subject's normal behaviors at the outset of the interview. Thus, the investigator should evaluate the subject in the areas of intelligence, sense of social responsibility, degree of maturity, possible influence of drugs, general nervous tension, emotional condition, cultural differences, and preexisting neurological disorders.
- The initial evaluation should be done by asking non-threatening background questions.
- Both truthful and deceptive subjects can exhibit reticence, nervousness, impertinence and anger. Signs of despair and resignation are more common in guilty subjects.

Continued...

- The investigator should not allow behavior analysis to outweigh the evidence and case facts.

- Investigators should be highly skeptical of the behavior symptoms of a person with a psychiatric history.

- An investigator must keep in mind the many factors that can influence the misinterpretation of behavior symptoms.

Excerpted from Essentials of the Reid Technique: Criminal Interrogation and Confessions *by Fred E. Inbau, John E. Reid, Joseph P. Buckley, and Brian C. Jayne. Jones and Barlett Publishers, Inc., 2005. Reprinted with permission.*

Holding Truth Hostage: The Staged Kidnapping for False Justice

In November 1987, the author resided in New York City. During that month, an anonymous call was made to the sheriff's department of Dutchess County, located approximately 70 miles north. The caller said that a young girl carrying a garbage bag was walking around in a daze outside an apartment complex in the city of Wappingers Falls. A search of the area found an African American girl behind the building, curled in a fetal position inside a plastic bag. Fifteen-year-old Tawana Brawley had "nigger" and "KKK" written in charcoal across her torso. Feces were smeared along her body. Her hair had been chopped off.

As she was treated in a nearby hospital, Brawley offered sketchy information about her ordeal. Four days earlier, the teen said, she had been abducted and sexually assaulted by six White men. One of the men had a badge.

Brawley's mother, Glenda, offered additional information: On the morning of November 24, Mrs. Brawley said, her daughter was on a bus returning from nearby Newburgh. She was approached by a man with a badge, whom she assumed to be a police officer. The man asked her to get into a dark green car. Inside the car was another man. She was struck in the head and driven to a wooded area where four more men were waiting and where all six sodomized her.

The allegation magnetized New York activists and polarized race relations in a city already stressed to its civil limit. One year earlier, racial tension exploded when three Black men stumbled into the predominantly White enclave of Howard Beach, Queens, and were beaten by a gang of bat-wielding White youth. One of the victims was chased to his death when he was hit by a car while attempting to escape. After a highly publicized and tense trial, three of the White youth were convicted of second-degree manslaughter and first-degree assault. A fourth defendant was acquitted of all changes. The convictions did little to ease racial tensions, which would once again ignite as Brawley's story unfolded.

"You will not do to another Black girl in America what you did to Tawana Brawley and get away with it," the Reverend Louis Farrakhan, the Black Muslim minister, declared.

Attorneys Alton H. Maddox, Jr. and C. Vernon Mason signed on to represent Brawley. Reverend Al Sharpton assumed responsibility for publicity.

For nearly a year following Brawley's allegation, investigators sought to find evidence and information through a morass of obstruction, political posturing, and racial protests.

The one investigative avenue not available was interviewing Brawley herself; her attorneys, citing a racial conspiracy throughout the New York law enforcement community, refused to cooperate with investigators.

Then New York Governor Mario Cuomo appointed Attorney General Robert Abrams as special prosecutor to handle the sensitive case. In an unusual demand, Brawley's attorneys refused to cooperate unless a prosecutor of their choosing was assigned. At first, Maddox and Mason demanded that Abrams personally handle all aspects of the investigation, rather than delegating tasks to a subordinate. Within several weeks, the attorneys demanded that Abrams be removed from the case, stating that his ownership of a house in Dutchess County posed a conflict of interest. The attorneys demanded Abrams be replaced by the attorney who had received the indictment of the White youth in the Howard Beach case. As the investigation proceeded, Reverend Al Sharpton further demanded that Brawley's own attorney, Alton Maddox, be named special prosecutor.

What Brawley's attorneys refused to discuss with the special prosecutor they disclosed at public rallies and to the media. Their often contradictory statements included the following:

- During her police interview in the hospital, Brawley identified one of the officers in her room as her attacker.
- Brawley nearly jumped off her exam table in fear when two White officers attempted to interview her. A Black officer was called and Brawley wrote a note saying she was attacked by "a white cop."
- Brawley wrote a note stating "I want him dead—I want Scoralick"—a reference to the Dutchess County sheriff.
- The rape tests, which tested negative for foreign fluid at both the FBI and New York State police laboratories, were mishandled.
- "Everybody in Wappingers Falls knows who did it—even I know who did it," Mr. Maddox claimed, refusing to name suspects.
- Harry Crist, Jr., a part-time police officer in the community, shot himself to death in his home a few blocks from the Brawley home 4 days after Brawley was found. Crist's father claimed his son was depressed after failing a state

Continued...

trooper exam and by the dissolution of his relationship with his girlfriend. Despite a suicide note claiming the test failure as the reason for his act, Brawley's lawyers claimed that Crist's car resembled one seen in the area on the day Brawley was found and that the timing of his suicide implicated him. The note, Brawley's attorneys claimed, was not authentic.

- A White man had sought out Brawley's lawyers with information about a racist cult which was responsible for Brawley's abduction and sexual assault.

Brawley herself continued her refusal to speak to investigators, and her attorneys remained steadfast in their refusal to speak with the special prosecutor. "That's like asking someone who watched someone killed in the gas chamber to sit down with Mr. Hitler," Al Sharpton remarked.

Despite a lack of cooperation from the alleged victim, investigators compiled information which allowed Abrams to convene a grand jury.

On the evening before juror selection was to begin, Brawley, her mother, Glenda, and her aunt Juanita joined Brawley's attorneys and Al Sharpton for another protest of the proceedings. Speaking to a crowd of more than 800, Sharpton reiterated the group's latest demand that the governor replace special prosecutor Robert Abrams with Brawley's own lawyer Alton Maddox.

"Give Maddox the power and we'll lock up all six men by six o'clock tomorrow," Sharpton said.

Instead, on February 29, 1988, the special prosecutor empaneled a jury to hear the testimony of investigators, neighbors, friends, and potential witnesses to Brawley's ordeal. Despite a lack of cooperation from the alleged victim and her family, the testimony presented to the grand jury was extensive. Over the course of the next 8 months, jurors would piece the information together to form the first cohesive story of the events surrounding Brawley's alleged abduction.

On the night of November 23, 1987—one day prior to Brawley's disappearance—a sister of Brawley's 17-year-old former boyfriend called her at home. The former boyfriend, who was serving a 6-month sentence at the nearby Orange County jail at Goshen for reckless endangerment after firing a gun at another youth, wanted to see Brawley.

The next day, Brawley left her house wearing blue jeans, a black blouse, black shoes, a yellow sweater, and a denim jacket. She carried a stack of books and a green and black miniskirt.

At 7:00 a.m., a 17-year-old friend of Brawley's arrived at her home in his gray car intending to drive her to the high school where she was a junior. Instead,

Brawley asked him to take her to the apartment of her former boyfriend's sister in nearby Newburgh. At 7:30, he left her knocking on the sister's door.

The sister was apparently surprised to see Brawley; although she had told Brawley that her brother wanted her to visit him, "I didn't tell her what day to come."

"I asked her why she wasn't in school," the girlfriend testified. "She lied to me and said that she was on Thanksgiving break. I didn't argue with her. I was too sleepy."

The sister told Brawley that her mother was going to visit her brother in jail that day and that the two should travel together. The sister's boyfriend drove Brawley to her mother's nearby apartment. She arrived at the mother's house just after 9:00 a.m.

Over the next hour, the mother of Brawley's former boyfriend readied herself for the trip. She characterized Brawley's mood during this time as unusual. "She didn't seem like the Tawana I knew. She wasn't jolly or nothing, like she normally is."

The mother added that Brawley's mood changed as the time to depart approached. She changed into her miniskirt and "was really excited," bouncing on the sofa.

Brawley carried the mother's 15-month-old granddaughter down to the taxi that awaited them. At 10:15 a.m. they departed on the Short Line bus to Goshen, arriving at 1:00 p.m.

Once at the jail, the mother lied and said Brawley was her son's sister who had traveled from New York City and had forgotten her identification; as an underage non-relative, Brawley would not have been granted access.

At approximately 2:30 p.m., the mother, her granddaughter, and Brawley left to catch a 3:00 p.m. bus back to Newburgh.

They arrived back at the mother's apartment at 5:30 p.m. She prepared dinner for her family as Brawley watched television.

At Brawley's home in Wappingers Falls, her mother, Glenda, grew concerned that Brawley had not returned from school. She called Brawley's aunt, Juanita, with whom Brawley was extremely close and who lived in Newburgh. Juanita called some of Brawley's friends, who reported that Brawley had not been in school and that they had seen her in the vicinity of her former boyfriend's apartment.

Concerned, Juanita went to the Newburgh police station to report that Brawley was missing.

"She was very distressed and preferred to come inside rather than talk to Sergeant Engle through the bullet-proof glass," said Deputy Police Chief William Bloom, who witnessed Sergeant William Engle's contact with Juanita.

Sergeant Engle told Juanita to file the report with the local police department in Brawley's home community of Wappingers Falls. For unknown reasons, the report was not filed until shortly before Brawley was found.

Continued...

Brawley remained at her former boyfriend's home. "She seemed like she wanted to stay," the boy's mother said. "I didn't know her mother, I didn't want her to get mad at me for keeping her out. I said, 'Tawana you might get into trouble.' And she said, 'I'm already in trouble.'"

Brawley told the mother that her stepfather was angry with her for staying out until 5 a.m. the previous Saturday after a Friday night party.

Although apparently reluctant to do so, Brawley called a cab at 7:30 p.m. after changing out of her miniskirt and back into the jeans she wore when she left her family's apartment earlier in the day. A 8:10 p.m., she boarded the Short Line bus to Wappingers Falls. The bus driver recognized Brawley; her stepfather was a fellow Short Line driver. Brawley sat at the front of the bus, and the two spoke for most of the 20-minute ride.

"She was in good spirits. She was smiling. She didn't appear to be down in any sort of way. And she did not appear to be intoxicated or anything like that," the driver reported.

Brawley asked the driver to drop her two blocks from her home, rather than at the scheduled stop more than a mile away. The driver explained that he could not do so because he needed to continue on his route for the other bus passengers.

He dropped her off at a busy street in the Wappingers Falls commercial strip, which was occupied by a service station, bank, shopping mall, fast-food outlets, and auto-repair shops. The service station and several fast-food restaurants were open for business during the time she alighted.

According to the disjointed account given by Brawley during her hospital stay, she was seized immediately after leaving the bus. Her family stated that she first crossed a six-lane highway and began walking down one of the side streets. Thereafter, Brawley claimed, a dark car pulled over, and the man in the passenger seat dragged her into the back seat. Her family stated that the man grabbed her by the hair and pulled her into the car. They stated that she struggled and screamed for her parents and the police; her abductor then allegedly informed her that he was a police officer.

Brawley described her abductor as a tall White man with sandy blonde hair and a light brown mustache who was wearing a badge, a dark jacket, and a holster. She said that she did not get a clear view of the driver before the passenger struck her on the head. She did not know what the passenger used to knock her unconscious.

Brawley said that when she regained consciousness, she was in a wooded area where at least one other man was waiting; she said she did not know the exact number of men but that it was more than three. Her aunt Juanita put the number of men at six. Brawley did not know where the wooded area was located.

Brawley said the men sexually abused her and that one urinated in her mouth. When asked by a doctor if she had been raped, Brawley indicated that she had not been, although she initially told a detective that she had. Her family stated that she was repeatedly raped and sodomized.

Brawley did not provide any additional information regarding what occurred from the time she was allegedly assaulted in the woods until the time she was found. She did not say what happened to her schoolbooks and purse, which were missing when she was discovered.

The day after she went missing, Glenda and Juanita Brawley reported driving around Wappingers Falls in search of Brawley, but that they did not see her.

The following day was Thanksgiving. A resident of the Pavilion apartments— where the Brawley family had previously lived—told *The New York Times* that he had seen Brawley at 8:00 a.m. that day, approaching her former apartment.

"She was acting very strange," said the man. "She was kind of cradled against the building over there. It looked maybe like she was looking for somebody or was looking in the apartment. She was kind of creeping along the wall. It's the kind of thing you notice and the kind of thing you remember. It looked like she went in. Her hair looked like she had slept in it, like she had just woken up."

Two other residents reported seeing Brawley at the apartment complex during the time she was missing. One couple indicated that they heard voices in the vacant apartment which had been previously occupied by Brawley's family. They said the tone of the voices was conversational.

The Brawley family retained a key to the vacated apartment; it was not known if Brawley herself had a copy.

On the Saturday Brawley was found, Glenda was seen at her former apartment at approximately 1:30 p.m. where she was apparently retrieving mail that had not been forwarded to her new address. She was seen sitting in her parked car in front of the building for approximately 15 minutes, examining the mail. She then went to the Wappingers Falls Police Department to file a missing persons report on her daughter at 2:02 p.m., 17 minutes after Brawley was found.

The family claims that they had filed previous reports with the Wappingers Falls Police Department; the department denies that any report, save the one on the day Brawley was found, had been filed. Also after Brawley had been found, Juanita returned to the Newburgh Police Department with a picture of Brawley and told the officer on duty that friends had seen Brawley in Newburgh between the Tuesday and Saturday she was missing.

At 1:45 p.m., neighbors saw Brawley on the grassy courtyard approximately 15 feet from her former apartment. They reported that she was trying to climb into a big plastic bag.

At 2:30 p.m. Dutchess County sheriffs' deputies arrived at the building after receiving an anonymous call that a young girl was walking around the building

Continued...

holding a plastic bag. Upon finding Brawley, deputies contacted the Dutchess County Fire Bureau, who called the Sloper-Willen Community Ambulance Service.

Brawley was not wearing the clothing she had worn when she left her Wappingers Falls home 4 days earlier. Her denim pants were scorched on the inner thighs, although she was not burned. She was wearing a pink sweatshirt, a dark sweater around her head and neck, and one shoe. On her torso, above and below her breasts, was written the words "nigger," "KKK," and "nigger ete shit," with "ete" apparently a misspelling of "eat." The words were written in block letters in charcoal or a fine tip marker.

The ambulance performed tests which revealed that Brawley was free of narcotics.

Upon arrival at St. Francis Hospital in Poughkeepsie at 2:55 p.m., Brawley was given a series of standard medical tests. Samples were taken from several parts of her body to determine if she had been raped or sexually abused. In accordance with the hospital's standard operating procedure, the specimens were sealed and turned over to the FBI for processing.

Medical staff indicated that Brawley had been smeared with non-human feces (most probably dog feces). They also indicated that she was not suffering from exposure, malnutrition, or any serious injury, indicating that she had not been beaten, kept outdoors, or deprived of food.

Brawley was treated for a minor bruise on her scalp. Although she was not physically hurt, she did appear traumatized. When White police officers attempted to question her, she remained silent. When a Black officer asked who had attacked her, she wrote "a white cop" on a piece of paper.

Shortly before 11:00 a.m. on Saturday, Brawley was released from the hospital. Glenda and Juanita took her to the Wappingers Falls apartment where they claimed that they learned the specifics of Brawley's ordeal over the next several hours.

The following day, Juanita relayed Brawley's story to three detectives from the Dutchess County Sheriff's office and a social worker who visited the Brawley home.

On the following Monday, Brawley herself gave a sketchy account, communicated primarily through nodding, shaking her head, and writing notes, to the two Dutchess County Assistant District Attorneys, an FBI agent, and a sheriff's detective whom the family invited to their home.

Brawley claimed to recall nothing from the time she was attacked in the woods until the time she was in the hospital. She could not say what had happened to her books or purse, when or how her hair had been cut, or who put the racial slurs on her body. She could not remember how she became smeared with feces. She could remember nothing about her attackers, save her original vague description of a tall blonde man.

An investigation of Brawley's former apartment yielded a denim jacket and pants in a washing machine which may have been the ones Brawley was wearing when she vanished. Parts of the clothing, which had not been washed, were smeared with feces. Clippings of hair and residue of burnt clothing were also found.

On October 7, 1988, after an 8-month investigation, 6,000 pages of testimony from more than 180 witnesses, and an estimated cost of $2,500 per day, the Dutchess County grand jury issued a 170-page report on its findings in the case of Tawana Brawley. "Tawana Brawley was not the victim of a forcible sexual assault by multiple assailants over a four-day period." The Grand Jury further concluded that "there is nothing in regard to Tawana Brawley's appearance on November 28 that is inconsistent with this condition having been self-inflicted."

It was later reported that Brawley staged her kidnapping in an effort to avoid punishment by her stepfather for breaking her curfew.

REFERENCES

Cullen, Murray C., and Bradley, M. T. (2004). Positions of Truthfully Answered Controls on Control Question Tests with the Polygraph. *Canadian Journal of Behavioural Science, 36*(3), 167–176.

DePaulo, Bella, Malone, Brian, Lindsay, James, Muhlenbruck, Laura, Charlton, Kelly, and Cooper, Harris. (2005). Cues to Deception. *Psychological Bulletin, 129*(1), 74–118.

Douglas, John E., Burgess, Ann W., Burgess, Allen G., and Ressler, Robert K. (1992). *Crime Classification Manual: A Standard System for Investigating and Classifying Violent Crimes.* San Francisco: Jossey-Bass, 253–255.

Ekman, P., O'Sullivan, M., and Friesen, W. V. (1991). Face, Voice and Body in Detecting Deceit. *Journal of Nonverbal Behavior, 15*(2), 125–135.

Faigman, David, Fiengerg, Stephen, and Stern, Paul. (2003, Fall). The Limits of the Polygraph. *Issues in Science and Technology,* 1–8.

Gronau, Nurit, Ben-Shakhar, Gershon, and Cohen, Asher. (2005). Behavioral and Physiological Measures in the Detection of Concealed Information. *Journal of Applied Psychology, 90*(1), 47–158.

Gunter, Kohnken, Schimossek, Elke, Aschermann, Ellen, and Hofer, Eberhand. (1995). The Cognitive Interview and the Assessment of Credibility of Adults Statements. *Journal of Applied Psychology, 80*(6), 671–684.

Inbau, Fred E., Reid, John E., Buckley, Joseph, P., and Jayne, Brian C. (2005). *Essentials of the Reid Technique: Criminal Interrogation and Confessions.* Sudbury, MA: Jones and Bartlett Publishers, Inc., p. 115.

Mann, Samantha, Vrij, Albert, and Bull, Ray. (2004). Detecting True Lies: Police Officers' Ability to Detect Suspects' Lies. *Journal of Applied Psychology, 89*(1), 137–149.

Masip, Jaume, Garrido, Eugenio, and Herrero, Carmen. (2004). The Nonverbal Approach to the Detection of Deception: Judgemental Accuracy. *Psychology in Spain*, 8(1), 48–59.

Navarro, Joe, and Schafer, John. (2001, July). Detecting Deception. *FBI Law Enforcement Bulletin*, 70(7), 9–12.

Palermo, George B., and Kocsis, Richard N. (2005). *Offender Profiling: An Introduction to the Sociopsychological Analysis of Violent Crime.* Springfield, IL: Charles C Thomas Publisher, Ltd., 108–109.

Turvey, Brent E. (2000, December). Staged Crime Scenes: A Preliminary Study of 25 Cases. Part 2 of 2. *Journal of Behavioral Profiling*, 1(3). Epub: http://www.profiling.org/journal/index.html.

U.S. v. Edward R. Hughes, 211 F.3d 676; 2000 U.S. App. Lexis 9151.

U.S. v. Michael Sean Gianakos, 404 F.3d 1065; 2005 U.S. App. Lexis 6812.

Vrij, Aldert, Akehurst, Lucy, Soukara, Stavroula, and Bull, Ray. (2004). Let Me Inform You How to Tell a Convincing Story: CBCA and Reality Monitoring Scores as a Function of Age, Coaching and Deception. *Canadian Journal of Behavioural Science*, 36(2), 113–126.

Yeschke, Charles L. (2003). *The Art of Investigative Interviewing*, 2nd ed. Boston, MA: Butterworth-Heinemann.

Zuckerman, Miron, Amidon, Mary D., Bishop, Shawn E., and Pomerantz, Scott D. (1982). Face and Tone of Voice in the Communication of Deception. *Journal of Personality and Social Psychology*, 43(2), 347–357.

Zuckerman, Miron, Kernis, Michael, Driver, Robert, and Koestner, Richard. (1984). Segmentation of Behavior: Effects of Actual Deception and Expected Deception. *Journal of Personality and Social Psychology*, 46(5), 1173–1182.

Zuckerman, Miron, Koestner, Richard, and Alton, Audrey. (1984). Learning to Detect Deception. *Journal of Personality and Social Psychology*, 146(3), 519–528.

Zuckerman, Miron, Koestner, Richard, Colella, Michael, and Alton, Audrey. (1994). Anchoring in the Detection of Deception and Leakage. *Journal of Personality and Social Psychology*, 47(2), 301–311.

Chapter | nine

Political Kidnapping

CHAPTER CONTENTS

WHAT DEFINES THE POLITICAL KIDNAPPING

The political kidnapping is generally perpetrated for one of four reasons: (1) to demonstrate that the government cannot protect its own citizens; (2) to ascertain publicity for a specific cause; (3) to cause civil discontent; or (4) to demand the release of incarcerated group members. Political kidnappings are not typically tried in the United States Court system and, as a result, were not included in the review process. Nonetheless, their prevalence, and the commonality shared by incidents of this kidnapping subtype, rendered it worthy of inclusion. The following case studies are taken from media accounts of the incidents listed. All information presented appeared in more than one source.

The Achille Lauro

At 8:45 a.m. on October 7, 1985, four members of the Palestine Liberation Front (PLF)—23-year-old Youssef Magied al-Molqi, 23-year-old Hammid Ali Abdullah, 20-year-old Abdel Atif Ibrahim, and 17-year-old Hallah al-Hassan—fired machine guns into the Achille Lauro's dining hall. The 21,000-ton cruise ship and its more than 400 passengers and crew members, including 19 Americans, were traveling Egyptian waters. In accordance with a plan devised by PLF leader Abu Abbas, the ship was to dock at Ashdod, Israel, where the hijackers would complete a suicide mission. Instead, the gunmen were discovered by a ship steward and seized control of the vessel.

In a ship-to-shore communication, the PLF gunmen demanded release of 50 Arab comrades held in Israeli prisons. The group ordered the ship's crew to set a course for the Syrian port of Tartus, in the mistaken belief that the Syrian government would be sympathetic to their cause.

Turned away from Syria, the hijackers steered toward Egypt's Port Said on Tuesday, October 8. Contrary to the will of the U.S. authorities, the Egyptian government opened negotiations with the hijackers through Palestinian Liberation Organization leader Yasser Arafat. The gunmen agreed to surrender the ship if granted immunity from prosecution and flown, along with hijacking mastermind Abbas, to Tunis.

On Wednesday, October 9, it was reported that the immunity would also extend to the group's murder of American Leon Klinghoffer, a wheelchair-bound retired appliance manufacturer from Manhattan. Klinghoffer was shot in the chest and head by the gunmen, his body tossed into the sea.

At 5:30 p.m. on Thursday, October 10, then President Reagan authorized the USS Saratoga to utilize seven F-14 Tomcats to divert the Egyptian aircraft to a NATO base in Sicily. After initial Italian resistance, the Egyptian aircraft landed, and the American troops prepared to escort the Palestinians to a U.S. aircraft for transportation to the United States. Once grounded, however, Italian and American authorities fought for custody of the prisoners. President Reagan ordered the American Delta Force commander to stand down.

Four of the kidnappers were ultimately convicted of hijacking in the Italian courts. The group's leader, Abu Abbas, was inexplicably released after the aircraft landing, and was convicted in absentia. Bassam al-Akar was granted parole in 1991 and died in 2004. Ahmad Marrouf al-Assadi disappeared in 1991 while on parole. Yousesef al Molqui was sentenced to 30 years in prison. He escaped to Spain during a 12-day furlough and was extradited back to Italy.

In 1996, Abbas issued a public apology for the hijacking and murder, and advocated peace talks between Palestinians and Israelis. His apology was rejected by both the United States and Leon Klinghoffer's family. Abbas was captured by U.S. forces in 2003 during the U.S. military invasion of Iraq. He died in U.S. custody a year later.

The Achille Lauro caught fire off the coast of Somalia on November 30, 1994. Abandoned, it sank on December 2.

The Iranian Hostage Crisis

At 6:30 a.m. on November 4, 1979, a group of between 300 and 500 Iranian students gathered to prepare for an attack on the U.S. Embassy in Iran. The attack was designed to lodge the students' displeasure at then U.S. President Jimmy Carter's admittance of ousted Iranian Shah Mohammad Reza Pahlavi into the United States. One female student was given a pair of metal cutters to hide beneath her chador. She was allegedly instructed to approach the Embassy gates, pull the cutters from her garment, and break the chain that held the gates closed. Thereafter, the remaining students were to storm the Embassy, overrunning soldiers and staff.

The plan was effectively executed. Six American diplomats avoided capture and took refuge at the nearby Canadian and Swedish embassies from which they escaped to Canada 3 months later. The remaining hostages were blindfolded and paraded before photographers.

In mid-November, the group released 13 women and African Americans, claiming kinship with the "oppressed minorities." Eight months later, an additional hostage was released after he was diagnosed with multiple sclerosis. The remaining hostages were held captive until January 1981.

The students, who called themselves the Muslim Student Followers of the Imam's Line, initially justified their hostage taking as an appropriate response to the United States' admission of Iran's former leader. They demanded that the Shah be returned to Iran for trial and execution. After President Carter applied economic and diplomatic pressure on Iran, the Followers' demands evolved to include the release of $8 billion in Iranian assets frozen by the United States. The group also demanded an apology for interference in Iranian internal affairs, refusing to accept the U.S. explanation the Shah entered the United States solely for medical reasons. The Shah's death less than a year later did not dissuade the kidnappers from their position that the United States was "the Great Satan" determined to overthrow Iran's new fundamentalist regime.

Carter rejected the group's demands and approved a secret rescue mission known as Operation Eagle Claw. On the night of April 24, 1980, C-130 transport planes rendezvoused with eight RH-53 helicopters in the Great Salt Desert of Eastern Iran. The mission failed when two helicopters broke down in a sandstorm and a third was damaged on landing. A fourth helicopter clipped a C-130 and crashed, killing eight U.S. servicemen and injuring several more.

Iran's new leader, Ayatollah Khomeini, credited divine Islamic intervention for the failure.

Six months later, a second rescue attempt failed when a highly modified YMC-130 H Hercules aircraft misfired during a demonstration test.

In November 1980, Ronald Reagan defeated Jimmy Carter in the United States presidential race. Analysts cited Mr. Carter's inability to rescue the American hostages as the cause of his loss.

The Americans had been held captive for more than 400 days when an Algerian diplomat opened negotiations between the United States and Iran. On January 19, 1981 the countries finalized the Algiers Accords. The United States agreed not to "intervene, directly or indirectly, politically or militarily, in Iran's internal affairs." The United States also agreed to unfreeze the $8 billion in Iranian assets.

On January 20, 1981, 444 days after being seized and minutes after Ronald Reagan was sworn in as president, the hostages were released into U.S. custody.

In 2000, the hostages and their families attempted to sue Iran under the Antiterrorism Act. They initially won their case when Iran failed to provide a defense. The U.S. State Department appealed the case, fearing that it would compromise international relations. A federal judge subsequently ruled that, under the Algiers Accords, damages could not be claimed.

Kidnappings in Iraq

On September 16, 2004, Englishman Kenneth John Bigley and Americans Jack Hensley and Eugene Armstrong were abducted by the Islamic group Tawhid and Jihad, or "Oneness of God and Holy War." The victims were civil engineers for Gulf Supplies and Commercial Services, one of the companies working on reconstruction projects throughout Iraq following the U.S. invasion. In exchange for their victims' release, the kidnappers' leader, Abu Musab al-Zarqawi, demanded the release of Iraqi women held prisoner by coalition forces. al-Zarqawi stated that the victims would be beheaded if his demands were not met within 48 hours of the abduction. He made his announcement through a videotape that showed the three hostages kneeling before a Tawhid and Jihad banner.

Shortly after the demand, the British government issued a statement that it held no Iraqi women prisoners. The only two women known to be in United States custody, the statement continued, were the British-educated Dr. Rihab Taha and U.S.-educated Dr. Huda Salih Mahdi Ammash. Both women were found to have participated in the Iraqi biological weapons program by the United Nations weapons inspectorate.

The Iraqi provisional government announced that the women's release had been imminent because no charges had been brought against them. The U.S. government quickly denied this and refused the prisoners' release.

On September 20, the kidnappers beheaded Eugene Armstrong. Twenty-four hours later, victim Jack Hensley was beheaded. Both murders were videotaped and aired on Islamic websites, as well as on one shock site specializing in violence and pornography.

Kenneth Bigley remained in the group's custody. On September 22, Tawhid and Jihad issued another video in which Bigley pleaded to British Prime Minister Tony Blair: "I need you to help me now, Mr. Blair, because you are the only person on God's earth who can help me."

Blair asserted that he was doing everything short of direct negotiation with the kidnappers to ensure Bigley's release. When it was learned that Bigley was a citizen of Ireland, rather than England, the Irish government made an appeal on al-Jazeera for Bigley's release; as an Irish citizen, they argued, Kenneth was not aligned with the government that invaded Iraqi, as Ireland was not a member of the coalition forces. On September 24, the British Foreign Officer distributed 50,000 leaflets requesting information on the victim's whereabouts. The Muslim Council of Britain also appealed for the victim's release and sent a senior two-man team to negotiate on his behalf. On September 29, Tawhid and Jihad issued a third video. In it, the victim was wearing an orange boiler suit, presumably meant to resemble those worn by inmates at the U.S. facility in Guantanamo Bay, Cuba. He was chained inside a small chicken-wire fence.

On October 7, 2004, Tawhid and Jihad issued a final video. In it, the victim was again clad in the orange jumpsuit as one of his kidnappers stepped forward and beheaded him with a knife.

Following the victim's death, analysts suggested that the video did not occur in real time and that the beheading may have been staged. Some suggested that the victim actually died from a gunshot wound to the head.

Shortly after his death, it was revealed that the victim had briefly managed to escape with the help of two agents of Syrian and Iraqi origin. The men attempted to drive the victim out of the town in which he was held but were spotted at an insurgent checkpoint and returned. The two agents were later beheaded.

The victim's body was never recovered. The chicken-wire cage in which he was filmed was later found in a house in the Iraqi town of Fallujah.

CHARACTERISTICS OF THE POLITICAL KIDNAPPING

Victimology

The victims of the political kidnapping are chosen for what they represent, rather than for who they are. A single political kidnapping can involve victims from multiple nations, as in the case of the Achille Lauro; a single nation, as in the Iran Hostage Crisis; or a coalition of interests, as has occurred in many of the political kidnappings that have followed the onset of the Iraqi War.

Abduction Site

While political kidnappings can occur in any country (as became all too evident following the September 11 hijacking of three airliners originating within the United States), the abduction sites are typically in countries experiencing political unrest or instability. In 2007, for example, the United States State Department advised Americans against travel to 23 countries deemed high risk for crimes against Westerners, including kidnappings.

Modus Operandi

The Achille Lauro, Iranian, and Iraqi kidnappings typify the approach applied by many political kidnappers; i.e., they tend to be perpetrated by groups of modestly to extremely organized individuals. Blitz attacks which overpower victims via physical force are common. The victim or victims are equally likely to be secured in an undisclosed location as in known locations that are precarious to breach.

Outcome

Within 2 days of the Achille Lauro hijacking, the hijackers killed one victim and submitted to the negotiated release of the others. The majority of the victims of the American Embassy seizure in Iran were held for 444 days prior to release. All the victims of the Gulf Supplies and Commercial Services kidnapping in Iraq were murdered within 1 month of their abduction.

The length of time victims of political kidnappings are held involves a complex calculus that includes the willingness of the victim(s)' country of origin to negotiate, that county's power to sanction or coerce the sovereignty in which the kidnapping occurred, and public outcry. These factors also bear on the outcome of the political kidnapping, which typically ends at one of two extremes: the victim(s)' release or the victim(s)' murder. As demonstrated in the case of victim Kenneth Bigley, rescue efforts that do not involve negotiation with the political kidnappers represent a higher risk intervention whose outcome is extremely uncertain and frequently results in the death of the victim.

IMPLICATIONS FOR PREVENTION AND INVESTIGATION

The United States Code Title 18 Section 1203 defines *hostage taking* as

> ... whoever, whether inside or outside the United States, seizes or detains and threatens to kill, to injure, or to continue to detain another person in order to compel a third person or a governmental organization to do or abstain from doing any act as an explicit or implicit condition for the release of the person detained....

The Code excludes acts of kidnapping by one U.S. citizen of another, unless the goal of the kidnapping is to influence the U.S. government.

In the volatile, post-9/11 world, hostage taking has become a popular method of lodging protest against governmental decisions. During 2006, for example, the U.S. State Department reported 1,334 such kidnappings occurred, an increase of 16 percent over the previous year. More than 50 percent of U.S. kidnapping victims were abducted in Iraq. The withdrawal of U.S. or coalition forces was a common demand made by the abductors.

Despite the higher probability of victimization by the political kidnapper in countries rife with political and social unrest, many clients or protectees have business- or government-related interests in these countries that necessitate exposure. In these instances, several factors should be considered.

Political kidnappers are typically organized groups of individuals who surveil their target prior to the abduction. Heightening pre-travel security efforts may serve as a deterrent to the kidnappers, particularly if these individuals are considering multiple potential targets: The political kidnapper will presume the target with greater pre-travel security will likely have greater security during travel, thereby rendering him or her less desirable.

Pre-travel precautions should also evaluate the application of security practices to multiple, interrelated areas of vulnerability, including

- *Site-Specific Safety:* Residences, hotels, airports, workplaces, and other business locations.
- *Interpersonal Safety:* Personal and professional interactions, protecting family members and maintaining privacy protocols.
- *Communication/Data Safety:* Telephone, cell, fax, electronic messages, postal materials, and proprietary data.
- *Transitional Safety:* Personal and rental vehicles, mass transit and commercial or chartered travel.

Additional pre-travel precautions parallel those appropriate for all high-profile targets, including

- Limiting access to the target's itinerary;
- Instituting a varied routine;

- Conducting a crime analysis for the destination and immediate vicinity for the prior 3- to 5-year period;
- Conducting a thorough review of activities related to the target to identify any corporate or organizational conflicts that can result in a potentially exploitable vulnerability;
- Conducting an industry-specific review of problems and crimes.

Assessment of risk to foreign destinations should also include a review of the Consular Information Sheets and applicable Travel Warnings issued by the U.S. State Department, and review of local laws and customs of the country to which travel will occur.

September 11 provided a stark reminder of the willingness of terrorists to utilize public transportation as the site of abductions. When the individual with whom security or law enforcement works plans to travel via public airlines, basic defensive travel tactics should be applied. Specifically, travel through high-risk airports should be avoided whenever possible; indirect routes are preferable to those that include layovers in volatile areas. Seats toward the center of the airplane, furthest from restrooms, exits, and the cockpit, should be preferred. Window seats should be chosen over those on the aisle because they offer greater protection against potential terrorists as they move throughout the plane.

While a comprehensive risk assessment and risk management strategy decreases the probability of a political kidnapping, security and law enforcement professionals should also allocate resources to train the potential target in techniques that maximize chances of survival should an abduction occur. As in any abduction, the most likely time for escape is during the first few minutes. If a window of opportunity exists, potential victims should be trained in the situational awareness and self-defense tactics that will support escape. Whenever possible, victims should also be trained to scream and draw the attention of bystanders. While it is unlikely that such actions will dissuade the political kidnapper, awareness of the event by bystanders may result in a report to authorities and can aid in the investigation.

Although rescue efforts for private citizens and public officials tend to move down different paths, the survival tactics are universal. Potential victims should be trained to remain calm during their ordeal, particularly in the initial hours and days, when the threat of actual violence is highest, and when the victim will most likely be moved to multiple locations before arrival at a final destination. Training in mental strategies that offer a sense of control, such as keeping track of time, distance traveled, offender(s) characteristics, and any sensory information, such as unusual smells and sounds, can assist the victim to avoid panic behaviors that can precipitate violent action on the part of the kidnappers.

Depending on the length of the kidnapping, the potential victim must also be mentally prepared to endure long periods of isolation and boredom while rescue efforts proceed. Potential victims should also be cautioned regarding attempts to establish rapport with or to speak to an abductor. Many experts believe that such efforts are actually counterproductive and that potential victims should be instructed to remain silent and compliant, offering only small amounts of useful information if coerced.

In the post-9/11 reality, religious fundamentalism has emerged as a significant catalyst for the political kidnapping. Abductors target the infidel, or those who represent societies whose beliefs and values differ from the abductor's own. In some cases, the captor insists that the victim appear in a video denouncing a particular faith or lifestyle. Many security professionals recommend that the victim remain compliant with the demands but resist efforts to "convert" to the captor's beliefs as such a conversion may, ironically, render the victim expendable.

Once the victim has been located, the delicate process of negotiation begins. In the political kidnapping, negotiation is influenced by many variables including the ability of officials from the victim's government of origin to pressure intervention by the sovereignty in which the abduction occurred, the availability of local intelligence and trusted local resources, and public sympathy for the victim, particularly among local residents who might offer information regarding the victim's location.

In circumstances in which direct negotiations with the kidnapper proceed, security professionals representing corporations that insure the victim may enter into discussions regarding a financial exchange. Governments aligned with the victim may threaten sanctions or other punitive actions that will result in direct or indirect pressure upon the kidnappers.

Trained negotiators can also exploit the potential Stockholm Syndrome that may develop between the victim and his or her captors.

The name *Stockholm Syndrome* was coined following the 1973 robbery of Kreditbanken in Stockholm, Sweden. From August 23 to August 28, two robbers held four bank employees hostage in the bank's vault. During their captivity, the victims became so emotionally attached to their captors that they defended them following the ordeal.

Contrary to many of the dynamics of other kidnapping subtypes, the dynamics of the political kidnapping lend themselves to the development of Stockholm Syndrome between kidnapper and victim. Research generally agrees on several conditions favorable to the development of this paradoxical phenomenon: (1) the victim and the kidnapper are strangers to one another; (2) the kidnapping is of significant length or intensity; (3) the victim is held in isolation; and (4) the kidnapper behaves kindly toward the victim, i.e., refrains from abusive behaviors. In the presence of these factors, the victim may regress to an infantilized state, resulting in adaptive behavior such as compliance and positive regard toward the kidnapper who wields the power of life and death.

Stockholm Syndrome also generally results in the favorable regard of the kidnapper toward the victim. Negotiators encourage this phenomenon through a delicate balance of humanizing the victim to the kidnapper, while continuing to fuel the kidnapper's need to remain the "center of attention." Tactics such as offering messages from family members ("Please tell him his wife loves him and knows they can work out their conflicts when he is released") can help attain this balance by disclosing personal details and subtly acknowledging the captor's control of the victim's liberty.

The negotiator must also be aware of the detrimental aspects of Stockholm Syndrome to his or her rescue efforts. Specifically, victims who feel favorably toward their kidnappers may be less likely to assist, and may even resist, interventions to secure their freedom. Breach planning must therefore include contingencies for the resistant victim. Additionally, victims of Stockholm Syndrome are typically less likely to participate in efforts to prosecute their offenders. In the Kreditbanken incident, for example, several victims refused to testify against their abductors.

Clearly, the negative aspects of Stockholm Syndrome are far outweighed by the syndrome's protective value to the life of the victim. Additionally, the syndrome's effects may be mitigated in relation to post-incident prosecutions by mental health interventions that assure the victim that his or her response is entirely normal, help reduce feelings of isolation, and support the victim to regain a sense of personal control through daily activities and participation in post-incident planning activities.

We Do Not Negotiate with Terrorists: The Theoretical and Practical Considerations of Negotiating with the Political Kidnapper

There is a great deal of controversy surrounding negotiations with the political kidnapper. On one end of the continuum, experts argue that such negotiations accord these kidnappers legitimacy, reward them for violence, and undermine the efforts of those who pursue peaceful political change. On the opposing side, experts state that a willingness to negotiate with everyone alleviates concerns regarding legitimacy; if we'll talk to anyone, dialogue with the political kidnapper cannot confer special status. These experts further point out that even countries that adopt a non-negotiation stance typically do open negotiations through diplomatic or other means.

The primary objective of governments faced with the political kidnapper is to proceed in a manner that prevents loss of life without setting a precedent that encourages further kidnappings and undermines political stability.

While sharing these concerns, the primary consideration of the security expert working the political kidnapping is successful recovery of the victim. Typically, recovery efforts involve the very type of negotiations which many governments publicly reject.

In cases in which a tactical removal is deemed impractical or too high risk, determining the kidnapper's willingness to compromise is essential; i.e., can the negotiator effect an arrangement in which return of the victim improves the kidnapper's position to a greater extent than harming the victim would do?

For "traditional" political kidnappers who seek to exchange the victim for funding that supports their cause, a negotiation that attaches financial reward to victim safety may prove a direct avenue to recovery.

Political kidnappers who seek to establish their legitimacy as sovereigns may also be motivated to return the victim unharmed; the act of kidnapping serves as a demonstration of power, while the return of the victim is symbolic of the mercy the kidnappers would presumably exhibit as rulers.

Negotiation is rendered more difficult with religiously motivated kidnappers, particularly if the abductors are acting individually or are lower level agents who insulate the sect's leader. Providing these individuals with a rationale for releasing the victim must occur quickly because the expected value of the abduction is often measured in terms of dramatic action, including the victim's murder.

Does the willingness of security professionals to negotiate with the political kidnapper undermine the non-negotiation stance of governments such as the United States?

Most agree it's unlikely. The near inevitability that individuals will continue to engage in political kidnapping renders the most effective response to be varied and unpredictable. The willingness to negotiate in some instances and refusal to do so in others may actually serve as a protective risk factor for the victim. The kidnapper who is unsure of outcome may be more willing to negotiate for a victim's life than one who is sure of success or certain of failure.

Training to Be a Victim

While the emphasis of most kidnapping training programs is logically focused on prevention and avoidance strategies, time must also be spent on the grim topic of how to survive if taken hostage. Threat management expert Mike Gillette describes such training in the following excerpt:

Ideally, this training should include simulated hostage scenarios to provide participants with a sense of the overwhelming fear and complete loss of control that characterizes these events.

The endurance of the captivity phase of a hostage event best determines one's long-term success in surviving the incident on a psychological level. To that end, effective training must discuss coping strategies for the inherent boredom, despair, and helplessness that accompanies the hostage experience. This includes such vital steps as

- Managing time by creating schedules for simple tasks, exercising, and housekeeping. This facilitates goal setting and a feeling of accomplishment throughout each day.
- Maintaining physical health; eating any food provided without complaint, even if it is unappetizing. Requesting medical treatment or medications if needed.
- Maintaining mental health. Keeping the mind active; reading anything available. Taking any opportunity to write, even if those writings are routinely confiscated. If such materials are not provided, mentally composing fiction, keeping a daily journal, or recalling scripture to keep the mind engaged.

The overarching priority for hostages is to ensure that they feel as though they are controlling as much of the experience as possible. This means maintaining a sense of dignity and managing their behavior. This difficult task is made easier with the right training.

REFERENCES

Beaumont, Peter. (2004, November 14). The Final Battle, *The Observer*.

Burke, Jason. (2004, November 21). Theatre of Terror, *The Observer*.

De Fabrique, Nathalie, Romano, Stephen, Vecchi, Gregory, and Van Hasselt, Vincent. (2007, July). Understanding Stockholm Syndrome, *FBI Law Enforcement Bulletin*.

Ensor, David. (2003, April 26). U.S. Captures Mastermind of Achille Lauro Hijacking. *CNN.com*.

Farrell, Michael B. (2006, June 27). 444 Days in Captivity as the World Watched. *Christian Science Monitor*.

Fuselier, G. Dwayne. (1998). Hostage Negotiation Consultant: Emerging Role for the Clinical Psychologist. *Professional Psychology: Research and Practice*, *19*(2), 175–179.

Gillette, Michael. E-mail to Diana Concannon, September 26, 2007.

National Counterterrorism Center: Annex of Statistical Information, April 13, 2007.

Serrill, Michael S. (1985, October 21). In Pursuit of Justice, *Time Magazine*.

Appendix A

Summary of Subtype Characteristics by Percentage

		Domestic Kidnapping (n = 15)	Predatory Kidnapping– Adult Victim (n = 18)
Victimology & Offender Characteristics	1. The victim was under 18 years of age.	33%	0%
	2. The victim and the offender were strangers to one another.	0%	56%
	3. The victim and the offender had a relationship prior to the abduction.	100%	39%
	4. The offender and the victim were of different genders.	80%	94%
	5. The offender and the victim are of different ethnicities.	NA*	NA*
	6. The victim was low risk, i.e., not likely to be immediately missed or reported as missing.	0%	11%
	7. The offender was unemployed at the time of the abduction.	NA*	NA*
	8. The offender was employed at the time of the abduction.	NA*	NA*
Abduction Site	1. The abduction occurred in a public place.	27%	67%
	2. The victim was abducted from a private location (such as home, school, workplace).	73%	33%
Modus Operandi	1. The abduction was perpetrated by more than one offender.	27%	11%
	2. The victim was chosen randomly or opportunistically.	0%	61%
	3. Physical force was used to abduct the victim.	60%	56%
	4. The victim was abducted following verbal threats of harm to himself or herself and/or others.	40%	17%
	5. The victim's abduction was the result of persuasion or deception.	33%	39%
	6. The offender used a firearm to facilitate the abduction.	60%	22%
	7. The offender used a knife to facilitate the abduction.	20%	17%

Continued...

Summary of Subtype Characteristics by Percentage—continued

	Domestic Kidnapping (n = 15)	Predatory Kidnapping— Adult Victim (n = 18)
8. The offender used a weapon, other than a knife or a firearm, or did not use a weapon, to facilitate the abduction.	27%	28%
9. The offender sexually assaulted the victim during the abduction.	33%	94%
10. The offender physically assaulted the victim during the abduction in a manner that did result in death.	33%	17%
11. The offender physically assaulted the victim during the abduction in a manner that did not result in death.	53%	56%
12. The offender did not assault or physically harm the victim during the abduction (excludes sexual assault).	13%	28%
13. The offender transported the victim during the abduction.	87%	78%
14. The offender did not transport the victim during the abduction.	13%	22%
15. The offender exhibited obvious psychotic symptoms (delusions, hallucinations, etc.).	7%	0%
16. The offender held the victim captive for greater than 24 hours.	53%	17%
17. The offender held the victim captive for less than 24 hours.	40%	83%
18. The kidnapping occurred in the morning (midnight–8 a.m.).	33%	28%
19. The kidnapping occurred during the day (8 a.m.–4 p.m.).	13%	6%
20. The kidnapping occurred in the evening/at night (4 p.m.–midnight).	27%	50%
21. More than one victim was abducted.	20%	11%
Outcome 1. The abduction was witnessed.	53%	39%
2. The victim was released by the offender.	7%	56%
3. The victim escaped.	20%	6%
4. The victim was released following law enforcement intervention.	40%	22%
5. The victim was not found.	0%	0%
6. The victim was found dead.	33%	17%
7. The victim was discovered in a public place.	33%	56%
8. The victim was discovered in a private place (a home, school, or workplace).	67%	44%

Continued...

Summary of Subtype Characteristics by Percentage—continued

	Domestic Kidnapping (n = 15)	Predatory Kidnapping– Adult Victim (n = 18)
9. Witness testimony contributed to the offender's apprehension/conviction (not limited to event witnesses).	87%	67%
10. Physical evidence contributed to the offender's apprehension/conviction.	53%	44%
11. Accomplice statements contributed to the offender's apprehension/conviction.	13%	0%
12. Victim testimony contributed to the abductor's apprehension/conviction.	67%	83%

*NA-Insufficient data to render determination.

Summary of Subtype Characteristics by Percentage

		Predatory Kidnapping– Child Victim (n = 14)	Profit Kidnapping (n = 32)
Victimology & Offender Characteristics	1. The victim was under 18 years of age.	100%	16%
	2. The victim and the offender were strangers to one another.	57%	57%
	3. The victim and the offender had a relationship prior to the abduction.	43%	41%
	4. The offender and the victim were of different genders.	93%	38%
	5. The offender and the victim are of different ethnicities.	NA*	NA*
	6. The victim was low risk, i.e., not likely to be immediately missed or reported as missing.	0%	13%
	7. The offender was unemployed at the time of the abduction.	NA*	NA*
	8. The offender was employed at the time of the abduction.	NA*	NA*
Abduction Site	1. The abduction occurred in a public place.	64%	16%
	2. The victim was abducted from a private location (such as home, school, workplace).	36%	78%
Modus Operandi	1. The abduction was perpetrated by more than one offender.	36%	88%
	2. The victim was chosen randomly or opportunistically.	60%	34%

Continued...

Summary of Subtype Characteristics by Percentage—continued

		Predatory Kidnapping– Child Victim (n = 14)	Profit Kidnapping (n = 32)
	3. Physical force was used to abduct the victim.	36%	72%
	4. The victim was abducted following verbal threats of harm to himself or herself and/or others.	29%	41%
	5. The victim's abduction was the result of persuasion or deception.	29%	9%
	6. The offender used a firearm to facilitate the abduction.	21%	63%
	7. The offender used a knife to facilitate the abduction.	14%	6%
	8. The offender used a weapon, other than a knife or a firearm, or did not use a weapon, to facilitate the abduction.	36%	22%
	9. The offender sexually assaulted the victim during the abduction.	93%	13%
	10. The offender physically assaulted the victim during the abduction in a manner that did result in death.	36%	53%
	11. The offender physically assaulted the victim during the abduction in a manner that did not result in death.	50%	25%
	12. The offender did not assault or physically harm the victim during the abduction (excludes sexual assault).	14%	22%
	13. The offender transported the victim during the abduction.	100%	88%
	14. The offender did not transport the victim during the abduction.	0%	12%
	15. The offender exhibited obvious psychotic symptoms (delusions, hallucinations, etc.).	0%	0%
	16. The offender held the victim captive for greater than 24 hours.	14%	31%
	17. The offender held the victim captive for less than 24 hours.	79%	63%
	18. The kidnapping occurred in the morning (midnight–8 a.m.).	0%	25%
	19. The kidnapping occurred during the day (8 a.m.–4 p.m.).	29%	9%
	20. The kidnapping occurred in the evening/at night (4 p.m.–midnight).	57%	22%
	21. More than one victim was abducted.	14%	41%
Outcome	1. The abduction was witnessed.	29%	38%
	2. The victim was released by the offender.	29%	19%

Continued...

Summary of Subtype Characteristics by Percentage—continued

	Predatory Kidnapping– Child Victim (n = 14)	Profit Kidnapping (n = 32)
3. The victim escaped.	14%	3%
4. The victim was released following law enforcement intervention.	14%	25%
5. The victim was not found.	0%	0%
6. The victim was found dead.	36%	53%
7. The victim was discovered in a public place.	57%	47%
8. The victim was discovered in a private place (a home, school, or workplace).	43%	53%
9. Witness testimony contributed to the offender's apprehension/conviction (not limited to event witnesses).	71%	53%
10. Physical evidence contributed to the offender's apprehension/conviction.	93%	63%
11. Accomplice statements contributed to the offender's apprehension/conviction.	0%	56%
12. Victim testimony contributed to the abductor's apprehension/conviction.	57%	47%

NA-Insufficient data to render determination.

Summary of Subtype Characteristics by Percentage

		Revenge Kidnapping (n = 18)	Staged Kidnapping (n = 3)
Victimology & Offender Characteristics	1. The victim was under 18 years of age.	22%	0%
	2. The victim and the offender were strangers to one another.	11%	0%
	3. The victim and the offender had a relationship prior to the abduction.	89%	100%
	4. The offender and the victim were of different genders.	50%	67%
	5. The offender and the victim are of different ethnicities.	NA*	NA*
	6. The victim was low risk, i.e., not likely to be immediately missed or reported as missing.	13%	0%
	7. The offender was unemployed at the time of the abduction.	NA*	NA*
	8. The offender was employed at the time of the abduction.	NA*	NA*

Continued...

Summary of Subtype Characteristics by Percentage—continued

		Revenge Kidnapping (n = 18)	Staged Kidnapping (n = 3)
Abduction Site	1. The abduction occurred in a public place.	33%	33%
	2. The victim was abducted from a private location (such as home, school, workplace).	61%	67%
Modus Operandi	1. The abduction was perpetrated by more than one offender.	72%	33%
	2. The victim was chosen randomly or opportunistically.	34%	0%
	3. Physical force was used to abduct the victim.	61%	33%
	4. The victim was abducted following verbal threats of harm to himself or herself and/or others.	11%	33%
	5. The victim's abduction was the result of persuasion or deception.	39%	67%
	6. The offender used a firearm to facilitate the abduction.	28%	67%
	7. The offender used a knife to facilitate the abduction.	17%	0%
	8. The offender used a weapon, other than a knife or a firearm, or did not use a weapon, to facilitate the abduction.	44%	0%
	9. The offender sexually assaulted the victim during the abduction.	22%	0%
	10. The offender physically assaulted the victim during the abduction in a manner that did result in death.	78%	100%
	11. The offender physically assaulted the victim during the abduction in a manner that did not result in death.	17%	0%
	12. The offender did not assault or physically harm the victim during the abduction (excludes sexual assault).	5%	0%
	13. The offender transported the victim during the abduction.	72%	67%
	14. The offender did not transport the victim during the abduction.	28%	33%
	15. The offender exhibited obvious psychotic symptoms (delusions, hallucinations, etc.).	17%	0%
	16. The offender held the victim captive for greater than 24 hours.	11%	0%
	17. The offender held the victim captive for less than 24 hours.	83%	100%

Continued...

Summary of Subtype Characteristics by Percentage—continued

		Revenge Kidnapping (n = 18)	Staged Kidnapping (n = 3)
	18. The kidnapping occurred in the morning (midnight–8 a.m.).	28%	0%
	19. The kidnapping occurred during the day (8 a.m.–4 p.m.).	0%	0%
	20. The kidnapping occurred in the evening/at night (4 p.m.–midnight).	44%	100%
	21. More than one victim was abducted.	28%	0%
Outcome	1. The abduction was witnessed.	67%	33%
	2. The victim was released by the offender.	11%	0%
	3. The victim escaped.	5%	0%
	4. The victim was released following law enforcement intervention.	5%	0%
	5. The victim was not found.	0%	0%
	6. The victim was found dead.	78%	100%
	7. The victim was discovered in a public place.	61%	33%
	8. The victim was discovered in a private place (a home, school, or workplace).	39%	67%
	9. Witness testimony contributed to the offender's apprehension/conviction (not limited to event witnesses).	89%	67%
	10. Physical evidence contributed to the offender's apprehension/conviction.	67%	67%
	11. Accomplice statements contributed to the offender's apprehension/conviction.	44%	33%
	12. Victim testimony contributed to the abductor's apprehension/conviction.	22%	0%

NA-Insufficient data to render determination.

Appendix B

SUMMARY OF SUBTYPE CHARACTERISTICS BY ELEMENT

DOMESTIC KIDNAPPING

Based on the previously detailed research, the following elements were found to be common to the Domestic Kidnapping subtype.

Victimology

- Offenders are more likely to abduct partners and estranged partners than to abduct children of the relationship with partners or estranged partners.
- A prior victim/offender relationship will exist.
- Offender and victim(s) are most likely of different genders.

Abduction Site

- The offender will most likely abduct from a private location (such as the victim's home, school, or workplace) that is not readily accessible to the general public.

Modus Operandi

- Although not common, the offender may enlist the aid of another to accomplish the abduction.
- The victim is targeted, i.e., not chosen randomly or opportunistically.
- Physical force is likely used to accomplish the abduction.
- Although not common, the offender may use verbal threats to himself or his victim to accomplish the abduction, or use persuasion or deception (e.g., falsely claiming that he will return children following visitation).
- The offender will likely use a firearm to accomplish the abduction.
- The offender will likely physically assault his victim(s) during the abduction. (*Note:* Offender is less likely to engage in physical assault with child victims.)
- The offender will likely transport the victim during the abduction.
- The victim is typically held greater than 24 hours.

- The abduction is most likely to occur between midnight and 8 a.m.
- Although not common, the offender may exhibit obvious psychotic symptoms (i.e., delusions, hallucinations, etc.).

Outcome

- The abduction is likely witnessed by others.
- The victim is most likely to be recovered following law enforcement intervention.
- The victim is most likely to be recovered in a private location (a home, school, or workplace) that is not readily accessible to the public.
- Witness testimony is most likely to contribute to the offender's apprehension and conviction, followed by victim testimony, physical evidence, and accomplice testimony, respectively.

PREDATORY KIDNAPPING–ADULT VICTIM

Based on the previously detailed research, the following elements were found to be common to the Predatory Kidnapping–Adult Victim subtype.

Victimology

- The victim will be age 18 or older.
- No prior victim/offender relationship will likely exist, although in a minority of cases, the victim and offender may have had past contact which the offender believes is of significance.
- The offender and victim are most likely to be different genders.

Abduction Site

- The offender is most likely to abduct from a public location that is readily accessible to the general public.

Modus Operandi

- The offender is unlikely to enlist the aid of another to accomplish the abduction.
- The victim is chosen randomly or opportunistically.
- Physical force is likely used to accomplish the abduction.
- The offender is most likely to use a firearm to accomplish the abduction.
- The offender will likely sexually assault his victim.

- The offender will typically physically assault his victim beyond the sexual assault.
- The offender will likely transport the victim during the abduction.
- The victim is typically held for less than 24 hours.
- The abduction is most likely to occur between 4 p.m. and midnight.
- The offender is not likely to exhibit obvious psychotic symptoms (i.e., delusions, hallucinations, etc.).

Outcome

- The abduction is not generally witnessed by others.
- The victim is most likely to be released by the offender.
- The victim is most likely to be released to a public location that is readily accessible to the public.
- Victim testimony is most likely to contribute to the offender's apprehension and conviction, followed by witness testimony and physical evidence, respectively.

PREDATORY KIDNAPPING–CHILD VICTIM

Based on the previously detailed research, the following elements were found to be common to the Predatory Kidnapping–Child Victim subtype.

Victimology

- The victim will be under 18 years of age.
- No prior victim/offender relationship will likely exist, although in a minority of cases, the victim and offender may have had past superficial contact through a family member, community member, or school-related interaction.
- The offender and victim are most likely to be different genders.

Abduction Site

- The offender is most likely to abduct from a public location that is readily accessible to the general public.

Modus Operandi

- The offender is unlikely to enlist the aid of another to accomplish the abduction.
- The victim is most likely chosen randomly or opportunistically.
- Physical force is likely used to accomplish the abduction.

- The offender will likely use a weapon other than a knife or firearm (e.g., stun gun) or will not utilize a weapon to accomplish the abduction.
- The offender will likely physically assault his victim during the abduction.
- The offender will likely sexually assault his victim during the abduction.
- The offender will likely transport the victim during the abduction.
- The victim is typically held less than 24 hours.
- The abduction is most likely to occur between 4 p.m. and midnight.
- The offender is not likely to exhibit obvious psychotic symptoms (i.e., delusions, hallucinations, etc.).

Outcome

- The abduction is not likely to have been witnessed.
- The victim is most likely to be recovered following release by the offender.
- The victim is most likely to be recovered in a public location that is readily accessible to the public.
- Physical evidence is most likely to contribute to the offender's apprehension and conviction, followed by witness testimony and victim testimony, respectively.

PROFIT KIDNAPPING

Based on the previously detailed research, the following elements were found to be common to the Profit Kidnapping subtype.

Victimology

- The victim will likely be over 18 years of age.
- No prior victim/offender relationship will likely exist, although the offender will likely have researched the victim.
- The offender and victim are most likely to be the same gender.

Abduction Site

- The offender is most likely to abduct from a private location (i.e., a home, school, or workplace) that is not readily accessible to the general public.

Modus Operandi

- The offender will likely enlist the aid of another to accomplish the abduction.
- The victim is most likely targeted and will not be chosen randomly or opportunistically.
- Physical force is likely used to accomplish the abduction.
- The offender will likely use a firearm to accomplish the abduction.
- The offender will likely physically assault his victim during the abduction.
- The offender will likely transport the victim during the abduction.
- The victim is typically held less than 24 hours (although the victim is more likely be held for greater than 24 hours than in any other subtype save the domestic kidnapping).
- The abduction is most likely to occur between 4 p.m. and midnight.
- The offender is not likely to exhibit obvious psychotic symptoms (i.e., delusions, hallucinations, etc.).

Outcome

- The abduction is not likely to have been witnessed.
- The victim is most likely to be recovered following law enforcement intervention.
- The offender will frequently physically assault the victim in a manner that results in the victim's death.
- The victim is most likely to be recovered in a private location (i.e., a residence, school, or workplace) that is not readily accessible to the public.
- Physical evidence is most likely to contribute to the offender's apprehension and conviction, followed by accomplice testimony, witness testimony, and victim testimony, respectively.

REVENGE KIDNAPPING

Based on the previously detailed research, the following elements were found to be common to the Revenge Kidnapping subtype.

Victimology

- The victim will likely be age 18 years or older.
- A prior victim/offender relationship will likely exist.
- The offender and victim are as likely to be the same gender as to be different genders.

Abduction Site

- The offender is most likely to abduct from a private location (i.e., a home, school, or workplace) that is not readily accessible to the general public.

Modus Operandi

- The offender is likely to enlist the aid of another to accomplish the abduction.
- The victim is most likely targeted, i.e., not chosen randomly or opportunistically.
- Physical force is likely used to accomplish the abduction.
- The offender will likely use a weapon other than a knife or firearm (e.g., stun gun) or will not utilize a weapon to accomplish the abduction.
- The offender will likely physically assault his victim during the abduction.
- The offender will likely transport the victim during the abduction.
- The victim is typically held less than 24 hours.
- The abduction is most likely to occur between 4 p.m. and midnight.
- Although uncommon, the offender may exhibit obvious psychotic symptoms (i.e., delusions, hallucinations, etc.).

Outcome

- The abduction is likely to have been witnessed.
- The victim is unlikely to survive the abduction.
- Victim survivors are most likely to be released by the offender.
- The victim is most likely to be recovered in a public location that is readily accessible to the public.
- Witness testimony is most likely to contribute to the offender's apprehension and conviction, followed by physical evidence, accomplice testimony, and victim testimony, respectively.

STAGED KIDNAPPING

Based on the previously detailed research, the following elements were found to be common to the Staged Kidnapping subtype.

Victimology

- The victim will likely be age 18 years or older.
- A prior victim/offender relationship will exist.
- The offender and victim are likely to be different genders.

Abduction Site

- The offender is most likely to abduct from a private location (i.e., a home, school, or workplace) that is not readily accessible to the general public.

Modus Operandi

- The offender is not likely to enlist the aid of another to accomplish the abduction.
- The victim is targeted, i.e., not chosen randomly or opportunistically.
- The offender is as likely to utilize persuasion or deception as a firearm to accomplish the abduction.
- The offender will likely physically assault his victim during the abduction.
- The offender will likely transport the victim during the abduction.
- The victim will generally be held for less than 24 hours.
- The abduction is most likely to occur between 4 p.m. and midnight.
- The offender is unlikely to exhibit obvious psychotic symptoms (i.e., delusions, hallucinations, etc.).

Outcome

- The abduction is unlikely to have been witnessed.
- The victim is unlikely to survive the abduction.
- The victim is most likely to be recovered in a private location (i.e., a home, school, or workplace) that is not readily accessible to the public.
- Witness testimony and physical evidence are most likely to contribute to the offender's apprehension and conviction, followed by accomplice testimony.

Appendix C

MENTAL HEALTH RESPONSE TO KIDNAPPING

Law enforcement, security professionals, and members of their interdisciplinary team are often also called upon to provide emergency mental health to the victims, family members, and witnesses of kidnappings.

Emergency mental health differs from traditional psychotherapy in several ways. First, emergency mental health is typically applied following a critical incident, i.e., an event or situation that causes a dramatic or profound change or disruption in an individual's or community's level of functioning, such as generally occurs in the aftermath of a kidnapping. Second, emergency mental health typically involves the application of intense and immediate crisis intervention during a limited period of time. Third, emergency mental health may be provided by individuals from varied backgrounds and disciplines, including mental health professionals, law enforcement, security professionals, paramedics, physicians, teachers, and faith-based leaders.

Emergency mental health also differs from the post-incident interview, in which the law enforcement or security professional works to illicit information to aid the investigation of the crime and apprehension of the offender. The solicitation of facts regarding the incident during the emergency mental health response, when extant, is solely for the purpose of supporting the acute and long-term mental health of the individual or individuals affected by the incident.

Research in the efficacy of various emergency mental health approaches continues to evolve. The most common emergency mental health interventions currently employed include the following.

Critical Incident Stress Debriefing: Developed by former firefighter Jeffrey T. Mitchell to support the recovery of emergency responders following traumatic incidents, CISD (also known as the "Mitchell Model") is one of the most widely applied emergency interventions utilized today. CISD is designed to be one element of a crisis intervention management system. CISD is generally conducted in a group setting (although there is a protocol for individual application) within the first week following the critical incident. Participants are asked to describe their experience of the trauma in detail and are facilitated to form a cognitive interpretation of the event, as well as to express their emotional experience. Such sharing is designed to normalize the individual's reaction, as well as forge supportive interactions with fellow group members. The intervention typically concludes with a discussion of coping strategies and education regarding possible future stress reactions that the participants might endure.

CIDS is envisioned as element four of the seven-component Critical Incident Stress Management system. It is designed to be preceded by pre-crisis preparation that improves coping skills and supports general stress management; consultation with staff and the dissemination of information of use to civilians, schools, and businesses; and defusing, which is a three-stage process that involves assessment, triaging, and acute symptom mitigation in the hours following the event. CISD is followed by one-to-one crisis intervention counseling, family crisis intervention and organizational support, and follow-up and referral provision.

Research on the efficacy of CISD has been mixed. Some studies have demonstrated the efficacy of this approach in limiting subsequent development of post-traumatic stress disorder (PTSD). Other studies have revealed that debriefing strategies, such as those employed in the CISD model, cause greater harm to the victim's psychological well-being. In general, practitioners who engage in debriefing with critical incident victims, such as those who have experienced a kidnapping, must proceed with caution and consider the victim's pre-event level of functioning, prior trauma exposure histories, and level of individual distress and risk for PTSD, each of which can influence the risk of re-traumatization following a debriefing.

Psychological First Aid: Psychological First Aid was developed by the National Child Traumatic Stress Network (NCTSN) and the National Center for PTSD (NCP). In contrast to CISD and other debriefing techniques, Psychological First Aid is a modular framework through which mental health and other professionals can provide individualized assistance that meets the specific needs of the victim(s). The Psychological First Aid Field Operations Field Guide, which can be downloaded at www.nctsn.org, recommends the following when performing this intervention:

1. Politely observe first; don't intrude. Then ask simple, respectful questions to determine how you may help.
2. Often, the best way to make contact is to provide practical assistance (food, water, blankets).
3. Initiate contact only after you have observed the situation and the person or family, and have determined that contact is not likely to be intrusive or disruptive.
4. Be prepared that survivors will either avoid you or flood you with contact.
5. Speak calmly. Be patient, responsive, and sensitive.
6. Speak slowly, in simple, concrete terms; don't use acronyms or jargon.
7. If survivors want to talk, be prepared to listen. When you listen, focus on hearing what they want to tell you and how you can be of help.
8. Acknowledge the positive features of what the survivor has done to keep safe.
9. Give information that is accurate and age-appropriate for your audience.
10. When communicating through a translator or interpreter, look at and talk to the person you are addressing, not the translator or interpreter.
11. Remember that the goal of Psychological First Aid is to reduce stress, assist with current needs, and promote adaptive functioning, not to elicit details of traumatic experience or losses.

Obtaining details regarding the kidnapping is, clearly, critical to the investigation and to the apprehension of the offender. The application of Psychological First Aid following the sensitive solicitation of such details may prevent further traumatization.

National Institute for Mental Health: In 2001, the NIMH convened a workshop of disaster mental health experts from around the world to determine the impact and efficacy of early psychological interventions. While the resulting guidelines focused specifically on mass violence, this was broadly defined as incidents such as school violence, shootings in the workplace, and terrorists acts. The experts identified key components of effective early intervention that are equally appropriate for use by the responder charged with supporting those affected by kidnapping:

1. Basic Needs
   - Provide survival, safety, and security.
   - Provide food and shelter.
   - Orient survivors to the availability of services/support.
   - Communicate with family, friends, and community.
   - Assess the environment for ongoing threats.
2. Psychological First Aid
   - Protect survivors from further harm.
   - Reduce physiological arousal.
   - Mobilize support for those who are most distressed.
   - Keep families together and facilitate reunions with loved ones.
   - Provide information and foster communication and education.
   - Use effective risk communication techniques.
3. Needs Assessment
   - Assess the current status of individuals, groups, and/or populations and institutions/systems. Ask how well needs are being addressed, what the recovery environment offers, and what additional interventions are needed.
4. Rescue and Recovery Environment Observation
   - Observe and listen to those most affected.
   - Monitor the environment for toxins and stressors.
   - Monitor past and ongoing threats.
   - Monitor services that are being provided.
   - Monitor media coverage and rumors.
5. Outreach and Information Dissemination
   - Offer information/education and "therapy by walking around."
   - Use established community structures.
   - Distribute flyers.
   - Host websites.
   - Conduct media interviews and programs and distribute media releases.

6. Technical Assistance, Consultation, and Training
   - Improve capacity of organizations and caregivers to provide what is needed to re-establish community structure, foster family recovery and resilience, and safeguard the community.
   - Provide assistance, consultation, and training to relevant organizations and other caregivers and responders and leaders.
7. Fostering Resilience and Recovery
   - Foster but do not force social interactions.
   - Provide coping skills training.
   - Provide risk assessment skills training.
   - Provide education on stress responses, traumatic reminders, coping, normal versus abnormal functioning, risk factors, and services.
   - Offer group and family interventions.
   - Foster natural social supports.
   - Look after the bereaved.
   - Repair organizational fabric.
8. Triage
   - Conduct clinical assessments, using valid and reliable methods.
   - Refer when indicated.
   - Identify vulnerable, high-risk individuals and groups.
   - Provide for emergency hospitalization.
9. Treatment
   - Reduce or ameliorate symptoms or improve functioning via individuals, family, and group psychotherapy; pharmacotherapy; and short- or long-term hospitalization.

A complete copy of the NIMH report, titled *Mental Health and Mass Violence: Evidenced-Based Psychological Intervention for Victims/ Survivors of Mass Violence,* can be found on the NIMH website at www.mentalhealth.gov/health/publications/massviolence.pdf.

Additional resources and training related to the provision of emergency mental health can be found at the following:

American Red Cross, www.redcross.org
American Red Cross Disaster Services, www.redcross.org/ services/disaster

Catastrophic Disaster Response Group, www.fema.gov/rrr/frp/frpconc.shtm

Center for Mental Health Services, http://mentalhealth.org/cmhs

International Critical Incident Stress Foundation, www.icisf.org

International Society for Traumatic Stress Studies, www.istss.org

National Center for Missing and Exploited Children, www.missingkids.com

National Center for Post-Traumatic Stress Disorder, www.ncptsd.org

National Organization for Victims Assistance, www.try-nova.org

Appendix D

DRILL EXERCISES

Preparedness is an essential element in any prevention effort. The following are Tabletop Drills ("What if" scenarios) that law enforcement and security professionals can use to support potential kidnapping victims prepare and better respond to a kidnapping threat. As with any Tabletop Drill, the exercises that follow allow participants to evaluate how they will respond during an actual event in a low-stress environment.

Each exercise includes a Scenario and Key Discussion Points. An Evaluation Form is provided that the Tabletop Drill facilitator can utilize to assist participants (or, in the case of children, their guardians) to assess response efficacy and to identify areas in need of improvement. Finally, a sample Certificate of Participation is included. It is recommended that this simple certificate is given to each course participant; it serves not only as an acknowledgment of the participant's willingness to invest in his or her own safety, but also as a powerful psychological reminder that he or she has trained and can cope in the event of an actual kidnapping.

DRILL 1: DOMESTIC KIDNAPPING

Target Audience:

Females estranged from a formerly violent partner.

Background for the Scenario:

During the past several years of your relationship, your ex-husband was increasingly withdrawn, often going days barely speaking or acknowledging either you or your son. At other times, he would explode, seemingly out of nowhere, yelling and throwing lamps or other items that were within reach. If he was drinking, he would grab you roughly, corner you, and scream loudly. His rants frequently included complaints of being taken for granted and not appreciated by the family for which he "sacrificed" so much. Once, he raised his hand as if he was going to hit your son.

You separated from your husband soon after this incident and temporarily moved into your sister's home. At first, your ex-husband would call you there, irate, or show up uninvited, yelling. Your threat to divorce him seems to have had an effect; now he calls to apologize (although you suspect he is most contrite after he's had more than a few drinks). He is also more polite, showing basic courtesy that he previously lacked. He now, for example, will ask you if it is a convenient time for you to speak when he telephones, instead of demanding that you listen to him. He claims that the possibility of divorce was "like a wake-up call."

He says that he realizes he won't win you back easily, but he wants to try. He even offers to allow you and your son to return to the family home, while he takes an apartment nearby. All he asks is that you give him another chance.

Discussion Points for Participants:

- What signs and behaviors on the part of your ex warrant caution?
- If you do decide to return to the home, are there actions you can take to support your safety?

Scenario:

You've decided to move back to the home, basing this decision on what is best for your son. Your ex relocates as promised and, for the first several weeks, continues to courteously call. During these conversations, he reports that he has stopped drinking during the week. He says that he realizes the source of his stress is work related, where he feels undervalued, and he recognizes that he has been taking his frustration out on you and your son. He even agreed to attend couple's counseling but had missed the first session because he had an interview at a different firm.

Discussion Points for Participants:

- What new signs and behaviors on the part of the ex warrant caution?
- What additional steps, if any, can you take to support your safety?

Scenario:

Several weeks later, you return home from a new part-time job you have secured. You pull into the driveway and note that your ex-husband's car is already parked there. Your ex-husband is not in sight. You enter the home and find him in the kitchen. He states that he needed to obtain an item for work. You confront him about entering the house in your absence, and he becomes agitated, calling you ungrateful for all that he is doing to accommodate you. He also demands to know where you were during the day. You tell him that you have been at your new job, and this makes him irate. He says that it is his responsibility to take care of his family, and he won't allow you to take that away from him. He moves as if to hit you but instead storms past and exits the house, slamming the door.

Discussion Points for Participants:

- What signs and behaviors on the part of the ex warrant caution?
- What steps should you consider to support your safety and that of your son?

Scenario:

A half hour later, you have calmed yourself and await the arrival of your son from school. You hear his bus stop down the block and move through the soothing ritual of preparing a snack while you wait for his arrival. Ten minutes later, he still has not arrived. You leave the house to look for him. Other children are approaching their homes. Your son is nowhere to be seen.

Discussion Points for Participants:

- What are the first steps you take?
- Whom do you contact?
- What information do you provide?

Scenario:

Quelling panic, you telephone your son's school, and one of your worst fears is realized: Your ex-husband has picked up your son from school. You realize that you don't even have a telephone number for your ex-husband and don't know his new address.

Discussion Points for Participants:

○ Whom do you telephone?
○ What information do you provide?
○ What additional support might you call upon?

Scenario:

Law enforcement arrives and immediately begins a search for your son, canvassing the community. Additional officers are dispatched to your son's school and to your ex-husband's place of employment. Officials learn that your ex-husband had been fired from his job 2 days prior. Law enforcement decides to issue a news bulletin including a description of your son and the car owned by your ex-husband. Within the hour, tips are called into the hotline. One is from a manager of a McDonald's restaurant 40 miles away, who reports that a boy fitting your son's description is with a man fitting the description of your ex-husband. Officers are dispatched, and your son is recovered unharmed. Your ex-husband is retained for questioning.

Discussion Points for Participants:

○ What are your next steps?
○ How do you evaluate the threat that your ex-husband poses currently and the threat he potentially poses in the future?
○ What steps can you take to safeguard yourself and your son?

Discussion Points for Drill Facilitators:

○ What information do you release to the media?
○ What do you do when you approach the suspect and the child to support the child's safety and emotional well-being?
○ What questions would you pose to the suspect?
○ How do you determine the custodial rights of each parent? Given that custody has not been legally determined, what are your options for dealing with the suspect?
○ What recommendations do you make to the mother to support her future safety and the future safety of her child?

DRILL 2: PREDATORY KIDNAPPING– ADULT VICTIM
Target Audience:
Potential female victims of the predatory kidnapper of adults.

Background for the Scenario:

This year, the office party was held at a local bar, owned by a friend of one of the employees. The private party was scheduled to end at 10:00 p.m., but a group of staff, including you, decide to stay longer and celebrate a very successful year. The bar begins to fill once more with members of the general public. You've limited your drinking to two glasses of wine and have switched to sparkling water. Your colleagues have not and are getting louder and less interesting. You decide it's time to leave and tell them you'll see them on Monday. You gather your purse and move through the crowd gathered to watch the game on the television above the bar. As you reach the exit, you try to remember where you parked your car. You turn back toward the bar, having the sensation that someone is watching you. No one appears to be, and you shrug it off as the type of behavior typical of guys in bars.

Discussion Points for Participants:
- What would you do in this scenario?
- If you decide to proceed to the parking lot, what precautions would you take?
- If you decide to ask for an escort, whom do you ask?

Scenario:

You open the door to the bar, and your car looks farther away than when you parked it earlier and the lot was filled with the cars of your colleagues. Nonetheless, the lot is relatively well lit, and a group of professionally dressed people is gathered in the opposite direction, talking and laughing. You proceed to your car, pulling your keys from your purse as you do so. Within 3 feet of your car, you push the remote to unlock your door. You approach the driver's side.

A man bumps you from behind, trapping you between his body and the car door. His arm comes around your neck.

Discussion Points for Participants:
- What would you do in this scenario?
- If you decide to resist, what do you do to support your safety?
- If you decide not to resist, what steps can you take to support your safety?

Scenario:

Almost before you can respond, the man momentarily stuns you, opens the door, and throws you into the front seat. He puts the keys in the ignition to start the car.

Discussion Points for Participants:

- ○ What would you do in this scenario?
- ○ If you decide to resist, what do you do to support your safety?
- ○ If you decide not to resist, what steps can you take to support your safety?

Scenario:

Your attacker says he has a knife and won't hesitate to use it if you resist. He drives the car, while pressing your head into the passenger seat. He eventually stops in a deserted alley and turns off the ignition. He begins to attack you. He has not shown you a knife, but he wears a bulky jacket that you believe may conceal one.

Discussion Points for Participants:

- ○ What would you do in this scenario?
- ○ If you decide to resist, what do you do to support your safety?
- ○ If you decide not to resist, what steps can you take to support your safety?

Scenario:

After the attack, your assailant exits the car and runs further into the alley, jumping over a chain link fence at the opposite end.

Discussion Points for Participants:

- ○ What would you do in this scenario?

Discussion Points for Law Enforcement and Security Personnel:

- ○ What steps will you take to assist the participant to identify her "line in the sand," i.e., the point at which—based on the situation, her personality, and her training—she will resist despite the potential consequences?

- What safety strategies will you suggest to participants to avoid the preceding scenario.

- What safety strategies will you suggest to participants confronted with the preceding or a comparable scenario?

- If a victim of the preceding or comparable scenario presented to you and was emotionally withdrawn, what would you do?

- If the victim of the preceding or comparable scenario presented to you as highly emotional, what would you do?

- If presented with a victim of the preceding or comparable scenario, what questions would you ask to support the successful apprehension of the assailant?

- What actions would you take to support the successful apprehension of the assailant?

DRILL 3: PREDATORY KIDNAPPING– CHILD VICTIM

Target Audience:

Potential victims of predatory kidnappings of children.

Background for the Scenario:

[*Note:* It is recommended that scenarios geared toward children be relayed through questions and stories.]

1. Raise your hand if you have friends.
2. Raise your hand if your friends are your age.
3. Raise your hand if you have friends who are younger than you.
4. Raise your hand if you have friends who are older than you.
5. If you've seen someone before, like your friend's older brother or a gardener at school, is he your friend?
6. If you've never seen someone before, is he your friend?

Discussion Points for Drill Facilitator:

- How do you help children to differentiate between friends, acquaintances (what child safety experts John Walsh and Julie Clark refer to as "Kinda Knows"), and strangers?

Scenario:

If someone asks you to do something and you don't want to, what can you do?

1. Yell "NO."

[*Note:* Children are often told to be quiet so often that they learn to be inhibited and not yell. Allow children to practice yelling "NO!"]

2. Run to your mommy or daddy.

3. Run to someone mommy and daddy has told you that you can run to if you need help, like maybe your teacher or your grandmother.

[*Note:* Children need to practice running away from a situation safely, i.e., not running blindly into greater danger, such as oncoming traffic. Allow children to practice running away safely.]

4. If someone you don't know offers you candy, what do you do?

5. If someone you don't know offers you toys, what do you do?

6. If someone you've seen before at your friend's house asks to play with you in the playground, what do you do?

7. If you're walking home from school and someone in a car asks you if you want a ride home, what do you do?

8. If you're walking home from school and someone in a car asks you for directions, what do you do?

9. If someone you've seen before on the playground has a puppy he wants to show you, what do you do?

10. If someone you've seen before on the playground says your mommy sent him to pick you up from school, what do you do?

[*Note:* Use a cartoon picture of a little boy and little girl to narrate a story of Super Safety Boy and Super Safety Girl. Have Super Safety Boy and Super Safety Girl experience the situations indicated in the preceding example and ask the children what Super Safety Boy and Super Safety Girl should do. Consider modifying the generic participant certificate at the end of this appendix to acknowledge the child's participation as Super Safety Boys and Super Safety Girls.]

DRILL 4: PROFIT KIDNAPPING

Target Audience:

Potential corporate adult victims of profit kidnappings.

Background Scenario:

John Taylor is senior vice president of General Design Concepts, Inc. Taylor is also a major stockholder in the company, which recently went public to great success. Taylor was scheduled to speak before a group of cardiologists about the non-invasive diagnostic tool the company is innovating. Shortly before the time he is scheduled to present, Judy, his secretary, receives a call from an adult male, stating that "they" have Taylor and will call back in 20 minutes. Only Taylor's assistant is to answer the phone; she is the only one to whom they will relate their demands.

Discussion Points for Participants:

- Does the company have an emergency response protocol for this scenario?
- Who are the people who can activate the emergency response protocol?
- Once the protocol is activated, what is the alert and notification process, and what personnel and outside resources are notified?

Scenario:

Exactly 20 minutes later, the direct line to Taylor's office rings. Judy answers, surrounded by the response team, several members of whom listen on extension lines. From the ambient noise, the caller appears to be phoning from a public location. He demands that Judy leave $500,000 cash beneath a public bench in the northeast corner of Community Park at 10:00 a.m. the following morning. A note indicating the location at which Taylor can be found will be under the bench. Taylor, the caller states, will be moved to the location only after "they" safely retrieve the money and confirm that it has been paid in full.

Discussion Points for Participants:

- How do you verify the threat?
- What steps do you take to analyze the threat?
- What questions should Judy ask of the caller?

Scenario:

When Judy asks to speak to Taylor, she is told that he is being held in a separate location. She then asks how she can be certain that the caller is, in fact, holding Taylor and that Taylor is unharmed. The caller provides Judy with details of the meeting Taylor was to attend as proof that he is holding and has spoken with Taylor. The caller disconnects from the line after stating that he will call again at 8:00 a.m. the following morning to confirm the pick-up.

Discussion Points for Participants:

- What further steps can be taken to verify the validity of the threat?
- Based on the threat analysis, what is likely to occur if the threat is ignored?
- Based on the threat analysis, what is likely to occur if the demand is met?
- What steps should be taken, if any, to identify individuals with access to Taylor's itinerary?
- What steps should be taken, if any, to speak with members of the group to whom Taylor was scheduled to speak?
- What steps should be taken, if any, to trace Taylor's movements?
- At what point does the corporation engage law enforcement?
- At what point does the corporation contact its insurance company?
- At what point does the corporation contact the family members of the alleged victim?
- Does the organization have a policy that provides guidelines as to how and when to negotiate, meet, or reject ransom demands?

Scenario:

As the response team prepares its next step, one of the members' assistants knocks on the door of the office in which they are meeting. She is uncomfortable but suggests that the team turn on the local television news. They do so and learn that an "unidentified employee of General Design Concepts" has reported that a senior officer in the company has been kidnapped.

Discussion Points for Participants:

- Does the leak of this event to the public alter the response that the team was considering?
- Does the leak alter the assessment of the threat?

Scenario:

Within a half hour of the news report, Taylor's direct line rings again. The caller states that, since the news of the kidnapping has been leaked, he will no longer wait until tomorrow morning to receive his demand. Instead, he wants it dropped at the park location within the hour. Per a script provided by the response team, Judy assures the caller that it is the company's policy to meet all reasonable demands, but that she is not qualified to speak for the company. She tells the caller that the company's Chief Financial Officer is standing beside her and is the only one authorized to release the money. The CFO must briefly speak to the caller before he can give him what he wants. The caller curses Judy but agrees to her demand when she remains apologetic but insistent. The CFO gets on the phone and reiterates the company's willingness to discuss reasonable demands. The CFO states, however, that he can release the funds only if he is assured that Taylor is still alive and unharmed. Once again, the caller asserts that Taylor is being held at a separate location. The CFO asks the caller for additional information about the location as a good faith gesture. The caller states that once he receives the money, "you won't have to travel too far." The caller hangs up.

Discussion Points for Participants:

- ○ Does the fact that the caller changed the timeline for meeting his ransom demand affect the assessment of risk? If so, how?
- ○ Does the caller's statement that "you won't have to travel too far" provide any additional information in the risk evaluation?

Scenario:

Based on the caller's recent statement, the response team telephones law enforcement. Security also suggests that they activate a building lockdown to search every room in case the caller's statement implies that the victim is in the facility. During the search, the victim's car is found parked in an unassigned spot inside the garage. Items found on the floor of the garage, as well as on the steps leading to the building's basement, lead security officers to the victim, who has been tied to an old water heater in a remote storage room. He is shaken but unharmed.

Discussion Points for Participants:

o After the victim has been secured, what additional steps would you take?

o Who deactivates the response team, and at what point does the deactivation occur?

o How do you release information to the public? What are some of the points that must be considered in any public statement to ensure that the public and the corporation's staff and stakeholders maintain confidence in the corporation's capabilities?

o What changes might you make to your security procedures based on this event?

Discussion Points for Drill Facilitators:

o How would you recommend that the organization establish a crisis management team, if one does not already exist?

o What type of training would you recommend that the organization embark upon to ensure that all staff members know whom to contact in the event of a crisis?

DRILL 5: NON-TRADITIONAL PROFIT KIDNAPPING: INFANT ABDUCTION

Target Audience:

Hospital staff who may need to respond to an infant abduction.

Background to Scenario:

A 40-year-old patient was rushed to the emergency room after being in a car accident, in which her vehicle was broadsided by a large truck. The woman survived with a broken leg and minor cuts and bruises. She also suffered a miscarriage. When she learned of the miscarriage, she became inconsolable and had to be heavily sedated. Staff later learned that she had undergone several fertility treatments to conceive her child. Weeks after her release, the woman returned with flowers for the staff who treated her so kindly. She continued to visit the staff every couple of months, bringing baked goods or plants from her garden. On one such occasion, she asked staff to "hold good thoughts"; she had begun fertility treatments again, she said. Staff wished her well and hugged her enthusiastically when she returned several months later to announce her pregnancy. She also informed them that she was accepted as a hospital volunteer and would be working to help others who might need "a little help and a little hope." The woman began to show up regularly during the evening and worked at the front desk, directing patients in need of assistance and answering basic questions.

Several weeks into her volunteer assignment, a staff member notes that the woman is checking the computer system and looking up patient names, though she has no one on the phone, and no one is standing before her. The staff member asks the woman to explain what she is doing and is told that the woman believed someone she knew had been admitted to cardiology and she wanted to be sure. The staff member explains the hospital's HIPAA regulations, and the woman seems genuinely contrite, promising not to seek patient data again. The staff member decides to report the incident, but the ER experiences a surge when a fire tears through a nearby apartment building, injuring many. The staff member doesn't think of the incident again until the following evening, when the woman is so friendly that she decides to let it go.

Discussion Points for Participants:

- ○ Should the staff member report the incident? If so, to whom?
- ○ If the incident is reported, what additional steps should be taken?

Scenario:

One month later, a patient in the maternity ward moves slowly and frantically to the nurses station, claiming that her newborn, who was sleeping in the bassinet beside her when she drifted to sleep, is missing.

Discussion Points for Participants:

- ○ What would you do in this scenario?
- ○ Who are the key people to activate the Hospital Command Center (HCC)?
- ○ Once the decision to activate is made, how are key personnel and outside agencies notified?
- ○ Which positions in the HCC should be activated and why?

Scenario:

A Code Pink is called, and the HCC is activated.

Discussion Points for Participants:

- o What are the immediate first steps taken after the Code Pink alert?
- o How is the hospital physically secured?
- o How is the search conducted?
- o Which staff personnel should be immediately interviewed regarding potential, suspicious activity, and what activities would be particularly significant (e.g., patient leaving the facility with an infant who is unaccompanied or not escorted in a wheelchair, missing uniforms, etc.)?
- o How critical is it to involve the media? What information should be disseminated?

Scenario:

The hospital is locked down, hospital security is conducting a search from the outer perimeter working inward, while designated hospital personnel are searching inward out. Law enforcement has been engaged, and an AMBER Alert has been issued. A security officer returns to the Command Center with one of the volunteers from the nursing station, who reports that a fellow volunteer has been on break for more than 40 minutes and has not returned.

Discussion Points for Participants:

- o What next steps should be taken in relation to this information?
- o What information about the volunteer should be obtained, and how should it be used?

Scenario:

The local news media release a photo of the child, and law enforcement receives several tips on the hotline established for this incident. In one such incident, a community member reports that a neighbor and her husband have placed "IT'S A GIRL" signs on their front lawn and are planning a brunch to introduce neighbors and friends to the child. The neighbor states that the infant, whom she saw briefly, looks like the photo in the media. Additionally, while the new mother had claimed to be pregnant for months, the presence of the infant seems abrupt to the neighbor. The hospital's volunteer coordinator confirms that the address reported by the neighbor is listed on the application of the volunteer who is missing. Law enforcement go to the house and discover the woman, her husband, and the unharmed newborn. They safely recover the infant and arrest the couple.

Discussion Points for Participants:
- ○ Who makes the decision to deactivate the HCC and on what basis?
- ○ What steps are taken to debrief?
- ○ What support is provided to the infant's family and to staff affected by the incident?
- ○ What post-abduction information is released to the media to restore patient, staff, and community confidence in the hospital?

DRILL 6: REVENGE KIDNAPPING
Target Audience:
Professionals who are potential revenge kidnapping victims.

Background Scenario:
Ryan has been a mediocre employee at your corporation for the past 6 years. Over the past several months, Ryan's coworkers have reported that he is complaining about everything from the company's health insurance plan to the number of tasks he is assigned. They are also concerned about Ryan's claims that he will be promoted to Section Chief when the person who currently holds the position retires next year. You are surprised to learn of Ryan's statements because you had actually been considering terminating him and replacing him with someone who will bring some enthusiasm to the position. Your resolve to terminate strengthens when an employee turns in a note that she claims is written by Ryan and that states, "This place sucks like a toilet and should be flushed."

You confront Ryan about the note and his recent statements. He denies writing the note or making the statements. He states that his colleagues are jealous of him and are "acting out." Because you have no proof to substantiate the claims against Ryan, you tell him to refrain from making any comments that might be misconstrued by others and let the matter rest.

Several months later, the Section Chief resigns. At his farewell party, the Division Manager announces that an individual from the company's corporate office will be replacing him.

The following day, Ryan calls off work. One of your staff brings you a facsimile that was sent anonymously to the office machine. "The toilet is stopped up with corporate paper. The toilet needs to be plunged."

Discussion Points for Participants:

○ How much of a threat does Ryan pose?
○ What warning signs has Ryan exhibited?
○ What steps would you take at this point?

Scenario:

The next day, Ryan returns to work. His eyes are puffy, and his face seems bloated. He complains of a headache. You suspect that he is hung over, but he states that he is recovering from a stomach flu. Later in the day, he tells a coworker that he dragged himself to work to prove that "they" couldn't beat him. He tells the coworker that you're the reason why he didn't get the promotion to Section Chief and that you have always been jealous of him. The coworker reports Ryan's words to you.

Discussion Points for Participants:

○ What would be your next step?
○ What factors would you consider in evaluating the risk posed by Ryan?
○ What precautions might you take?

Scenario:

You confer with the Human Resources Manager, who suggests that you have a joint conversation with Ryan. You agree, and the two of you walk to Ryan's cubicle. Ryan is absent from his desk. A coworker says that he said he wasn't feeling well again and left abruptly. The Human Resources Manager agrees to join you and meet with Ryan the following day. You leave the office later that evening, and as you drive home, you believe you spot Ryan's car behind you, following you. You take an alternative route, and the car does not follow. You stop at the market and continue home. A car that looks like Ryan's is parked up the street from your house.

Discussion Points for Participants:

- What would you do if you saw a car that might by Ryan's?

Scenario:

You decide to exit your car and proceed cautiously to your house. Once inside, you lock the door and immediately reset the alarm. You check the house and find no evidence of an intruder. You check your answering machine. There is a message from Ryan, whom you were not aware had your home number and has never called you at home before. The message was left in the late afternoon. Ryan apologizes for leaving the office early, but says he's sure you can understand how "sick he has been lately." He ends the call by stating that "one way or another," I'll call you tomorrow.

Discussion Points for Participants:

- How do you assess the risk posed by Ryan at this point?
- How do you rate the risk he would pose if allowed to continue working for you?
- How do you rate the risk he would pose if he was to be terminated or placed on administrative leave?

Scenario:

The following day, you arrive at the office early. Ryan is also at the office and knocks on your door, requesting to speak with you. Few others have arrived to start the day.

Discussion Points for Participants:

- What precautions would you take when speaking with Ryan?
- What would be some of the things you might say to him to de-escalate a potentially dangerous situation?

Scenario:

As there is no one to call upon, you invite Ryan to sit in your office, noting that by doing so you maintain the desk between you, and prevent him from standing between you and the door. You decide to be understanding but direct. You tell Ryan that you've been concerned he has been upset as a result of not being promoted to Section Chief. Ryan initially denies having any resentment but then rants about the choice and your role in it. You allow him to rant for a few moments and then explain as reasonably as possible why the organization needed to bring in an outsider. You also explain that Ryan may be eligible for future positions given his loyalty to the company and carefully explain steps he might consider to better position himself in the eyes of the "higher-ups." Ryan begins to show alignment with you and seems to believe that you are on his side in advancing. He states that he has felt in the past that you did not like him, that the staff do not like him, but he feels that everything will change now. He commits to trying to get along better with others and to apply himself more to his job.

Discussion Points for Participants:
- What do you gain by keeping Ryan on the job?
- What do you risk by keeping Ryan on the job?
- What steps can be taken to minimize the risk going forward?

Discussion Points for Drill Facilitators:
- How can you assist employers and supervisors to evaluate new employees prior to time of hire?
- What additional information would you suggest employers and supervisors obtain about an employee who may potentially act in an irrational or dangerous manner following a professional or personal disappointment or challenge?

DRILL 7: POLITICAL KIDNAPPING

Target Audience:
Professionals required to travel to "hot spots" as part of their job responsibilities.

Background for Scenario:
Your company has won a major contract to aid reconstruction efforts in Iraq. Approximately 50 staff have been dispatched over the past 6 months for what is anticipated to be a 24-month job. You are scheduled to travel to their temporary work site to conduct a semi-annual quality assurance check.

Discussion Points for Participants:
- What information do you want to know prior to arrival at the location?

Scenario:

You are assigned a private security detail which is coordinated through the corporate office in cooperation with the facility in Iraq. You have your itinerary and prepare for your upcoming department.

Discussion Points for Participants:

- What steps do you take to safeguard your itinerary?
- Whom do you tell of your impending departure?
- What additional information do you want to access regarding the assignment you are to review and the individuals with whom you will be meeting?
- What information do you want regarding the area in which you will be staying?

Scenario:

You arrive at Baghdad airport with the security detail and are met by security on the ground. You are informed that you will be transported by Humvee to the location and that the route has been relatively quiet during the past week. The journey is uneventful, and you arrive safely at your hotel.

Discussion Points for Participants:

- What should you be noting during the trip and upon arrival at the hotel?
- What steps can you take to ensure your hotel room is secure/ remains secure?

Scenario:

You exit the hotel the next morning and await transport to the corporate facility. You make note of several armed individuals outside the hotel lobby who are engaged in speaking to young civilians. The men leave moments later, and you and your security detail enter a Humvee for the drive to the corporate facility. The driver explains that you will be taking a previously agreed upon but circuitous route to avoid armed gunman known to travel the more populated thoroughfare. Approximately 4 miles into your travel, you experience an explosion which seems to have occurred to one side of your vehicle. The Humvee is swarmed by armed men and boys who disarm your security detail after an exchange of fire and drag him beyond your sight. A boy of about 14 kills your driver. You are dragged from the Humvee at gunpoint and hustled into an awaiting vehicle.

Discussion Points for Participants:

- What actions, if any, do you take to protect yourself?
- Do you attempt communication with your captors?
- What environmental cues should you note and remain aware of?

Scenario:

You are in the vehicle for what feels like an interminable time, while the men around you speak in a language you assume to be Arabic. No one has spoken directly to you, nor have they harmed you in any way. The vehicle eventually comes to a stop and a man beside you ties a dirty bandanna around your eyes. You are roughly taken from the vehicle and shoved into a room. The door is closed and latched behind you. Your hands have not been tied, and you remove the bandanna to find yourself in a small, cement building, with a cot, a gallon of water, and a small bucket.

Discussion Points for Participants:

- What information do you have to assess your situation?
- What strategies can you use to remain calm and alert?

Scenario:

Several days pass. You are provided food at infrequent intervals. Thus far, your captors have not spoken to you, save to gesture at you the day before when they took a photograph of you beside the daily newspaper. You fight boredom, fear, and fatigue. The next morning, the monotony is interrupted by what sounds to be the arrival of a vehicle outside your location. You note that two doors slam. An armed man whom you have not seen before enters and, in English, orders you to turn toward the wall. You do so, and he ties your hands and places tape over your eyes. He pushes you toward the doorway and tells you to walk.

Discussion Points for Participants:

- Do you attempt to communicate with the man? If so, what do you say?
- Do you attempt to resist? Are there actions that the armed man might take that would cause you to resist?

Scenario:

You allow yourself to be led by the man into the vehicle you presume is the one that arrived earlier. You travel in the vehicle for what you believe to be close to one hour, before the vehicle slows considerably. The man, who is seated beside you, opens your car door. "Get out!" he states as he shoves you from the slow-moving vehicle. You roll to a stop and are surrounded once more. A hand pulls the bandanna from your eyes, and you look into the face of a small child. A second child runs away.

Discussion Points for Participants:

- What steps can you take to support your safety?
- What situational cues can you utilize to determine your course of action?

Scenario:

As you survey the environment and decide on your options, the second child returns, followed by what appear to be British soldiers. They untie your hands and ask your identity. They move you to a secured location, where you await the arrival of a representative from your corporation's insurance company for a debriefing.

Discussion Points for Participants:

- What information do you believe important to relay during a debriefing?
- What actions do you want to take following your recovery to ensure your ongoing safety while within the region?

Discussion Points for Drill Facilitators:

- What techniques can you offer to help the potential political hostage combat the fear and boredom that may result during captivity?

○ What recommendations will you offer in relation to speaking or refraining from speaking with captives?

○ What information would you seek to obtain during a debrief?

DRILL EXERCISE EVALUATION FORM

The following evaluation questions are designed to assist you to assess your current level of knowledge and preparedness if confronted with a situation comparable to that addressed by the drills. Your responses can also provide you with information regarding additional skills and training you may consider acquiring in support of your safety.

1. Did you identify event precursors and warning signs that may have been useful in averting the event?

❑ Yes   ❑ Somewhat   ❑ No   ❑ Not Applicable

2. Did you identify actions that you could take to minimize the threat to your safety as the situation became more dangerous?

❑ Yes   ❑ Somewhat   ❑ No   ❑ Not Applicable

3. Did you identify ways in which you could verbally de-escalate the situation?

❑ Yes   ❑ Somewhat   ❑ No   ❑ Not Applicable

4. Did you identify your "line in the sand," i.e., the event that—given your personality, level of training, and the unique situational circumstances—would cause you to resist the individual threatening you?

❑ Yes   ❑ Somewhat   ❑ No   ❑ Not Applicable

5. Did your proposed post-event actions support your ongoing safety?

❑ Yes   ❑ Somewhat   ❑ No   ❑ Not Applicable

6. Name three concrete steps you can take to support your safety:

A. _____

B. _____

C. _____

NAME OF ORGANIZATION/LOGO

Name of Participant

Has Successfully Completed a

Tabletop Drill

To Prevent Victimization

*Instructed by:*_____

*Date:*_____

*Course Location:*_____

Epilogue

In the month preceding the completion of this book, media reports of kidnappings abound.

In St. Louis, Missouri, the man accused of abducting two young boys, age 11 and 13, pled guilty to kidnapping, attempted murder, and forcible sodomy. Michael Devlin abducted the 11-year-old boy at gunpoint in 2002 and the 13-year-old in January 2007. A tip from a classmate who was able to describe the white pickup truck in which Devlin drove off with his second victim led law enforcement to the apartment in which he held both boys. His guilty plea will save the two young victims from being forced to testify.

In Kansas City, Missouri, the former husband of Lisa Montgomery testified that his wife claimed to be pregnant twice prior to the couple's separation. It had earlier been revealed that she had also claimed to be pregnant on three occasions by her current husband. Her claims contradicted medical evidence that Montgomery had a tubal ligation in 1990. Montgomery is on trial for the kidnapping and murder of a 23-year-old pregnant neighbor whom she killed by crudely cutting the fetus from her womb. Later on the day of the murder, Montgomery telephoned her husband, claiming to have given birth at a nearby birthing center. The following day, the couple showed off the baby at a diner, a bank, a courthouse, and the convenience store where Montgomery worked. Law enforcement arrested Montgomery the day after the murder, tracing her through e-mails she had sent the victim related to the purchase of a dog. If Montgomery is convicted, prosecutors say that they will seek the death penalty.

In Pretoria, South Africa, the wives of four men kidnapped at a checkpoint in Iraq met with the media to raise interest in the fate of their missing husbands. Andre Durant, Callie Scheepers, Johann Enslin, and Hardus Greef were abducted as they protected a convoy of water and food en route to an American army base in December 2006. The wives have not received any communication from the men since an initial telephone call 11 days following the kidnapping.

In Afghanistan, two Italian soldiers were rescued following an operation by NATO's International Security Assistance Force. The two men were kidnapped while participating in a mission to maintain contacts between military and civilian leaders in the region. Reports indicated that both soldiers were wounded, one severely. The nine Afghan abductors were killed during the rescue operation.

In Auckland, New Zealand, police issued a murder and kidnapping warrant for the father of a missing 3-year-old after finding the body of the child's mother in the trunk of a car. The warrant was issued based on images captured by a security camera, which showed the suspect, Xue Naiyin, abandoning his daughter at a train station in Australia. The child was rescued and later identified. Naiyin is believed to have boarded a flight for Los Angeles.

In Logan, West Virginia, court hearings proceeded against six White suspects accused of the kidnapping and torture of a 20-year-old Black woman. During the time the defendants held the woman in a remote trailer, they allegedly sexually assaulted her, stabbed her with a butcher knife, beat her with wooden sticks and fly swatters, and forced her to eat animal feces. The woman was rescued after law enforcement received an anonymous tip. Deputies had not yet determined how long the woman was held.

In Seoul, South Korea, 19 Christian aid workers were reunited with their families after being held by the Taliban as they traveled in eastern Afghanistan. The kidnappers had previously executed two of the hostages and released two others. The remaining victims were released following a deal between the South Korean government and the Taliban in which South Korea agreed to adhere to its decision to withdraw its 200 non-combat troops from Afghanistan and halt all Christian missionary work in the country.

In Polk County, Florida, a manhunt was under way for 46-year-old William Joe Mitchell, a registered sex offender accused of luring a 15-year-old girl from her home. The two had met on the Internet. Mitchell transported the girl 400 miles, allegedly threatening to kill her before abandoning her at a DeFuniak Springs Wal-Mart.

And in Las Vegas, Nevada, O.J. Simpson and three others were charged with 11 counts including two counts of first-degree kidnapping after allegedly pointing guns at two men who were selling memorabilia that had belonged to Simpson. Simpson and the other accused men reportedly entered a hotel room at the Palace Station Hotel and Casino to demand the return of the items. Simpson claimed to be simply retrieving what belonged to him.

These kidnappings represent but a portion of the abductions that undoubtedly occurred during the same limited time frame. These crimes absorb the resources of the law enforcement and security professionals engaged in the investigations and cause incredible suffering for the victims, their families, and members of the local communities.

It is likely that kidnappings will continue to require the resources and resourcefulness of professionals well into the future. Informed risk assessment and risk management strategies are critical to allocating limited resources to the prevention and investigation of these crimes.

Advances in technology will certainly aid in resource allocation. Several manufacturers, for example, now market Global Positioning System (GPS) tracking devices, such as car tracking systems. These systems allow immediate, real-time identification of vehicle location. Several companies also market child tracking devices that can be attached to a child's clothing or shoelaces. Child tracking systems typically utilize radio frequency to alert a parent if a child goes beyond a user-defined distance and to provide the child's location.

In 2004, the Food and Drug Administration approved radio frequency identification (RFID) implants for humans. Since that time, several companies have implanted silicon chips in employees to control access to corporate assets. In Europe, several nightclubs have implanted the technology in clubbers to grant easy access to frequent patrons.

Less intrusive has been the enhancement of the national emergency network system by the Federal Communications Commission. Known as E911, the system allows emergency responders to automatically read the telephone number and location of 911 calls made from wireline and cellular phones. Calls to 911 are routed to a Public Safety Answering Point (PSAP). Calls from wireline devices are filtered through a reverse directory which provides location data. Wireless phones are tracked via radiolocation or by the GPS built into the phone itself.

As has been made all too apparent in the post 9/11 reality, the pendulum that swings toward advances in personal security generally swings away from individual privacy. Law enforcement and security professionals have the opportunity to assist communities, civilians, and protectees to understand the risks they face in a manner that supports a balance between personal safety and individual liberty, and thereby encourages compliance with prevention and investigation efforts.

As with any assessment of risk, past acts are critical predictors of future behaviors. It is hoped that knowledge of the victimology, abduction site choices, modus operandi, and outcomes of past kidnappings will support effective and balanced risk management strategies that will prevent and assist in the investigation of future kidnappings.

REFERENCES

19 Freed South Koreans Arrive Home, CNN.com, September 1, 2007.

Cops: Polk Teen Left in DeFuniak Springs by Man She Met on Web, OrlandoSentinel.com, October 3, 2007.

Kidnap Wives' Long Wait in Hell, CNN.com, October 7, 2007.

Man Accused of Kidnapping Boys Expected to Plead Guilty, CNN.com, October 6, 2007.

Missing Italians Freed in Afghanistan, CNN.com, September 24, 2007.

Prosecutors Charge O.J. Simpson and Three Others, CNN.com, September 18, 2007.

Six Face Kidnap Charges in Torture Case, CNN.com, September 19, 2007.

Trial Begins in Bizarre Fetus-Snatching Case, CNN.com, October 1, 2007.

Woman in Trunk Was Pumpkin's Mom, CNN.com, September 20, 2007.

Woman Accused in Fetus-Snatching Death Faked Pregnancies, CNN.com, October 10, 2007.

Index